A Life Cut Short at the Little Big Horn

A Life Cut Short at the Little Big Horn

U.S. ARMY SURGEON GEORGE E. LORD

Todd E. Harburn

Foreword by
Paul L. Hedren

University of Oklahoma Press · Norman

Library of Congress Cataloging-in-Publication Data

Names: Harburn, Todd E., 1956– author. | Hedren, Paul L., writer of foreword.
Title: A life cut short at the Little Big Horn : U.S. Army surgeon George E. Lord / Todd E. Harburn ; foreword by Paul L. Hedren.
Description: Norman : University of Oklahoma Press, 2023. | Includes bibliographical references and index. | Summary: "Portrays the making of an army medical professional (George Edwin Lord) in mid-nineteenth-century America, including his education and training, his time as a contract physician, his appointment as a post surgeon, and his untimely death at the Battle of the Little Big Horn"—Provided by publisher.
Identifiers: LCCN 2022032494 | ISBN 978-0-8061-9158-4 (hardcover)
ISBN 978-0-8061-9484-4 (paper)
Subjects: LCSH: Lord, George E. (George Edwin), 1846–1876. | Little Bighorn, Battle of the, Mont., 1876—Biography. | United States. Army—Surgeons—Biography. | Surgeons—United States—Biography.
Classification: LCC E83.876 .H288 2023 | DDC 973.8/2092 [B]—dc23/eng/20220707
LC record available at https://lccn.loc.gov/2022032494

The paper in this book meets the guidelines for permanence and durability of the Committee on Production Guidelines for Book Longevity of the Council on Library Resources, Inc. ∞

Copyright © 2023 by the University of Oklahoma Press, Norman, Publishing Division of the University. Paperback published 2024. Manufactured in the U.S.A.

All rights reserved. No part of this publication may be reproduced, stored in a retrieval system, or transmitted, in any form or by any means, electronic, mechanical, photocopying, recording, or otherwise—except as permitted under Section 107 or 108 of the United States Copyright Act—without the prior written permission of the University of Oklahoma Press. To request permission to reproduce selections from this book, write to Permissions, University of Oklahoma Press, 2800 Venture Drive, Norman OK 73069, or email rights.oupress@ou.edu.

Dedicated to Paul L. Hedren, distinguished historian
and my friend, with many thanks for his friendship,
guidance, and sharing his passion for understanding
the human experience of the American West

Contents

List of Illustrations	ix
Foreword, by Paul L. Hedren	xiii
Preface	xvii
Acknowledgments	xxiii
1. From Maine to Chicago	1
2. Dakota Territory and Beyond	28
3. All in the Line of Duty at Fort Buford	61
4. To the Little Big Horn	96
5. Aftermath	121
Epilogue: A Note on Thomas Lord at the End of His Life	137
Notes	143
Bibliography	203
Index	219

Illustrations

FIGURES

West Auburn Congregational Church (Auburn, Maine) circa 1841 and present	5
Lewiston Falls Academy (Lewiston, Maine)	6
Bowdoin College (Brunswick, Maine) campus view, 1870s	9
George Edwin Lord, Bowdoin College portrait	10
Bowdoin class of 1866 in front of Bowdoin College Chapel, 1864	12
George Edwin Lord, class of 1866, Bowdoin College	13
George Edwin Lord, 1866, at North Abington schools (Abington, Massachusetts)	14
Hosmer Allen Johnson, MD	21
Edmund Andrews, MD	22
Chicago Medical College building, 1870	23
Mercy Hospital (Chicago, Illinois), circa 1880s	24
Elbert Judson Clark, MD	25
Fort Randall Hospital, 1870s	35
Elliott Coues, MD	36
Fort Snelling, circa 1870s	56
George Edwin Lord with Custer hunting party at Heart River hunting camp site, 1875	58

Holmes Offley Paulding, MD	59
First Lieutenant George Edwin Lord, MD, assistant surgeon, U.S. Army, 1875	67
Lord's oath of office as assistant surgeon	68
Colonel William Babcock Hazen	70
Fort Buford, restored 1870s commandant's house	71
Fort Buford, reconstructed soldiers' barracks	77
Fort Buford Hospital, 1870s	88
Fort Buford Medical Log original page, March 1876	89
Colonel Orlando Hurley Moore	95
Brigadier General Alfred H. Terry	98
Colonel John Gibbon	99
Brigadier General George Crook	100
Henry Rinaldo Porter, MD	107
James Madison DeWolf, MD	108
Lieutenant Colonel George Armstrong Custer	113
Captain Frederick W. Benteen	114
Major Marcus A. Reno	115
Lord's death site at Last Stand Hill	126
George E. Lord's dress uniform, chapeau, and pocket surgical kit	130
George E. Lord's surgical case	131
Thomas W. Lord's headstone at Arlington National Cemetery	141

Maps

George Lord in the West, 1871–1876	32
Northern Boundary Survey Commission 1873–1874	40
Little Big Horn Campaign	106

Illustrations xi

The Valley Fight at the Little Big Horn 117
Seventh Cavalry Movements at the Little Big Horn,
    June 25, 1876 119

Foreword

THREE PHYSICIANS rode with George Custer's troops on that fateful day in June 1876 when they descended into the Little Big Horn Valley and charged an immense Lakota and Northern Cheyenne Indian village. Of those doctors, Henry Porter and James DeWolf were contract physicians, what the army called acting assistant surgeons. It was a slightly dismissive label. They were simply doctors for hire, whether for specific places, timeframes, or campaigns. Porter survived that terrible battle. DeWolf perished in Major Marcus Reno's Little Big Horn Valley fight.

The medical anomaly that fateful day was the third of those physicians, George Lord. Unlike his civilian counterparts, Lord was a commissioned medical officer, an assistant surgeon with the rank of first lieutenant. In the day, that alone was a simple but proud statement that Lord possessed not only the requisite medical training and skills essential for an army practice, but also the necessary classical education equally critical for surmounting the army's rigorous examination for entrance into its carefully monitored commissioned ranks. In the Old Army, mere medical training itself, regardless of quality or institutional branding, was not enough for permanent standing in its extremely well-educated and elite medical corps.

Lord, an elite officer? Quite so. Connected to Custer and the Little Big Horn? Indeed. But why, then, in a world where everything about Custer and Little Big Horn has been dissected repeatedly, is there so little on George Lord before this book? The answer becomes apparent in the present pages. While Porter survived and enjoyed a prosperous and highly visible post–Little Big Horn medical and civic career, and DeWolf bequeathed to history an extraordinary diary and letters, George Lord's documentary legacy is a nearly empty page. Exploring a life, career, and dramatic death absent a trove of paper is ordinarily any historian's nightmare. But to our good fortune, Todd Harburn has creatively turned every possible stone and serves up a tale of a scholar, soldier, and doctor worth remembering.

George Lord was a tireless overachiever. He was the adopted child of Reverend Thomas and Mary Lord, and Thomas was a Congregational pastor in Maine and Massachusetts. George was classically educated at Bowdoin College in Maine, his father's alma mater, where he graduated in 1866. With little pause, George Lord continued his education at the Chicago Medical College, the eventual Northwestern University School of Medicine, where he graduated in 1871.

Lord was drawn to military service, almost certainly influenced by his older brother, another Thomas, who was a Civil War veteran and in the 1870s a captain in the Twentieth U.S. Infantry then stationed at Fort Snelling, Minnesota. As a contract surgeon first, George Lord served stints at small military posts in Minnesota and the Dakota Territory and with the Northern Boundary Survey Commission, then busily detailing an international border across Dakota and Montana in 1874. All the while Lord eyed an invitation from the Army Medical Board to take the challenging exam for admission to those ranks, an achievement realized in 1875.

Lord was promptly dispatched to Fort Buford, in far northwestern Dakota at the confluence of the Yellowstone and Missouri Rivers, where he was assigned as post surgeon. From Buford in the spring of 1876, Lord was drawn to the Great Sioux War, detailed initially as the medical attendant at several of the small Yellowstone River supply depots established to support Brigadier General Alfred Terry's oncoming Dakota Column, one of three forces aiming for the heart of Sioux Country. In turn, when Terry reached the Yellowstone in mid-June, Lord was reassigned to that burgeoning command. That was a fateful move, and it sealed the young doctor's eventual demise at Custer's side on June 25, 1876.

Through it all, George Lord tells us very little of this. He never married, and no letters to family members are known to survive. His

Foreword xv

official "Appointments, Commissions, Personal File," maintained originally by the Adjutant General's Office and now preserved in the National Archives, is lean but helpful. So too are scattered papers at Bowdoin College and Northwestern University. What more exists to illuminate an interesting life and short army career was the plain hard work of a creative, modern-day Michigan surgeon turned historical sleuth, and the sum comprises a good tale.

Todd E. Harburn of Twin Lake, Michigan, has devoted the better part of his adult life to the intrigues of history, whether in the Straits of Mackinac or the American West. By night, weekend, and vacation moment, Todd was and still is a familiar figure in the historical doings at Michilimackinac and Fort Mackinac, in his home state, and at the Little Big Horn Battlefield and ever-popular Real Bird Last Stand Reenactment in southeastern Montana. Incongruity, you wonder? Perhaps, especially considering that by workday, Harburn enjoyed a long and satisfying career in sports medicine as an orthopedic surgeon, college football team physician, and long-time orthopedic surgery residency instructor at the Lansing/East Lansing program associated with Michigan State University. He mostly retired in 2019.

Marry these diverse outside interests and personal career and it is perhaps only natural that Harburn began exploring the world of doctoring in the Old Army, and particularly in George Custer's Little Big Horn army. Already Harburn had authored the definitive accounting of DeWolf's life in a skillfully introduced and lavishly annotated edition of that doctor's campaign diary and letters (*A Surgeon with Custer at the Little Big Horn*, University of Oklahoma Press, 2017).

For George Lord, Harburn gives us all there is. He adds to the foundational biography exhaustive endnotes highlighting virtually every character and side note in Lord's life. He dissects every shred of information on Lord's movements in the Little Big Horn battle, imagining—logically—that the young doctor fought not with revolver but bandage in hand. And he closes with an exploration of brother Thomas's own pathetic ending. The lives of two brothers, both adopted, speculatively blood related, ended tragically.

Here, then, is the story of George Lord, the surgeon who literally rode and died with Custer. It's a tale cast broadly in the world of army medicine in the 1870s, and craftily told by Todd Harburn, who has carved for himself his own niche as today's acknowledged authority on this unique dimension of the Little Big Horn story.

Paul L. Hedren
Omaha, Nebraska

Preface

NEARLY EVERYONE who has an interest in the Battle of the Little Big Horn of June 25, 1876, is likely familiar with the name of Dr. George Edwin Lord. Lord and his two colleagues, Dr. Henry Rinaldo Porter and Dr. James Madison DeWolf, composed the medical staff involved in the horrific and now famous battle in which Lieutenant Colonel (Brevet Major General) George Armstrong Custer and five companies of the Seventh United States Cavalry were annihilated and the rest of his command defeated by a large force of combined Lakota and Northern Cheyenne Indians. Of the three physicians, Porter was the only one to survive the overall engagement. DeWolf was killed in the early stages of the battle during the desperate retreat from the Timber area after the initial attack on the huge Indian village along the banks of the Little Big Horn River had been thwarted. Lord fell on Last Stand Hill, where Custer and the remaining soldiers of his section made their final defense against the overwhelming force of Indians.

While one might think that everything that could be written about the Custer fight has already been done, historians and researchers continue to find new and varied aspects for further study about the actions on the banks of the Little Big Horn River and the people involved. So why a book on Lord? In the last three to four decades, information has been discovered and brought to light about many of the participants on both sides in the battle. Aside from some of the more famous army officers and Indian leaders, most of the Indian warriors and the individual soldiers were simply ordinary individuals who found themselves inevitably caught up in the war campaign—the Indians fighting to preserve their homeland

and cultural way of life and the soldiers doing their duty as directed by the U.S. government's policy of Manifest Destiny and forced resettlement of the Indians on the reservations. George Lord was among the latter. His story adds additional overall perspective to this more humanistic look at the tragedy that occurred and the individuals who were involved, adding to the traditional military studies that have been and continue to be written.

The men of the army medical department were highly educated individuals, although not all had military experience. Nor did all of them leave diaries or journals. Yet, those who did leave some type of written record, whether in the form of an actual journal or perhaps letters or even medical logs, had much to say about their profession and military events, social class, and life at the isolated posts on the western frontier. One needs only to read, for example, the published journals and correspondence of John Vance Lauderdale by distinguished historian Robert Utley, or the work of Peter Josyph and Jerry Green, or the journals of Isaac Coates, edited by W. J. D. Kennedy, to gain a rich understanding of this era of western military and medical history.[1]

Unlike his colleagues Porter and DeWolf, George Lord had no military fighting experience prior to the Little Big Horn campaign. DeWolf had served as an artillerist during the Civil War from 1861 to 1865 and as an army hospital steward during the Snake Indian War years of 1865 to 1868. As a civilian contract surgeon for the army, Porter had experienced actions in Arizona against the Apache Indians with Lieutenant Colonel George Crook from 1872 to 1873. Despite the lack of actual experience "under fire," Lord proved to be a well-educated, competent physician and was seen as a gentleman well respected by his peers and those who knew him. An obituary notice described him as a "young man of promise and held in universal esteem."[2] Having served as the post surgeon at Fort Buford in Dakota Territory from August 1875 to mid-May 1876, his surviving writings in the medical log from that time provide evidence of his competency as well as interesting insight as to some of the afflictions treated at frontier army posts. Sadly, his life followed a similar path to that of DeWolf's in that a promising career in medicine was cut short by destiny on Last Stand Hill at the Little Big Horn.

Not least, a full-length biography on Lord completes "the trilogy" regarding the surgeons involved in the Little Big Horn battle. Two biographies of Henry Porter have been written, L. G. Walker Jr.'s 2009 interesting general biography and Joan Nabseth Stevenson's detailed 2012 book focused on Porter's heroic efforts in attending wounded soldiers during the Little Big Horn battle at the field hospital he established on Reno–Benteen Hill. DeWolf's 2017 biography (by this author) included an extensive editing and annotation of his surviving Little Big Horn diary and letters. Aside from articles by prominent Custer historians, including two biographical sketches by C. Lee Noyes (the more extensive being a very informative and well-researched piece in the Custer Battlefield Historical and Museum Association's journal *Greasy Grass* in 2000), J. W. Vaughn's brief sketch in the *New York Westerners Brand Book* in 1962, Edward S. Petersen's 1974 article in the *Chicago Westerners Brand Book*, and John M. Carroll's sketch in the *Little Big Horn Associates Research Review* in 1984, there was no full-length biography published about this compelling medical officer.[3]

While a couple of personal letters written by George Lord have survived, he did not leave a journal, and there is also no surviving correspondence with his brother, Thomas. However, a review of the existing information about him suggests that he and his brother remained close throughout their lives despite the sometimes distance and events that prevented more frequent visits or a family reunion. To further understand and appreciate his life, a comparison with that of his brother is reasonable. Both experienced the emotional highs and lows that all human beings engage during their lifetimes. Yet, while both enjoyed some successes in their military careers, Thomas in marriage and George in his college and medical school education, their lives were destined to be ones defined by tragic events. Thomas was to suffer the loss of a leg during the Civil War and an eventual mysterious death, while George endured disappointment in romance and eventual death at the Little Big Horn.

In writing this narrative on the life of George Lord, I chose to pattern my monograph to that of my previous biographical presentation of the diary and letters of Lord's Little Big Horn colleague James DeWolf. The first chapter presents newly discovered information gained from tracing his early years and family history and his college and medical school education. The middle chapters pertain to his military career and personal events, including the presentation and updated annotation of his two surviving letters, and editing and annotation of the medical log maintained during his tenure as post surgeon at Fort Buford in late 1875 to early 1876. The fourth and fifth chapters relate the events on the campaign leading to his death at the Little Big Horn, while tracing, exploring, and reviewing the arduous effort by his brother (and later historians) to discover those details. A final chapter shares some more recently discovered information concerning George's brother, Thomas Lord, and a comparative discussion that places their lives in perspective. Once again, I have chosen to use the term "Little Big Horn" in keeping with the U.S. Army's historically preferred spelling for the region and battle instead of the modern popular terms "Little Bighorn" and "Custer's Last Stand."[4]

There may be some readers who question why I included Lord's full portion of the Fort Buford Medical Record while making only a few references to those similar records maintained at the Whetstone Indian Agency and Fort Randall. I chose to include and edit Fort Buford's log fully from his time there because Lord was the appointed post surgeon during his entire tenure at that post. While he was at the latter two stations for a somewhat extended time, he was the official post surgeon for only three months at Fort Randall and therefore was not the author of the official medical log for his entire tour. Moreover, Lord's time at Buford was closer to the Little Big Horn campaign and readers would be familiar with and have interest in many of the people, activities, and preceding events he wrote about just prior to that episode. Also, while some of the recorded events and statistics in the Fort Buford Medical Log regarding the daily military life at the post might seem mundane to some readers, a review of those specifics reveals that not to be the case. Finally, similar to my editing/annotation of the DeWolf diary and letters, I have chosen to leave sentence structure, punctuation, and spelling of the medical record exactly as they are in the original documents for historical authenticity and tradition.

George Lord was but one of three surgeons among hundreds of other individuals whose destinies brought them together in what would become the tragedy of the Little Big Horn, each with different backgrounds, personalities, and life experiences. We can read their names and view their images in photographs, yet until we search for and place all those aspects in perspective, we cannot know or understand the true essence of who they were and their human response to the events they experienced in life's journey. By combining a more in-depth study of some new and recently uncovered information regarding Lord's family, prep school, undergraduate and formal medical training, surviving personal letters, and Fort Buford Medical Log, I hope that a more complete picture emerges of his life, thus adding yet one more "piece of the picture" of the human experience in the history of this tumultuous time of the American West.

Acknowledgments

I AM EXTREMELY GRATEFUL for all the assistance and support that I have received from numerous people during this George Lord project.

First and foremost, one individual who has been invaluable in support and assistance to me from the very beginning, when I confidentially announced to him that a biography on George Lord was to be my next book project, is Paul Hedren of Omaha, Nebraska. Paul is a retired National Park Service administrator, a well-known distinguished historian and author of numerous books and articles regarding the Great Sioux War and military history in the American West. He is not only one of those simply "good guys," but is moreover one of those naturally gifted writers whose meticulously researched narratives seem to flow easily from his pen, and which appeal to and satisfy both the academic society and the general public's interest. Among his many published scholarly books are *After Custer*, *Powder River: Disastrous Opening of the Great Sioux War*, and *Rosebud, June 17, 1876*. In addition to graciously accepting my request to write the foreword, Paul reviewed drafts of the manuscript, at various times directed me to some "buried" lesser-known source, and saved me from making a few embarrassing, inadvertent errors. Importantly, he again held me to his high standards of historical scholarship, just as he did for my James DeWolf biography. Although I have known this gentleman for only a few years, I consider Paul my good friend as well. I will be forever grateful to him for his expertise, professionalism, support, and belief in me, but most of all, his friendship.

Once again, I owe a very special thank you to Sarah Walker, now head of reference services at the State Historical Society of North Dakota, for her tremendous assistance to me in my research requests. Ever since I first met her in 2009 when I started working on my DeWolf book, she has always been most gracious in taking time out of her extremely busy work schedule to answer my numerous email inquiries and locating some obscure source within the SHSND collections as well as always making me feel welcome during my research visits to the archives and history center. That she enjoys her career is readily evident and I do not recall ever seeing her without a smile on her face. I consider her a friend and she has been a huge contributor to my book endeavors.

Another gentleman who has been of great encouragement and assistance to me is Dr. James Brust of San Pedro, California. Aside from his medical practice as a psychiatrist, Dr. Brust's longtime interest in historical photos resulted in his discovering the first photograph ever taken of the Little Big Horn battlefield and subsequently coauthoring a book regarding photos of the battlefield that featured the image. I am grateful to him for allowing me to include it among the illustrations for my book. His critique of drafts of my manuscript was extremely helpful, not only with regard to the medical aspects but also because of his writing expertise. Our friendship, which developed in recent years, resulted from our being kindred spirits as neither of us are professional historians as to the Little Big Horn in the sense that we have written about it as an adjunct interest to our medical careers. So, I extend my thanks to Jim for sharing both those endeavors with me.

I will be forever grateful to members of the publishing committee and faculty advisory board of the University of Oklahoma Press, editorial director J. Kent Calder, and former senior acquisitions editor Katie Hall for their extreme generosity and kindness in accepting my second submission to the press, this Lord project, which followed their publication of my DeWolf book in 2017. Katie was a pleasure to work with, including her most pleasant personality, her expertise, and professionalism. Kent, a true professional himself, has been enthusiastic and supportive of this project from

Acknowledgments

the beginning and has my sincere appreciation for his guidance and oversight throughout the publication process. I also want to acknowledge the expertise, dedication, and contributions of managing editor Steven Baker, editorial intern Josh Mika, promotions manager Amy Hernandez, and copyeditor Kerin Tate. Kerin diligently made sure that endnotes adhered to the proper form as well as made grammatical suggestions for a smooth flowing narrative in several areas. OU Press is truly a team effort, which I value as a result of my own college football playing days and orthopedic surgery career philosophy.

I owe thanks to the following individuals for their tremendous assistance. Randy Kane, Crawford, Nebraska, kindly made a special trip back to his former site of employment to obtain copies of information regarding nearby Fort Buford from the library collections at Fort Union. Rod Lassey, Cartwright, North Dakota, lent me his copies of the transcribed Private Wilmot P. Sanford's Fort Buford diary. Brian Duggan, Turlock, California, has a passion for dogs that resulted in his excellent and captivating book on George and Libbie Custer's famous canines, and he consistently surprised me with copies in the mail of lesser-known, hard-to-locate articles relating to army medical history of the Indian Wars. Ron Nichols, Lake Forest, California, once again kindly allowed me to use maps from his biography of Major Marcus Reno. At the Little Bighorn Battlefield National Monument, both Sharon C. Smith, curator and White Swan Library administrator, and Cindy Hagen, retired former cultural and digital resources specialist, were extraordinarily helpful. Other historians who have encouraged and supported my Lord book project include Sandy Barnard, Wake Forest, North Carolina; James Donovan, Dallas, Texas; Brian Dunnigan, Spring Arbor, Michigan; John A. Houlding, Diepersdorf, Germany; Paul Andrew Hutton, Albuquerque, New Mexico; Phil Porter, Mackinac Island, Michigan; Timothy J. Todish, Grand Rapids, Michigan; Gregory J. W. Urwin, Doylestown, Pennsylvania; Charles E. "Chuck" Rankin, Helena, Montana; Doug Wamsley, Ridgewood, New Jersey; and Agnes and Keith Widder, East Lansing, Michigan.

I would be extremely remiss if I did not acknowledge the four historians who "paved the way" in providing the initial information about George Lord and who made my endeavor in "tackling" his biography a somewhat smoother process. The meticulous research of C. Lee Noyes of Morrisonville, New York, and three late historians, John M. Carroll, J. W. Vaughn, and Edward S. Petersen, MD, was extremely helpful. The collective published articles of these authors were essential in my attempt to complete Lord's story and provided me with much direction in discovering some of the information that was lacking and not available to them at the time of their writings. I extend additional thanks to Lee Noyes for always being willing to answer my questions and unselfishly sharing information with me.

The wonderful map depicting the locations of George Lord's life journey in the American West was created by the very talented Robert Pilk, Lakewood, Colorado, whose maps have been featured in many books relating the Plains Indian wars history. I greatly appreciate Robert fitting me in to his busy schedule. My thanks also for photographic assistance to Greg Teysen, Mackinaw City, Michigan; Richard "Dick" Creighton, Auburn, Maine; and Charles Warner, Milton, Pennsylvania.

Of course, no book project can ever be completed without the assistance of administrators, curators, librarians, archivists, and research assistants at various historical museums and libraries. Among these dedicated public servants are John Deeben, National Archives and Records Administration in Washington, D.C., who has assisted me for both of my Little Big Horn books, and Kelly McAnnaney, National Archives and Records Administration at New York City. Others include Sylvia Marcotte, administrator of the *Maine Orphans Not Forgotten* website; Katherine Ann Lattal, Galter Library, Northwestern University Feinberg School of Medicine, Chicago, Illinois; Donna Wallace and Kayla Chase, Auburn Public Library, Auburn, Maine; Roberta B. Schwartz, George J. Mitchell Department of Special Collections and Archives, Bowdoin College Library, Brunswick, Maine; Merlyn Liberty, Dyer Memorial Library, Abington, Massachusetts; Renee Giusti and Pam Rousseau, Androscoggin County Historical Society, Auburn, Maine;

Acknowledgments xxvii

Lowell Smith, Geraldine, Alabama, Little Big Horn Associates; Heidi Hellar, Gale Family Library, Minnesota Historical Society; Rodney C. Foytick, Karl K. Warner III, Jennifer T. Loredo, and director John "Jack" Giblin, U.S. Army Heritage and Education Center, Carlisle, Pennsylvania; Kirk F. Mohney, Maine Historic Preservation Commission, Augusta, Maine; and Zoe Ann Stolz, Montana Historical Society.

My sincere appreciation is also extended to executive vice president Robert C. Leeds, director George C. Wunderlich, Francis Trachta, and Charles E. Franson of the Army Medical Department Museum (AMEDD) and Foundation, Fort Sam Houston, Texas, for their generosity in providing and granting permission to use the photographs of Dr. George Edwin Lord's large surgical case; Alan Hawk, historical collections manager, National Museum of Health and Medicine, Silver Spring, Maryland, for providing the photographs of Lord's regimental dress coat, pocket surgical kit, and chapeau, and his kind permission to use them. I also extend special thanks to Carolyn Bird, register of probate and Hannah J. Dickinson, deputy register, Sagadahoc County, Maine; Kelly J. DeMers, register of probate, York County, Stanford, Maine; Renee Des-Roberts, McArthur Library, Biddeford, Maine; Catherine Moore, register of probate, and Tori Lorom, Lincoln County Probate Court, Wiscasset, Maine; Jay Robbins, historian, Wiscasset, Maine; Dawn Thistle, Gardiner Public Library, Gardiner, Maine; and Madison Vlass, Museum of Old Newbury, Newburyport, Massachusetts.

The are many friends to whom I am extremely grateful for their encouragement and support to me in this Lord book project, or for just listening to my rambling on about it. They know this; however, due to space limitations, I am unable to include their names here, and for that, I offer my sincerest apologies.

Finally, I again want to acknowledge the support of my family: my brother, Tadd, and his wife, Julia, my two daughters, Shannon and Stacey, and their husbands, Luke and Michael. Although our two beautiful grandchildren, Nora and Josiah, are too young as yet to understand the details, they know that their "Bumpa" has been working on some type of history project. Last but not least, I owe my wife, Shirley, tremendous thanks and more than I can perhaps ever repay her. I am very grateful for her tolerating yet another long-haul book project and for listening to my long, boring recitations from the manuscript drafts. But, more important, what I am most grateful for is her unwavering love, her faith and, once again, her always being there for me.

Todd E. Harburn
Twin Lake, Michigan

CHAPTER I

From Maine to Chicago

CLEAR, BRIGHT AND FULL OF LIFE AND ENERGY....
HE WAS HIGH MINDED AS A YOUNG MAN.
*Auburn, Maine, resident Henry M. Packard's
remembrance of George Lord in the Lewiston (Maine)
Evening Journal, April 3, 1907*

GEORGE EDWIN LORD was born on February 17, 1846, in Boston, Massachusetts, according to his autobiography statement, which also noted that his biological "parents soon after moved to the state of Maine."[1] His childhood years were not of the traditional family mode, as he and his older "brother," Thomas William Lord (1844–1903), were both adopted (although from different families). They were brought up in a loving family as the sons of a Congregational minister, Reverend Thomas Newman Lord (1807–84), and his wife, Mary E. Tupper Lord (1803–88), who added the two boys to the Lords' daughters, Julia A. Lord (1836–1919) and Maria Lord (1838–1927; also spelled Mariah). Historians who have previously written about George Lord stated that there is no information about his biological parents. However, newly discovered genealogical information has now identified Lord's biological parents as Robert Newman Lord (b. 1809) and Mary E. Damon Lord (1813–46; also spelled Dammon). Robert was the brother of Reverend Lord. His marriage to Mary Damon resulted in their only child, George E. Lord. Tragically, Mary died eight days after childbirth, and George was eventually taken in by her parents, blacksmith Chandler Dammon (1780–1857) and Betsy

1

Jackson Dammon (1779–1858), back in her original hometown of Wiscasset, Massachusetts.[2] By February 1858, both of George's grandparents were dead, dying within two months of each other. George then was adopted by his uncle, the Reverend Thomas Lord, and his wife, joining adopted brother Thomas and the two Lord sisters in the family.

Although both boys are listed as having been born in Massachusetts, whether a biological relationship existed between George and Thomas is not known. The U.S. Census of 1850 for Biddeford, Maine, where Reverend Lord was pastor of the local Second Congregational Church, lists only Thomas, Mary, and Julia as children of the Lord household.[3] In a 1907 article published in the *Lewiston* (Maine) *Evening Journal*, brief reminiscences of several West Auburn residents who went to school with the Lord boys and knew them well were reported. A Henry M. Packard stated that the adopted Thomas was Reverend Lord's nephew.[4] As this interview occurred long after the death of both Lord brothers, the possibility exists that Packard's memory was somewhat blurred on this particular detail. Although evidence has now been discovered confirming that George was an adopted nephew of Reverend Lord, nothing has been found confirming the same for Thomas.[5] As such, the biological parents, orphanages, or adoption circumstances of Thomas are not known, despite extensive searching by historians and genealogists.[6] Even if they were not remotely biologically related, evidence suggests they remained as close as natural siblings throughout their eventual military careers. The aforementioned Packard statement also provides some insight into the personality of the younger brother, George, as he was described as "clean, bright and full of life and energy. He was high minded as a young man."[7]

The brothers were fortunate to be adopted into a respected, socially established, close family and were given a good moral upbringing. Their father, Reverend Thomas N. Lord, was born in Newburyport, Massachusetts, on August 19, 1807,[8] but his family moved to Maine while he was yet a young man. He received his early formal education in the Maine towns of Farmington and Monmouth before enrolling in Bowdoin College in Brunswick, Maine, graduating in

1835.⁹ Shortly thereafter, Thomas married Mary E. Tupper, daughter of Dr. James Tupper of Hallowell, Maine, on September 3, 1835.[10] The first of the couple's children, daughter Julia A. Lord, was born the following year in Gardiner, Maine, and sister Maria was born two years later in 1838 in Topsham, Maine. Reverend Lord's brief biographical information in an 1882 publication of the history of Bowdoin College and its alumni asserts that one of the daughters was adopted but does not provide a name. The wording in this published history states that the reverend and his wife, Mary, "had one child, a daughter, but have adopted two sons and a daughter." Surprisingly, despite an extensive search of various Maine town historical societies and municipal, county, and state governmental records (including birth and probate records), no information has been discovered as to which daughter was adopted, although much is known about each of their life histories.[11] After obtaining his theological training in Winthrop, Maine, he began his long career of service to people as a clergyman, pastoring numerous churches in Maine, accepting callings, or being moved every few years, as is the historical practice of many church denominations.[12]

Aside from his chosen profession in the ministry, the fact that Reverend Lord and his wife were compassionate people, committed to the service of others, including their relatives, is evident by the fact that they had adopted the two young boys by 1860, providing two siblings for their own daughters. At this time, Reverend Lord and his family were living in West Auburn, Maine, where he had been serving as the acting pastor at the First Congregational Church of Auburn (the present-day West Auburn Congregational Church) since 1851, before being installed as the full-time pastor in 1858. His annual salary was initially $500, although that was increased to $600 in 1856.[13] He remained there until 1862. The Lord family was a respected pillar in the community.

Containing vast regions of heavy wilderness, which largely remain today, the state of Maine was experiencing rapid expansion in the mid-nineteenth century with regard to industrial development and population growth. The area comprising present-day Auburn on the Androscoggin River, where Reverend Lord and his family were residing, had originally been inhabited by the Androscoggin Indians (one of the geographic groups of the Abenaki Tribe).[14] In 1714, the region became a part of the Pejepscot Purchase and eventually, in 1736, was sanctioned for official settlement by the Massachusetts General Court. Although there were scattered settlers in the region in the ensuing years, the first permanent organized settlement occurred after the Revolutionary War in 1786. The settlement, originally named Bakersfield, was renamed Poland in 1795. A portion was then split off and named Minot in 1802.[15] Minot had a congregational meeting house and became a small settlement. This area was eventually further divided; West Auburn was established about 1835 (when the first shoe manufacturing company came to the area), and in turn was divided with a section being designated as the Town of Auburn proper in 1842 and named the county seat of Androscoggin County in 1854.[16] Auburn was initially a farming community, and then later with its sister city, Lewiston, just across the river, it became a cotton and wool textile manufacturing city with multiple mills also being constructed for grain and flour production. By the 1850s, when the Lords resided there (after the arrival of the railroads in 1848), the Auburn region had developed into a major boot and shoe manufacturing center, although the West Auburn and Minot communities remained agricultural.[17]

The First Congregational Church, located about four miles northwest of central Auburn, was founded in 1805 at Minot as a community meeting house. The meeting house also was used by the community's Congregationalists. In 1846 (some sources say 1841) a new church building was erected on the site, which still stands and is in use today. During his time there, Reverend Lord's faithful and diligent service (described in his obituary as "remarkably self sacrificing and humble as God's servant") resulted in the membership of the congregation greatly increasing.[18]

Being in a respected family and safe environment, George and Thomas, not surprisingly, were set on the path toward obtaining solid educations. Both brothers attended the prestigious Lewiston Falls Academy in Auburn. There, George "commenced" his education preparations for college, attending school from 1860 to 1862.[19]

The Lewiston Falls Academy was founded in 1834 by Edward Little, an attorney and philanthropist who came to Auburn in 1826 and was instrumental in the growth of that community and its sister city, Lewiston.[20] Little donated nine acres of his own land to establish the school, which was founded for the purposes of "advancing science and literature and promoting morality, piety, and religion."[21] Classes were held in the upper room of James Goff's nearby store. (Goff was also on the board of trustees of the school.) Two years later, in 1836, Little was the main contributor of funds for the first building of the academy, a large, three-story brick structure. A few of the upper floor rooms were made available for students who came from extended distances to attend the school with "room, wood, lights, and washing available for $1.50 per week." Tuition was four dollars per term, later increased by the time of the Civil War.[22] The academic year comprised four terms spanning forty-four weeks. In the early years, some forty students attended the school. Enrollment steadily and significantly increased by 1865 to 250 students.[23]

Left, West Auburn Congregational Church, Auburn, Maine, circa 1841. *Right*, West Auburn Congregational Church, present day. (Images courtesy of Androscoggin Historical Society and West Auburn Congregational Church, Richard Creighton, Deacon.)

Lewiston Falls Academy, Lewiston, Maine. (Courtesy of the Maine Historic Preservation Commission.)

When the Lord brothers attended the academy, they commuted to school since they lived with their parents and sisters in the church parsonage not far away.

In 1862, a year after the outbreak of the Civil War, Thomas decided to leave school and enlisted in one of the local Maine regiments. George remained at the Lewiston Falls Academy. Thomas joined the Seventeenth Maine Infantry on August 18, 1862, and was given the rank of sergeant in Company K.[24] The Seventeenth Maine was raised from Androscoggin, Cumberland, Franklin, Oxford, and York counties at Camp King in Cape Elizabeth, Maine. Assigned to the Third Brigade, First Division, Third Army Corps of the Army of the Potomac, the regiment left Maine on August 2, 1862, for Washington, D.C., where it served in the defenses of the city.[25] Thereafter, the Army of the Potomac was involved in the Virginia battles of Fredericksburg, December 11–15, 1862, and Chancellorsville, April 30 to May 6, 1863.[26] Official reports by the Union commanders of the Third Corps for both battles cited the officers and men of the Seventeenth Maine for "nobly performing their duties" at Fredericksburg and their "valuable assistance and gallant conduct on the night of May second" at Chancellorsville.[27] Serving as a second lieutenant, having been promoted from his initial rank of sergeant on February 11, 1863, Thomas was severely wounded at Chancellorsville on Sunday, May 3, 1863, which resulted in the amputation of his left leg.[28] The Official Report of the Battle of Chancellorsville by the commander of the Seventeenth Maine, Colonel Thomas A. Roberts, includes a mention of Lieutenant Thomas Lord with those cited "deserving of commendation for good conduct in the recent engagement."[29] Thomas was eventually admitted to the U.S.A. General Hospital in Annapolis, Maryland, on August 29, 1863. He recovered and was discharged for physical disability, being honorably mustered out on September 6, 1863.[30]

Sioux War historian J. W. Vaughn wrote in his 1962 article in the *New York Westerners Brand Book* that Thomas attended Bowdoin College with his brother, George, in 1863–64 while recuperating from his injury. A more recent in-depth examination of the college records shows this to be incorrect. During the start of his brother's sophomore year in the fall of 1863, Thomas did enroll as a freshman after recovering from his leg amputation. Yet, he "did not presecute [prosecute] his academic course." That is, he did not begin classes at all, as he chose to return to a military career instead.[31] He was appointed a second lieutenant in the Seventeenth Regiment of the Invalid Reserve Corps (eventually renamed the Veteran Reserve Corps) of the Union Army on December 8, 1863.[32] Near the end of the war, Thomas was cited for his "gallantry and meritorious service" in the Battle of Chancellorsville, received brevet recognition to the rank of captain March 13, 1865, and was promoted to first lieutenant in the Fifth Regiment Veteran Reserve Corps three months later. He was honorably mustered out of the service in October 1866.[33] Despite his unfortunate injury, that incident would ultimately result in the start of a long and dedicated administrative career in the army, and he eventually served as regimental and post quartermaster in the Twentieth Infantry.

While his brother was enduring the dangers and traumatic experiences of the Civil War, George completed his secondary education at the Lewiston Falls Academy and was accepted in 1862 at his father's alma mater, Bowdoin College, a small, well-known men's college in Brunswick, Maine, which was founded in 1794. Bowdoin also had its own medical school, the Medical School of Maine, in operation since 1821. By this time, the Lord family had moved to Brunswick, although his father would accept a call as acting pastor in Woolwich, Maine, the following spring in 1863, before moving to become pastor at the congregational church in North Yarmouth (twenty miles south of Brunswick) in 1864. While Bates College, a coeducational school established in 1855 in his former home area of Lewiston/Auburn, was a very good college as well, George's matriculation at Bowdoin was likely in part due to Reverend Lord being an alumnus of Bowdoin and George being a bright young student who had been well prepared at his prep school academy for the tough curriculum at either college.

Both Bates and Bowdoin were (and remain today) highly esteemed colleges with rigid admission requirements.[34] At Bowdoin, the terms of admission, as related in the college's 1863 catalog, declared the following:

> Candidates for admission into the Freshman Class are required to write Latin grammatically, and to be well versed in Geography, Arithmetic, six sections in Smyth's Algebra, Cicero's Select Orations (Johnson's edit.) or an equivalent in amount, the Bucolics, two Georgics, and nine books of the Æneid of Virgil, Sallust, (Andrew's edit.), Xenophon's Anabasis, six books* together with Latin and Greek Grammar and Prosody and the first thirty exercises of Arnold's Latin Prose Composition. They must produce certificates of their good moral character. . . . Particular attention to English Grammar and Composition is urged as essential to a satisfactory preparation for the College Course.
>
> *As an equivalent, Felton's Greek Reader is accepted; or Jacob's or Owen's Greek Reader with the two first Gospels of the Greek Testament. Beginners in Greek are advised to take first Harkness' First Greek Book, then the anabasis with Hadley's Grammar.[35]

Lord took the examinations for admission on Friday, August 8, 1862, and successfully passing those, he began the fall term commencing Wednesday, August 27, 1862. His entering class of 1866 officially numbered 41, which leveled to 24 and 25 during his last

Bowdoin College, Brunswick, Maine, campus view, circa 1870s. (Courtesy of the George J. Mitchell Department of Special Collections & Archives, Bowdoin College Library, Brunswick, Maine.)

two years, as the class roster varied from year to year due to students leaving for various reasons, including Civil War service. Bowdoin's total number of undergraduate students in 1862 was 181, with an additional 68 students enrolled at the medical school, although by George's senior year in 1866 the undergraduate enrollment had dropped to 131 while the medical school enrollment had increased to 108 students.[36]

After matriculating at Bowdoin, George lived at home in Brunswick for his first year, likely to help save money as his family had moved there between the pastoral assignments of his father. For his remaining undergraduate years, George lived in Appleton Hall, one of the three student dormitories on campus.[37] Annual expenses during his years at Bowdoin included "Tuition, $30.00, Room rent, $10.00, Incidental charges on the College bills, $12.00, Board, $2.75

George Edwin Lord, Bowdoin College student portrait. (Courtesy of the George J. Mitchell Department of Special Collections & Archives, Bowdoin College Library, Brunswick, Maine.)

to $3.50 per week; other expenses as wood, lights, washing, use of books and furniture, $35.00, total $220.00," as listed in the college's catalog.[38] Since students accepted for admission to Bowdoin were required to have successfully demonstrated proficiency in classical literature, humanities, and language composition during the admissions process, they would have been familiar with the classes they were required to take during the freshman course of study. Over the course of that academic year, these included such classes as Felton's extracts from the Greek histories, Arnold's Greek and Latin prose composition, the *Odyssey*, Greek grammar, Smyth's algebra, Paley's *Natural Theology*, Legendre's geometry, and exercises in elocution. By Lord's senior year, he would have taken the required advanced classes, including astronomy, Paley's *Evidences*, *Upham's Mental Philosophy*, moral science, chemistry, physiology, geology, physical geography, Butler's *Analogy*, Upham's *Treatise on the Will*, English literature, and Hebrew and Italian languages.[39] To teach these challenging courses, the college faculty included distinguished alumni such as Joshua Lawrence Chamberlain, a Maine native who later became a Gettysburg hero, governor of Maine, and president of his alma mater in 1871–83. Chamberlain was a professor of "rhetoric and oratory" and later of modern languages as well. George missed having Chamberlain as an instructor in his freshman year, as Chamberlain left the school on leave to serve in the Civil War, accepting a commission in August 1862 as lieutenant colonel in the Twentieth Maine Volunteer Infantry Regiment. George was fortunate in his senior year, however, to learn from the well-known professor and army hero when Chamberlain returned to his faculty position after the war, before embarking on a short political career as governor of Maine.

Although the curriculum at Bowdoin was intense, the demanding curriculum in literature and the humanities during his prep school years at the Lewiston Falls Academy had prepared George well. Lord proved fully capable of meeting the challenges of the college courses. He was a very good student and consistently ranked as "good" in the categories of attention to study and expression for rank, and as "cordial" in expression for conduct. His surviving academic transcripts over his four years preserved in the archive collections of the Bowdoin College Library document this and also show that he maintained an average of 24.5 (out of 30) for his weekly recitations in classes over the usual eleven-week terms shown for those four years, while only having a few unexcused absences from required prayers and public worship (chapel).[40] During his undergraduate years, he was also a member of the prestigious Delta Kappa Epsilon (DKE) Fraternity, a national collegiate fraternity founded at Yale University in 1844. Lord and his fraternity classmates strove to embody the mission of DKE to promote the development of "gentlemen, scholars and jolly good fellows."[41] Some of his class members served in the Civil War and returned to Bowdoin to complete their degrees with the class, although one was killed during the war.[42] An 1864 photo of Lord's class of 1866 shows him and some of his fraternity brothers posing on the steps of the college chapel. He also noted that his "winter vacations were spent in teaching."[43] This was likely to help pay for some of his college

Bowdoin class of 1866 in front of Bowdoin College Chapel, 1864. Lord is in the middle on the second-row step with a black top hat. (Courtesy of the George J. Mitchell Department of Special Collections & Archives, Bowdoin College Library, Brunswick, Maine.)

tuition in view of his father's meager annual pastoral salary as well as to prepare him for the teaching occupation that he "pursued for one year after graduation."

Lord graduated from Bowdoin in 1866, receiving his bachelor of arts degree at the commencement ceremonies held on Wednesday, August 1, 1866. Shortly thereafter, he secured a job as a principal of North Abington High School in Abington, Massachusetts, a position he would hold for only one year. Why he chose to go to that city for his first postgraduate job is unknown. Abington, an established town south of Boston, was officially founded in 1712. The area was first settled in 1668 as colonists ventured farther from the original Plymouth colony of 1620. By the 1860s, Abington had become a large manufacturing town for boots and shoes. Its high school principal position had experienced frequent turnover, as the predecessors had left for more prestigious positions in business or at other schools. After his formal interview and hiring, the town

George Edwin Lord, class of 1866, Bowdoin College. George Lord, back left. (Courtesy of the George J. Mitchell Department of Special Collections & Archives, Bowdoin College Library, Brunswick, Maine.)

council noted in its *Annual Report*, which included the *Annual Report of the School Committee*, that "the school found in him just the man it needed. The discipline has been mild and firm; the order good."[44] At some time during his year in Abington, Lord's brother, Thomas, apparently came to visit him while on military leave for a short period. During this visit, George and his brother built a miniature reproduction of Caesar's bridge, which was "one of the interesting features of the Historical Exhibit" on display at the Golden Anniversary reunion of the Abington High School Association on November 15, 1923.[45] At the close of the school year in the spring of 1867, George resigned as principal at North Abington, although no reason was cited in the school committee's *Annual Report*.[46]

George Edwin Lord, 1866, at North Abington High and Grammar Schools (Abington, Massachusetts). (Courtesy of Dyer Memorial Library & Archives, Abington, Massachusetts.)

During the year that George was overseeing the North Abington School District, his brother, Thomas, was serving as a second lieutenant in the U.S. Forty-Third Regiment, appointed on July 28, 1866, when the Veteran Reserve Corps was abolished earlier that year.[47] After being stationed at Richmond, Virginia, and passing an examination by the Army Board in New York City later that year in October, Thomas Lord was promoted to regimental adjutant, serving in that position from January 1, 1867, to April 8, 1869.[48] He was stationed at Fort Wayne in Detroit, Michigan, for the next two years from April 1867 to April 1869.[49] While there, he met his future wife, Mary Montgomery Eaton, daughter of a renowned Detroit philanthropist and businessman, Theodore Horatio Eaton, and they married on May 22, 1872.[50] While she and Thomas enjoyed a happy, albeit short eight-year marriage, as she died in 1880, George never experienced that type of bliss. He never married.

For unknown reasons, after resigning from his school principal job in Abington, George decided to make a career change and pursue a degree in medicine. After the summer, he "went to Chicago in the fall of '67 and commenced the study of medicine in the office of Hosmer A. Johnson, MD and attended lectures in the Chicago Medical College."[51] Another question that has puzzled historians while researching Lord's life pertains to why he decided to attend medical school in Chicago. He was certainly well familiar with his alma mater, Bowdoin College, having its own prestigious medical school during that era. The Medical School of Maine had been founded in 1821 by an "Act of the [Maine] Legislature" and "placed under the superintendence and direction of the Boards of Trustees and Overseers of Bowdoin College."[52] A new building, Adams Hall, had been constructed on the campus in 1861 to exclusively house all the departments of the medical school and the medical library, proclaimed by the school as "one of the best in the United States," with 3,550 volumes.[53] As an alumnus of good character and academic standing, Lord almost certainly could have gained admission there and remained in the east.

While no actual reason has been found that solves the mystery concerning the "why" of his decisions for a career change and Chicago instead of the Medical School of Maine, some reasonable explanations have been put forth. One theory is that he desired to be closer to his brother, Thomas, who was by this time stationed at Fort Wayne in Detroit, Michigan. While plausible, this might be questioned due to the distance between the two cities. As well, Detroit and nearby Ann Arbor had two medical schools, the Detroit Medical College and the University of Michigan Medical School, respectively.[54] Another possible reason suggested is a disappointment in romance, which Lord alluded to in a personal letter written some four years later, although the woman would remain unknown since he never revealed her name. Yet, one other possible reason may have been to simply get away from the Bowdoin community and the east, where he had been associated all his life, and to pursue a great new adventure out west. Whatever the reason, Lord went to Chicago in 1867 to study with Dr. Johnson, a renowned physician and surgeon and a cofounder of the Chicago Medical College, associated with Northwestern University.[55]

After relocating to Chicago and working with Dr. Johnson for over a year, Lord was awarded a master of arts degree from his alma mater, Bowdoin College, in 1869.[56] Postgraduate degrees at Bowdoin during this time were granted *pro merito*. In the third year after receiving their undergraduate degrees, students who preserved good moral character and paid a nominal fee to the treasurer for a diploma could request a master of arts degree. This requested degree, which did not involve a course of study, differed from the graduate program later established at Bowdoin in 1871 requiring a two-year course of study.[57]

Lord's mentor was an accomplished physician. In addition to his formal teaching duties at the medical school, Dr. Johnson, after having been a general surgeon, became one of the leading early laryngologists (a specialist in diseases of the throat and lungs) in the country while maintaining a general practice specializing in diseases of the chest. A graduate of Rush Medical College in Chicago and a faculty member there before the founding of the Chicago Medical College, he was involved in many local, state, and national organizations, including the Chicago Academy of Sciences (of which he was a cofounder), the Chicago Medical and Illinois State Medical societies, the American Medical Association, and the Chicago Historical Society. Dr. Johnson was also instrumental in helping to get legislation passed to legalize anatomical dissection for medical school education.[58] Overall, he was a highly respected gentleman described as "a magnificent man, possessing a clear, trenchant intellect and a great, noble heart. His reputation is without spot, and his honor without stain."[59] As a practicing physician he was described as being "clear-headed and kind-hearted" and having "that quickness of perception and sound judgment with that gentleness of manner and chasteness of expression."[60] Certainly, George Lord was fortunate to have such a revered and talented physician as Dr. Johnson for one of his instructors and preceptors during his years at the medical school.

The Chicago Medical College was originally established as a medical department for Lind University (today known as Lake Forest College in Lake Forest, Illinois, just north of Chicago) in 1859 by Dr. Johnson, Dr. Edmund Andrews, Dr. Ralph N. Isham, and Dr. David Rutter, who soon invited two colleagues, Dr. Nathan S. Davis and Dr. William H. Byford, to join them. All were prominent Chicago physicians who had been or were faculty members of Rush Medical College in Chicago and who had grown dissatisfied with the medical education system at their former school.[61] The name was changed to Chicago Medical College in 1863 when it reorganized after Lind University experienced financial difficulties in supporting the department. In 1870, the medical school affiliated with Northwestern University to serve as the university's medical department (although retaining its autonomy) and a new, ornate medical building for classrooms, laboratories, and administrative offices was constructed next to Mercy Hospital at the corner of Twenty-Sixth Street and Prairie Avenue in Chicago.[62] The school's name officially changed to Northwestern University Medical School in 1906 and currently is known as the Northwestern University Feinberg School of Medicine.[63]

During this time in the nineteenth century, a plethora of medical schools were appearing throughout the country. Many, unfortunately, were fraudulent financial schemes, often more commonly referred to as "diploma mills."[64] Yet, even among the legitimate medical schools, standards and regulations of education were sorely lacking. Medical school semesters or terms varied among institutions—either twelve or sixteen weeks with four to six daily lectures in each of the two required terms.[65] In addition, most medical schools, including Rush and the Chicago Medical College from their beginnings, and even the Medical School of Maine, required students to have three years of professional study "under the direction of a regular Practitioner of Medicine."[66] This preceptorship, which included the two full terms of formal curriculum, was usually started before enrolling in the school, but some students did this during and after the formal course sessions. After reforms in medical education eventually commenced by the Chicago Medical College, this clinical preceptorship was incorporated over a student's entire medical school career. Candidates who had a documented record of attendance, fulfillment of the clinical requirement, passing grades on the final examinations, and a final thesis presentation on some medical subject ("written by himself") were awarded their diplomas—after remittance of a fee.[67] For example, at the Medical School of Maine at Bowdoin College, "the Graduation fee, including an engraved Diploma on Parchment" was twenty dollars, the same as Chicago Medical College's fee, although the latter was noted to be an overcharged diploma since those "cost $1.55, including engrossing."[68]

Due to these concerns about the wide variance and longtime lack of standard regulations in the oversight of medical education, administrators and faculty members of medical schools, state legislatures, and national organizations across the country began to propose and implement reforms, although they had been attempting to accomplish this over the prior two decades.[69] Dr. Johnson, along with his cofounder colleagues (especially Dr. Davis, one of the founders of the American Medical Association) and other faculty members at the Chicago Medical College, were among top scholarly leaders and innovators in the country, and with organizations such as the American Medical Association, they advocated for and instituted higher educational standards for the medical profession. As a result, significant changes were implemented, which included the requirements for a medical degree being changed from two years to three in 1868. The Chicago Medical College was the first medical school in the country to do so, and it also increased lecture sessions from five to six months with a graded system and instituted attendance at hospital instruction for at least two of the terms (instead of one as it had done previously).[70] Other medical schools would implement the same reforms over the next three years, including, in 1871, Harvard Medical School, where Lord's eventual Little Big Horn fellow physician James DeWolf graduated in 1875. The Detroit Medical College increased the duration of its medical lecture terms from four to five months in 1872.[71] Although the three-year requirement was approved in 1869 at the Chicago college, the implementation of that specific change was a transitional one due to the logistics regarding scheduling. As such, the first couple of years thereafter, students were given the option to graduate in two years, which George Lord chose to do.

During Lord's official time at the Chicago Medical College, class enrollment his first year in 1869 was seventy-two students, down slightly due to the decision to change the degree requirement to three years. The total number increased in 1870 to 107 students.[72] Similar to the Medical School of Maine and other medical colleges, the annual lecture term was divided into sessions, although as part of the new changes at Chicago, these annual sessions were divided into three sessions instead of two. The first group (session), referred to as the "junior course," included lectures in the medical sciences, such as anatomy and physiology, materia medica, inorganic chemistry, and dissection. The second group, the "middle course," encompassed subjects such as surgery (including surgical anatomy), orthopedic surgery, organic chemistry, pharmacology (then referred to as toxicology), hygiene, medical jurisprudence, and clinical instruction in the hospital. The third group, known as the "senior course," included Principles and Practice of Medicine, Principles and Practice of Surgery and Military Surgery, Obstetrics and Diseases of Women and Children, Diseases of the Respiratory and Circulatory Organs, and Clinical Instruction in the Hospital (i.e., clinical medicine and surgery in the hospital).[73] Candidates were examined either daily or weekly on these varied subjects.

The annual lecture term ran from October to March. Additionally, there was a "summer reading and clinical term" from April until the first week of July. The official medical school year totaled nine months.[74] The summer course included two lectures on some of the previous named subjects from the regular winter term, plus one clinic every day. The dissecting room was available as desired by the students. The cost of attendance for the several courses of lectures at Chicago in 1869 was a total of $50 for both, although a $5 matriculation fee and anatomy demonstrator's fee of $5 was charged for the first-year students and a $6 hospital fee was required for those taking the senior lectures. This compared favorably to the "$70 for the year and a Matriculation or Library fee of $5 payable for each course" at the Medical School of Maine.[75] The cost of room and board in Chicago after the Civil War had risen appreciably, and for board and lodging provided by the medical school, the students were informed that it "will probably average $5.00 a week." Those who otherwise desired to obtain living arrangements themselves in the city faced prices varying from six to ten dollars a month.[76] Some students worked in between medical terms to earn money to pay for the cost of their education. Even Lord's preceptor, Dr. Johnson, had taught part time for this purpose at a local school during his own medical college years. No information has been found to indicate if Lord had to do the same during his Chicago years as he did during his undergraduate time at Bowdoin College, although reasonable speculation suggests that he probably did not need to do so since he likely may have had enough money saved from his time of employment at the North Abington High School back in Massachusetts.

There were many and varied medical textbooks available in America, all of which were acceptable standard texts during this era. Each medical school, of course, had its own recommended, preferred, and required lists of textbooks for the curriculum. Students were provided with a list of the suggested textbooks to purchase on their own. They could also check out the books at their medical school library, although, of course, that potentially presented logistical problems for the students. At the Chicago Medical College, Lord studied textbooks chosen from the list in the school catalog provided by Dr. Edmund Andrews, professor of surgery and corresponding secretary of the college faculty, which included such titles as Flint's *Principles and Practice of Medicine*, Gray's *Anatomy* (still in use today), Gross's *Surgery*, Virchow's *Cellular Pathology*, Wood's *Pharmacology or Materia Medica*, Dalton's *Human Physiology*, and Chicago Medical College faculty member William H. Byford's *Obstetrics* and *Medicine and Surgery of Women*.[77] As an example of the variance and leeway of multiple accepted medical books allowed at the different medical schools, several of these medical treatises were different from Harvard Medical School's recommended textbooks that James DeWolf used while a student there, such as Billroth's *General Surgical Pathology* and Huxley's *Lessons in Elementary Physiology*.[78]

Lord attended classes at Chicago Medical College's new building, constructed in 1870 next to Mercy Hospital. The building was substantial compared to some of those at other medical colleges. It contained two large lecture halls seating 240 and 260 students, the usual dissecting rooms and laboratories, a museum for anatomical and pathological specimens, a library and reading room, and examination rooms for patients seen in the free dispensary clinic.[79] The clinic was operated by the hospital under the direction of faculty physicians, and it could be observed by the medical students. Mercy Hospital had been associated with the medical school since its beginning, providing additional clinical instruction opportunities for the students under the supervision of faculty physicians and other community physicians who served as preceptors for the students. The hospital building was located at the corner of Calumet Avenue and Twenty-Sixth Street next to the college's new medical building and had beds for one thousand patients. Its three departments were headed by faculty physicians of the medical college. Dr. Davis and Dr. Johnson oversaw the medical department, Dr. Andrews, the surgical department, and Dr. Byford, the Lying-In and Gynaecology Department.[80] Students, especially those of the

Hosmer Allen Johnson, MD. (Courtesy of Galter Health Sciences Library & Learning Center, Northwestern University Feinberg School of Medicine, Chicago, Illinois.)

Edmund Andrews, MD. (Courtesy of Galter Health Sciences Library & Learning Center, Northwestern University Feinberg School of Medicine, Chicago, Illinois.)

senior class, had the opportunity to observe operations performed by the surgical faculty members, the surgeries being provided free of charge to the poor in the community. These clinical opportunities at Mercy Hospital and the college's dispensary were available one hour each day, four days per week, and were required for students during the junior and senior lecture sessions, in addition to one of the summer sessions required for graduation.

An interesting side note is that among the 107 students at the college in Lord's senior year, one of his classmates was Elbert Judson Clark. Clark, a native of New York, lived in nearby Rockford, Illinois. During their medical school years, while Lord had Dr. Johnson as his preceptor, Clark's assigned preceptor was Dr. Isham of the surgery and anatomy departments.[81] After graduating together in 1871, they would go separate ways. Clark went on to become a civilian physician for the U.S. Army, initially at the Cheyenne River Indian Agency post in Dakota. Lord and Clark probably never imagined their lives would cross paths again. However, both

Chicago Medical College building, 1870. (Courtesy of Galter Health Sciences Library & Learning Center, Northwestern University Feinberg School of Medicine, Chicago, Illinois.)

eventually became physician colleagues very briefly in the spring of 1876 in the early stages of the Great Sioux War at the start of the Little Big Horn campaign. As Lord left with Custer in mid-June for what would be the final trek of that campaign, Clark was reassigned to the Yellowstone supply depot, which spared him from the disaster that lay in the wind. He later returned to private practice in Winnebago, Illinois, from the 1880s through 1900 before he and his wife moved to Cleveland, Ohio. He died there in 1921, having had the good fortune of avoiding a fatal or devastating wound from either an arrowhead or bullet during his medical service in the army.[82]

As the reforms for improvement in medical education occurred at Chicago Medical College, successful navigation through the

Mercy Hospital, Chicago, Illinois, circa 1880s, from the *Northwestern University, Medical School, Chicago Medical College, Chicago, Ill. Circular of Information, for 1892–93*. (Courtesy of Galter Health Sciences Library & Learning Center, Northwestern University Feinberg School of Medicine, Chicago, Illinois.)

required medical school schedule was not easy, and that holds true at medical schools across the country today. As stated in the college's catalog, its system had a "comprehensiveness . . . a systematic order of progress, favorable alike to thorough acquisition of knowledge and desirable mental discipline," and all of these attributes were complemented by the daily hospital clinical instruction.[83] Although the new and expanded curriculum was difficult and challenging, George Lord was intellectually well prepared by the rigorous curriculums he experienced at the Lewiston Falls Academy and Bowdoin College. Lord was also fortunate to receive his medical training at one of the best medical schools in the country at the time and from faculty physicians (such as his clinical preceptor, Dr. Johnson) who were among the top leaders and innovators in improving standards in medical education and providing the best-trained physicians. Lord's determination and perseverance paid off. Having successfully completed the requirements for graduation, Lord received his

Elbert Judson Clark, MD, acting assistant surgeon, U.S. Army. Photograph by A. S. Atchley, 1871, Rockford, Illinois. (Courtesy of Dr. Doug Arbittier, American Civil War Medicine & Surgical Antiques, York, Pennsylvania.)

medical degree from the Chicago Medical College in March 1871 after the regular annual lecture term ended and after serving as a house physician at Mercy Hospital during the later portion of the term. He had chosen the option of finishing his training in two years instead of three during the college's new curriculum reform transitional period.

Prior to his last term at medical school, George decided to pursue a medical career in the military instead of entering private practice on his own. He applied for a position as a contract surgeon in the U.S. Army. Reasons as to why Lord opted for a military career are not known and create another puzzle for historians. Author and historian C. Lee Noyes has previously offered two possible explanations, one being the aforementioned disappointment in romance, and the other, again, being Lord's possible desire to be closer to his brother, Thomas.[84] Thomas had transferred from Fort Wayne in Detroit to Fort Snelling in St. Paul, Minnesota, after being assigned to the Twentieth Regiment and appointed regimental quartermaster in April 1871.[85] This latter reason seems likely, at least in part, because George had "respectfully" requested in his application letter to Major John Frasier Head, the medical director for the Department of Dakota in St. Paul, for a "detail with a detachment of troops on the Northern Pacific Road if practicable."[86] Whatever his reasons, George Lord would soon embark on a new medical career out west.

In the early 1870s, the army employed 175 civilian contract surgeons to help alleviate the shortage of medical officers to cover the 217 posts in the southern and western departments (by 1874 the number of forts had increased to 239), as only 161 surgeons or assistant surgeons existed for the entire military, despite the official authorized number being 222.[87] These contract surgeons were given the title of "acting assistant surgeon." While not entitled to wear army uniforms, they were considered part of the official army medical staff, and by army regulations they were to "receive . . . the fuel and quarters of an assistant surgeon of the rank of first lieutenant, and actual traveling expenses when traveling under orders and not with troops."[88] Having decided on this new career, Lord submitted his application to Major Head in early January. Although he was in the process of completing his last school term, he had done well in medical school and received a complete endorsement from his mentor and preceptor, Dr. Hosmer Johnson, and the other physicians he had trained under at the Chicago college and Mercy Hospital. In letters of recommendation submitted with the application to Major Head, these professors wrote highly of Lord regarding his character and skills and afforded pleasure in recommending him for the army position. Dr. Johnson, professor of diseases of the chest, wrote in his December 28, 1870, letter: "I have been personally acquainted with Dr. George E. Lord for the last three years and take pleasure in testifying to his good moral character and to his excellent literary and professional attainments. Dr. Lord has served with credit to himself and usefulness to the institution as house physician in the Mercy Hospital of this city. I have no hesitation in recommending him to the confidence of the public."[89]

Dr. Edmund Andrews, professor of surgery (and surgeon of the First Illinois Light Artillery) at the Chicago Medical College, wrote similarly: "This is to state that I am personally acquainted with Dr. George E. Lord, and that I consider him much superior to the average of physicians, both on account of his personal character, and the excellence of his medical education. I cheerfully recommend him for a contract surgeon in the Army."[90]

Likewise, Dr. Nathan S. Davis, professor of practical medicine, attested to Lord's "faithful discharge of his duties . . . being very thoroughly educated in all departments of the profession" and highlighted his "character for integrity, uprightness and industry as being very good," while Dr. William H. Buford, professor of obstetrics and diseases of women and children, noted Lord had "passed his professional studies on a creditable and regular manner" and described him as being a "young man of exemplary character in every respect."[91]

Soon after his graduation, George traveled to St. Paul, Minnesota, and undoubtedly visited his brother, now a lieutenant in the Twentieth Regiment, who was stationed at Fort Snelling as post quartermaster. Having submitted a required duplicate application letter to the army's surgeon general in Washington, D.C., in early April, Lord was informed that he was accepted for the army position and he signed a standard contract for civilian physicians on April 27, 1871. The position offered the pay of $100 per month.[92] Lord likely requested an assignment to a post in the same region as his brother, Thomas. Two days later, he was initially assigned for temporary duty at Fort Ripley, Minnesota, Department of Dakota, in conformance with Special Order No. 90, April 29, 1871, per Department of Dakota headquarters in St. Paul, in place of Assistant Surgeon Charles Knickerbacker Winne,[93] who took advantage of an authorized leave of absence.[94]

At age twenty-five, highly educated and with some valuable experience in service to the public through his previous teaching and medical house positions, George Lord was now ready to take on the next great adventure of his life.

CHAPTER 2

Dakota Territory and Beyond

TO HIS PERSONAL AND SOCIAL FITNESS FOR A MISSION
IN OUR CORPS—TO HIS ZEAL, ACCURACY, AND EFFICIENCY
AS AN ACT[ING] MEDICAL OFFICER— . . .
HE IS ONE OF THE RIGHT SORT.
*Dr. James F. Head, medical director, Department of Dakota,
to Dr. Joseph B. Brown, president, Army Medical Board,
New York City, January 9, 1875*

FORT RIPLEY was located about 121 miles northwest of St. Paul.[1] The fort had been built in 1848–49 on the west bank of the Mississippi River in central Minnesota to maintain peace around the newly established Winnebago (Ho-Chunk) Indian Reservation, where that tribe had been relocated to, and the region's indigenous Dakota (Sioux) and Ojibwe (Chippewa) Indians. The post later served as a refuge for displaced settler's families and a staging place for troops during several Indian outbreaks in the late 1850s and, particularly, the Dakota Sioux Uprising of 1862 in southwestern and central Minnesota.

Fort Ripley's importance as a military post was nearing its end by the time Lord received his initial assignment there in 1871, as the frontier conflicts with the Indians had since moved farther west. However, while further settlements in the outlying region had developed, the area was still an extensive wilderness. Distance between farms encompassed several miles and the journey to the fort from the fast-growing metropolis of St. Paul was a long, arduous one. A vivid description of Fort Ripley appeared in the *War*

Department Circular No. 4, A Report on Barracks and Hospitals, with Descriptions of Military Posts from 1870. The colorful depiction described the surrounding terrain:

> Fort Ripley is situated . . . upon the west bank of the Mississippi, elevated 20 feet above that river. . . . The post is built upon a sandy plateau, partially drained by shallow ravines . . . gradually sloping toward a narrow swamp about half a mile in rear of the fort. Beyond this is a range of thickly-wooded hills, rising to a height of 100 or 150 feet, which slightly shelter the post from the northwest winds of winter. . . . Above and below the fort the river is skirted by a narrow belt of swampy land, usually partially inundated in spring, supporting a growth of linden or basswood, elms, maple, and birch . . . with pine and poplar on the higher grounds. . . . On the east side of the Mississippi (here about 180 yards wide) a gently undulating, sandy, and barren prairie, from a few hundred yards to three miles wide, extends . . . southward.[2]

Prior to the fort's construction in 1848, heavy pine forests in the region had been logged and what remained was later ravaged by a series of forest fires. This resulted in scattered areas being enveloped with new pine, oak, and birch forest growth.

Outlying areas beyond were interrupted by farmlands that had been plowed as white immigrants continued to infiltrate the region, and settlements developed during the 1850s and 1860s along the Woods Trail leading northwest to the Red River region in Manitoba. Old Crow Wing, the site of a longtime eighteenth-century Ojibwe village and meeting place, which later became a European-American trading post, town, location of a Catholic mission, and county seat, was located about seven miles north of Fort Ripley at the confluence of the Crow Wing and Mississippi rivers.[3] The short-lived town had travelers and a growing multicultural community of Ojibwe, French Canadian, and American farming families. However, due to the combination of the U.S. government's 1868 relocation of the Ojibwes to a reservation farther north at Leech Lake, and the Northern Pacific Railroad bypassing the town area, Crow Wing was in decline by the time Lord came to Fort Ripley and was essentially abandoned by the late 1870s.

Despite the hostilities between settlers and several bands of eastern Sioux Indians during the recent Dakota Sioux War in southwest and central Minnesota and the simultaneously occurring Civil War, life at the post thereafter was quite mundane, with its geographic isolation, summer mosquitos, and severe winters being equal contributors. Luckily for Acting Assistant Surgeon George Lord, his first official assignment was designated as temporary at this post and ended up being shorter than he probably even imagined. As troops from the garrison assisted in distribution of supplies and payments each year at two nearby government Indian agencies, Lord was rather immediately detached on May 1, 1871, under the command of Lieutenant John A. Manley[4] of the Twentieth Regiment, to the Crow Wing Agency for the Chippewa (Ojibwe) tribe at Leech Lake, Minnesota.[5]

Soon, Lord was assigned to the military post at the Whetstone Indian Agency in Dakota Territory (present-day South Dakota), succeeding the contract surgeon at the agency, per Special Order No. 136 dated June 26, 1871, and he began duty in early July.[6] He remained at the Whetstone post for the next ten months. The original Whetstone Agency near Whetstone Creek, one of the Indian agencies established from an accord of the 1868 Fort Laramie Treaty, had been moved to the west bank of the Missouri River in 1869 during the closure of the North Platte River Agency in Nebraska. That treaty was signed at the conclusion of Red Cloud's War (1866–68), a bloodbath that occurred in the Powder River region of Wyoming Territory, a result of the encroachment of settlers on Sioux (Lakota) lands and the construction of the Union Pacific railroad. Treaty stipulations included abandonment of army posts along the Bozeman Trail in Wyoming and Montana Territories, and creation of the Great Sioux Reservation, consisting of twenty-five million acres, including the Black Hills in Dakota Territory. It also provided for the establishment of an agency system for the issuance of necessities such as food, clothing, and blankets, and the introduction of education and Christianity, all in an effort to transition the Sioux from hunters to agriculturalists, a process of "civilizing the Indians," as most government officials saw it.[7] The agencies were supervised by an Indian agent, a civilian appointed by the U.S. government to oversee the assimilation of the Indians to this American way of life and the distribution of the various amenities.

The Whetstone Agency was located thirty miles north of Fort Randall and served Brulé Sioux bands led by Swift Bear and Spotted Tail, who were relocated to the environs of the agency.[8] Fort Randall was the base of supplies for the agency, and it provided troops when needed for policing unscrupulous or rowdy local traders and for protection of settlers and travelers from the Indians. In addition to standard agency buildings (school, commissary, blacksmith shop, and sawmill), a military post with its usual structures for garrison use (quarters, guardhouse, magazine, stables, and storehouses) was constructed in 1870 for the protection of the agency.[9] A hospital was also built at the Whetstone military post, where Acting Assistant Surgeon George Lord had his quarters and attended the garrison, the lone Company D, Twenty-Second Infantry.[10]

Prior to Lord's service as Whetstone's post surgeon, seemingly ceaseless problems at the agency arose, including a lack of supplies for the Indians, poor soils in the area for farming, lumbering depletion of river bottom land, excessive river traffic, and the influx of an unsavory white population, all of which eventually led to the relocation of the agency westward in the spring of 1871.[11] Although the agency was moved to Big White Clay in the southwestern portion of the Pine Ridge Reservation in Nebraska, the Whetstone military post remained at the Missouri River location as the base of supplies and military protection for the new agency. However, that arrangement proved unfeasible, in part, due to the old agency storage buildings for the supplies having been gradually destroyed by settlers in the region. As a result, in the spring of 1872, the military post was abandoned, with the troops and agency support operations relocated back to Fort Randall.[12] When this occurred, Lord was reassigned to Fort Randall as the post surgeon, replacing contract surgeon J. Ottinger Boughten, who was transferred to the new post at the Northern Pacific Railroad crossing of the Missouri River.[13]

Fort Randall had been established in 1856 by the army to afford protection for settlers moving into the Nebraska and Dakota Territories

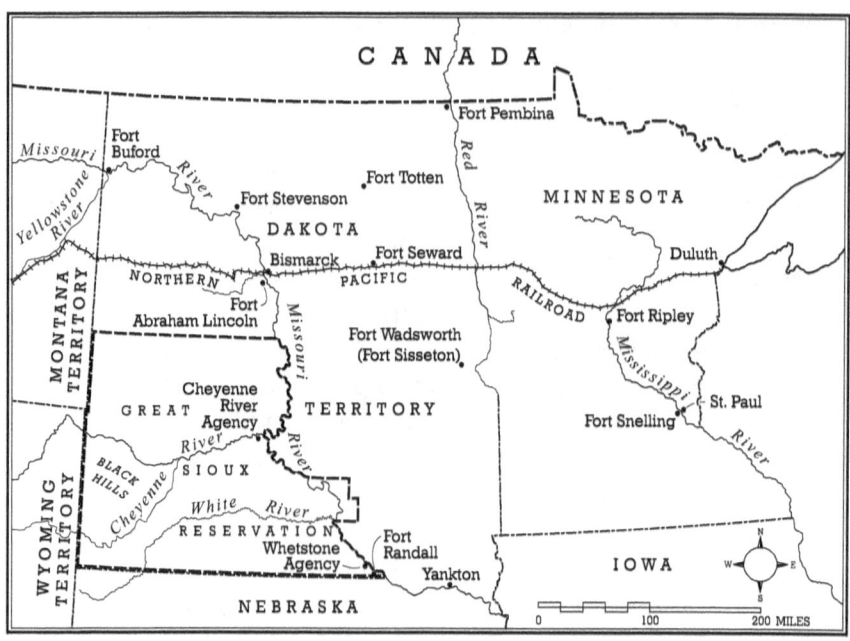

George Lord in the West, 1871–1876. (Prepared for Todd E. Harburn, Cartography by Robert Pilk.)

prior to the Civil War.[14] Following the conclusion of the Dakota War of 1862 and as permanent settlement pushed farther west, encroaching on Sioux lands, Fort Randall eventually became one of the major steamboat stopovers and staging areas for supplying military posts and Indian agencies, including the Yankton Agency in Dakota Territory (present-day South Dakota) and the Ponca Indian Agency in the Territory of Nebraska. Its location was seventy-five miles beyond Yankton and some 1,288 miles from St. Louis, the main source of goods and supplies.[15] A large sprawling post, the fort was originally constructed of logs using local cottonwood trees. An ingenious pipeline system supplied water from the Missouri River, a half mile distant, to the post. Some 12,000 gallons of water could be delivered daily using a two-inch suction pipe narrowing into a smaller pipe system, thus eliminating the need for wells inside the post proper.

By the time of Lord's transfer to Fort Randall, a major renovation of the fort's buildings was nearing completion. The original log structures had deteriorated and were progressively replaced over a two-year period from 1870 to 1872 with wooden framed buildings. Lord and his medical colleagues were immediately able to enjoy an entirely new post hospital, constructed in 1872 to replace the earlier dilapidated log building near the same site. The new structure was built according to a regulation U.S. Army Medical Department design for hospitals, with the "exception of having one wing omitted."[16] Built on a four-foot-thick stone foundation, it contained a single ventilating fireplace, wood-burning box-stoves, and an eight-foot-wide veranda.

Arriving at the post on May 27, 1872, Dr. Lord would serve at Fort Randall as a contract physician for the next seventeen months, enjoying a mere thirty-day leave of absence in the fall of 1872 during that period. The post commander, Lieutenant Colonel Elwell S. Otis,[17] oversaw five companies (B, D, G, H, and K) of the Twenty-Second Infantry. Over the year and a half that Lord was at Randall, he served in the head administrative position as post surgeon for three months from June to August 1872. For the remaining months he served as an assistant post surgeon to two other army doctors, the brilliant but somewhat eccentric ornithologist/naturalist and historian Elliott Coues[18] and James F. Weeds,[19] both captains.

When Coues was assigned as post surgeon at Fort Randall and arrived in October 1872, Lord's primary duties focused on tending the troops. The winter of 1872–73 was a hard one due to severe cold and heavy snows. When not attending to the needs of the post's hospital patients, evening activities helped pass the time. The medical and other garrison officers enjoyed playing poker. Just how good a poker player Lord was is not known, although Coues mentioned that Captain John Hartley[20] of the Twenty-Second Infantry at the post was the "best poker player he ever faced!"[21] For other evenings during that extremely harsh winter, "just going to bed to keep warm" was the activity in order, such as when the "post was almost buried under the snow we had in April," as Coues later mentioned.[22] In early May, Dr. Coues received assignment as medical officer and naturalist for the boundary commission, intending to survey the northern boundary in the eastern regions of the Red River of the Dakota-Manitoba border between Canada and the United States. In addition to his medical duties, this provided Coues an opportunity to expand on his observations and publications on North American bird species, which later established him as a leader in the field of American ornithology. He and Lord would serve together again when Lord was transferred to the medical staff of the same expedition in 1874, when the Northern Boundary Survey had moved farther west into the northern plains of the continent. George Lord appears to have made a good impression on his superior while at Fort Randall and on the subsequent survey mission, as Coues later wrote a letter of recommendation for him in his application before the Army Medical Board for an examination as an assistant surgeon in the army.

That he had decided on a medical career in the army after his graduation from medical school is further supported by the fact that as early as August 1872 George made inquiry to his superiors for this consideration. His brother, Thomas, then serving as a first lieutenant and regimental quartermaster in the Twentieth Infantry at Fort Snelling, had sent a letter on George's behalf to Department of Dakota medical director Major John Head expressing his brother's "wishes to attend medical lectures with view to exam for Assist. Surgeon and ask whether he could be assigned to duty in New York or Chicago."[23] However, due to the army's attempt to trim expenses in the years following the Civil War, and the overabundance of both civilian and military medical officers that had been accrued during that time to serve various assignments, the government imposed a moratorium on appointment of new army surgeons and assistant surgeons. Thomas Lord was initially informed that "no duty either in Chicago or New York City was available to which [his brother] could be assigned to."[24] George eventually received a personal reply several months later from Assistant Surgeon General Charles H. Crane in March 1873 informing him that "no Army Medical Examining Boards will be convened until the law (act approved March 3, 1869) prohibiting new appointments and promotions in the several Staff levels of the Army is repealed" but that his "application will be placed on file for future reference when a Board for the examination of candidates is convened."[25] No doubt Lord was disappointed in receiving this discouraging news, yet he would continue in his current civilian contract and his goal of pursuing an eventual regular army medical officer appointment.

One additional aspect to be noted regarding Lord's and Coues's concurrent time at Fort Randall, is that Coues spent most of the time concentrating on his self-centered interests of ornithology and wildlife collecting and writing. As such, Lord was the one who ended up performing the actual tasks of attending to the patients, although as post surgeon, Coues was responsible for writing the official medical record.[26] Coues even shamelessly admitted the same in a letter by noting that "I have an assistant surgeon to do pretty much all the [medical] work, and so my time is all my own."[27]

During the 1872–73 year, Lord and his medical colleagues encountered a much lesser volume of illnesses and diseases among the 206 enlisted men and officers of the garrison as compared to the preceding two years at the post. The official statistics for Randall for that period list only one case of typhoid fever, four cases of rheumatism,

Fort Randall Hospital, 1870s. (Courtesy of National Library of Medicine.)

Elliott Coues, MD, about age fifty, circa 1892. (Courtesy of National Library of Medicine, B05425.)

only one case of venereal disease (syphilis), no cases of consumption (tuberculosis), only ten cases of diarrhea and dysentery, with the majority of cases being minor catarrh (colds) and bronchitis (fifty-four), and twenty-eight "other accidents and injuries," including only one gunshot wound.[28]

Lord stayed on duty at Fort Randall for the remainder of the year until his contract was annulled at his request on November 6, 1873, with Major Head noting to the surgeon general that Lord's "character and efficiency as an Acting Assistant Surgeon have been very good."[29] Why Lord chose to resign at this time is not clear. He did not provide any hint, nor is there any surviving correspondence that provides any clues. As such, his reasons are left to conjecture. If he simply desired a temporary break from the varied yet extensive daily duties as post surgeon, he could have requested a leave of absence. Or he may have desired an extended visit back east to spend time with family. Regardless of his intentions, what is known is that George did spend time at home in Limerick, Maine, where his adopted family was residing at the time, his father Reverend Lord being the pastor at the local Congregational church. After spending nearly three months in the east, Lord still had intentions of seeking a formal army surgeon appointment. He requested and was offered a new contract as a civilian physician with the army, signing that on May 22, 1874.[30] Enclosed with the contract was the order to proceed without delay to St. Paul, Minnesota, and report to the medical director at Department of Dakota headquarters for assignment to duty.[31] As his brother, Thomas, was still stationed at Fort Snelling, it is likely that George visited him there. He also quickly resubmitted his application to the surgeon general and secretary of war for an invitation to appear before the Army Medical Examining Board. He received acknowledgment from Assistant Surgeon General Crane a week later that, again, his application had been placed on file for future action when the next board for examination of candidates was convened.[32] After arriving in St. Paul and reporting at Fort Snelling, he received notice of an assignment for duty with the escort to the Northern Boundary Survey Commission.[33]

The Northern Boundary Survey Commission was assigned the task of surveying and establishing the northern boundary between Canada and the United States along the forty-ninth parallel, as authorized by an act of Congress on March 19, 1872.[34] The boundary of the eastern region between Canada and the United States from the Atlantic coast to the northwest angle of the Lake of the Woods in northern Minnesota had been previously surveyed. However, the specific boundary of the mid-region from the northwest angle of Lake of the Woods westward to the Rocky Mountains had not been determined, and the former had even been in question as to the exact coordinates along the forty-ninth parallel.[35] An act of Congress authorized President Ulysses S. Grant to work with the British government in establishing a joint commission (the North American Boundary Commission) to undertake and complete the survey, and each government appointed a head commissioner and military engineers for their respective surveys.[36] Congress initially appropriated $50,000 for the first year, although this was viewed by commission members as "insufficient for a vigorous and economical prosecution of the work, particularly during the first year, as many purchases had to be made for an outfit."[37] Similar to the Northern Pacific Railroad Yellowstone surveys of 1871–73, the Northern Boundary Survey would be a three-year project and cover some 860 miles of rugged yet beautiful plains country. In addition, U.S. Army military escorts were assigned to accompany the expedition each year to provide protection from any potential attacks or harassment by the various Indian tribes in each region.

The first year of the survey played out from the middle of September to late November 1872, with Captain Abram A. Harbach[38] and Company K, Twentieth Infantry, from Fort Pembina[39] being assigned as the military escort.[40] Despite the short surveying season that closed at the onset of extreme cold weather, the first year's objective of establishing the true location of the forty-ninth parallel at an astronomical station marked on the western bank of the Red River was accomplished. Wagons and remaining supplies overwintered at Fort Abercrombie[41] and the U.S. commissioner and engineers wintered in Detroit, Michigan, where they had chosen to locate their office between the summer survey seasons.[42] The British commissioner and his staff located their winter quarters just north of Pembina.[43]

The second season for the boundary survey in 1873 had a considerably earlier start than the previous year, commencing in June at the preceding year's ending location at Lake of the Woods. The survey parties extended the boundary line westward past the Red River Valley and Mouse River to the western edge of Turtle Mountain in northern Dakota Territory. Operations ended in late October.[44] The boundary line was marked at intervals of one mile in this region, and later about every three miles in the regions farther west. Both the U.S. and British survey commissions agreed to make topographical map surveys five miles in width on their respective sides of the line.[45] Army engineer Captain William J. Twining had assumed the position of chief astronomer, as Captain Francis U. Farquhar had returned to his regular engineering duties back east in the St. Paul and Upper Mississippi region, per his request.

Dakota Territory and Beyond

Oversight of the military escort for 1873 had been assigned to Major Marcus Reno of the Seventh Cavalry and consisted of Companies D and I of that regiment and, again, Captain Harbach and his Twentieth Infantry company.[46] The season's work was curtailed by a massive snowstorm in late September, with the snow falling "to the depth of ten inches," although not before having completed the intended objective of surveying nearly four hundred miles. By early October, the military escort returned south to the designated winter quarters at Fort Totten at Devil's Lake in today's North Dakota, while the U.S. Survey commission party again returned to its winter offices in Detroit.[47] The British commissioners again spent the winter months at their offices at Fort Dufferin in Manitoba.[48] Although the Northern Assiniboine and Sioux inhabited these regions, no hostile encounters with Indians occurred for the U.S. troops and survey party during the season, unlike those occurring at the same time farther west in Montana Territory.[49] However, such was not the case for their thirty-five British counterparts as their survey party scouts, who were "50 miles in advance [of the American party and] were attacked by Indians in Turtle Mountain" on July 21, or so it was reported by the *Chicago Tribune* after receiving a letter from the American Party of the Northern Survey.[50]

The final year of the northern survey commenced in early June 1874. Major Reno was again given command of the overall military escort, employing Companies D and I, Seventh Cavalry in overseeing the safety of the survey and engineering staffs. For this survey, the lone Twentieth Infantry company was replaced with several companies of Sixth Infantry, per Special Orders 103 and 110, Department of Dakota.[51] The latter were stationed at Fort Buford, Dakota Territory, which had been designated as one of the bases for supplies, the other being Fort Benton, Montana Territory. Both bases were south of the region to be surveyed this year, which extended into Montana Territory and westward to the edge of the Rocky Mountains.[52]

When George Lord received his notice of assignment for duty with the escort in this final season of the survey, he was chosen as a solution to a problem. That problem was an extremely caustic quarrel

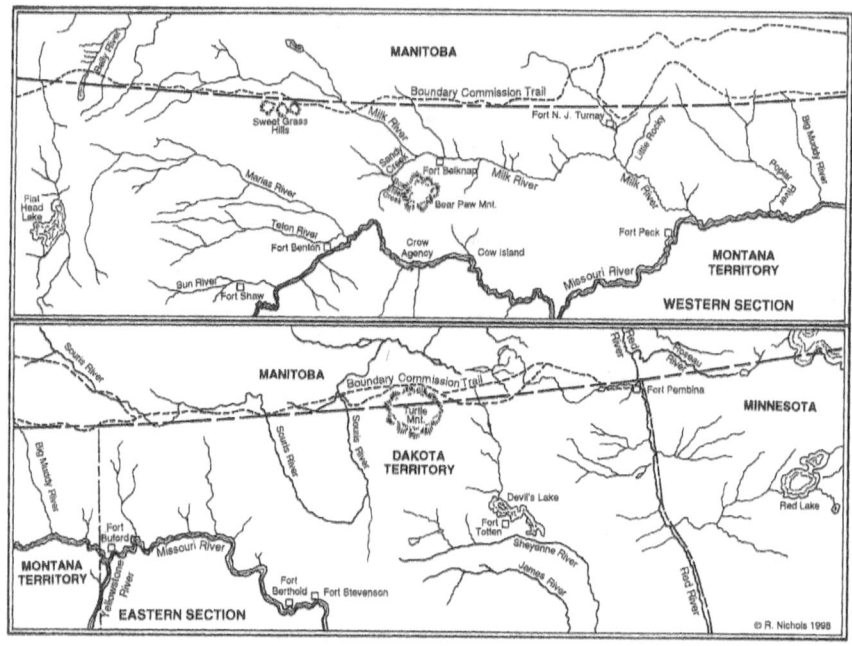

Northern Boundary Survey Commission, 1873–1874. (Courtesy of Ron Nichols and University of Oklahoma Press.)

between Major Reno and Francis O. Nash,[53] a civilian contract surgeon who had served as the medical officer for the military escort during the prior year. The antagonistic situation between the two began Wednesday, June 5, 1873, when they departed St. Paul by train via the St. Paul & Pacific Railroad to Breckinridge, Minnesota, en route to Fort Abercrombie to join the troops for the field.[54] Reno asserted in a letter to the department's assistant adjutant general, Oliver D. Greene, that the doctor had "reported for duty in the costume unbecoming a gentleman and without having made any provision as to his support during the summer" as well as chastising Nash for the reports in the St. Paul/Minneapolis newspapers that had "detailed disgraceful conduct on his part at his hotel . . . his bruised face gave every confirmation of it as a fact."[55] The latter incident referred to by Reno was described in the *Minneapolis Daily*

Tribune on June 6, 1873, the day after their departure in somewhat amusing account: "One of the medical staff of the Northwestern Boundary expedition undertook to bilk the landlord of the Merchants' Hotel this morning, and started down stairs with his baggage. He got reduced to his last shilling when landlord Schilling knocked him down. Our reporter applied for particulars but the *attaches* of the Merchants' were reticent."[56]

The personal dislike between Reno and Nash developed at a rapid crescendo over the ensuing two months, involving a juvenile continuum of back-and-forth spewing of sarcastic, vitriolic barbs at each other. Reno accused the acting assistant surgeon of being "party to the theft of some golden syrup from a sutler" and that "he was unable to understanding [*sic*] a simple prescription," so much so that Reno was "fearful that the man will poison somebody."[57] Nash retorted in his later defense, accusing Reno of having "an overstimulated brain" and declaring that there was "a keg on tap in front of the Major's tent."[58] Reciprocal accusations alleged that Nash was a drunkard himself who had also routinely used chloroform on the officers for the treatment of their hangovers.[59] This diatribe elevated to the extent that Major Reno suspended Nash twice before the doctor's contract was annulled and he was permanently barred from further employment by the U.S. Army Medical Department.[60] Major Reno then requested the other army medical officer on the 1873 survey campaign, Lord's former Fort Randall colleague, Dr. Coues, to oversee the medical duties for the troops for the remainder of the 1873 operation. However, as he was more interested in naturalist duties on the expedition in addition to considering himself as employed only for the boundary commission, not the troops, Coues refused the major's request.[61]

Oddly, although both Francis Nash and George Lord were graduates of Bowdoin College in Maine as well as acting attending surgeons within the Department of Dakota, those were likely the only aspects they shared. They were probably mere acquaintances, if that, as Nash graduated from the Medical School of Maine at Bowdoin two years after Lord completed his undergraduate degree at the school. Moreover, there is no evidence suggesting that they knew each other, and what was known by others in the army about their conduct at that time suggests they had entirely different personalities. Thus, it is not surprising that upon his being chosen to fill Nash's former position in 1874, there would be no disputes or confrontations between Major Reno and Dr. Lord.

After receiving orders for assignment with the survey commission escort, Lord left St. Paul with Reno by train, initially via the Lake Superior and Mississippi Railroad, before changing to the Northern Pacific Railroad for the remainder of the land trek. Eventually, they and the troops were transported by steamboat on the Missouri River heading initially for Fort Stevenson and then Fort Buford, where the expedition added additional troops. During the long river journey, Lord wrote the first of several letters to a lady with whom he enjoyed an apparent romantic relationship during his stay with the family in Limerick (perhaps one that had its beginnings several years prior). Only two letters are known to have survived, one at the beginning of the journey and the other following his return to Fort Snelling at the conclusion of the expedition.

In the first, a lengthy missive dated Sunday, June 7 and written on U.S. Northern Boundary Escort stationery, he penned a most enlightening narrative describing the current journey west for his military assignment while aboard the less than stellar steamer *Fontenelle*[62] on the Missouri River. Looking forward to the end of "this most disagreeable Steamboat trip," Lord noted to his lady friend Annie that she would see "many novel and amusing things" were she on the boat with him. He then painted a colorful picture of the varied sights, annoying sounds, and disgusting smells of the overcrowded conditions aboard the boat, one built more for an intended purpose as a supply transport vessel than as a luxury passenger boat. Among these sensory stimulations were numerous animals, including mules, horses, and dogs; tons of camp supplies such as tents, boxes of subsistence supplies (food), blankets, and beds; soldiers constantly shooting at ducks and geese on the river; a laundress; and "one greasy cook who never 'cleaned his body' and grit that would have, in days of yore, unpleasantly affected the mucous membrane of my stomach."[63]

Intertwined among these graphic descriptions of his current environment, young George Lord also expressed his lament on the recent passing of time and the forthcoming separation and loneliness of being apart from Annie for the next several months. He initially noted his extreme pleasure in her deeply expressed feelings for him and happiness in their time together. Reminiscing on pleasantries of afternoon visits back in Maine with her on her front porch and in the family parlor, and their final departing at the train depot as he left for the West, Lord reveals his own deep feelings for Annie in a rather sentimental proclamation. Lord avowed that "when I left you at the depot in Biddeford [Maine] I never felt so thoroughly alone and so entirely miserable; . . . the mournful contrast between the perfect happiness of the past twenty four hours and the dreariness of the many long hours to come—hours, days, weeks, months." He further passionately confessed to her, "The lump in my throat was a large one. . . . You did not see how hard it was for me not to kiss you but I knew I must resist the impulse. I wanted another last one. I shall never forget the one that was the last though: it was so earnestly passionate—the expression of feeling deep and fervent. I think it must have been love; . . . it will always be a pleasant remembrance."[64] Lord closed his letter to Annie by expressing his hope that "in the midst of flirtations and gaieties this summer, you will find time to write me often" and signed it "Lovingly yours, George."[65]

The 1874 survey season lasted from June to September. Company B, Sixth Infantry, from Fort Abraham Lincoln joined Companies D, E, I, and K of the same regiment already at Fort Buford, and all companies left there on June 16.[66] Lord, after arriving at Buford with Reno by steamboat, served with Companies E and I and eventually established camp at Quaking Asp River, Montana Territory, on June 30, after a month-long march of nearly 135 miles.[67] Successive duty took Lord to Camp Reno in the Sweet Grass Hills of central Montana,[68] and then to a camp on the Milk River, Montana Territory, by August 31.[69] During this time, Lord's former colleague at Fort Randall, Dr. Elliott Coues, had returned for a second year with the expedition. However, the two medicos never actually served together as Lord attended the troops while Coues busied himself with scientific duties in studying the ornithology, fauna, and other animal species encountered on the expedition.[70] As the summer faded away, Lord and the infantry contingent returned to Fort Buford by September 20 as the survey completed the year's assigned fieldwork.

With the end of those duties, Lord looked forward to a return east and continuing his relationship with Annie Hooper. These desires are evident in a second letter to her, penned on October 6 at the Merchants Hotel, where he stayed upon arriving in St. Paul. His opening salutation of "My Dear Cousin Annie," and noting later her "roving cousin, is he or is he not a cousin" might raise some confusion as to his relationship with her. One can reasonably speculate that this was either an odd attempt at humor or an inside joke they shared. Nevertheless, Lord stated that he would be even happier if he could immediately travel farther east "about 1500 miles to a certain house by the seas-side where them Hoopers do dwell," suggesting his feelings for Annie remained strong. He wrote further to "thank my dearest cousin" for keeping her promise to write him once a week (her letters having been forwarded to him in the field from Fort Benton, Montana Territory, that being the closest post to the escort's planned summer locations). Lord did confess that he had always been skeptical that women could keep such promises—this, again, perhaps a subtle hint at a prior failed relationship. Regardless, he expressed his extreme happiness to Annie that she had taken the time to write him and express her feelings for him.

In this letter, Lord also noted that after his arrival at the hotel in St. Paul on Saturday evening, he had dinner the following day with the medical director (of the Department of Dakota) before venturing out to Fort Snelling to visit his brother, Thomas, and his wife. To his disappointment, he found they were not at their residence and returned to the hotel. While undoubtedly happy that he had finally been invited to sit before the Army Medical Examining Board in November, George shared his apprehension with Annie that he would "be in New York City for that fearful examination which has been haunting me for the past three yrs." That he was still enamored of her is evident by his relating to her that after the exam, he would be "about O.O.B" (Old Orchard Beach, Maine, close to the Hooper home). Lord concluded his letter by promising to write her again in a couple of days or sooner, again signing off "With Love, George."[71]

These surviving letters are important for several reasons. First, Lord provides an interesting first-person description of the atmosphere and scenery experienced on military steamboat excursions on the Missouri River during the era. Aside from the potential dangers of the river itself, such as snags, sawyers, and sandbars (not to forget the possible threat from Indians in the region), from Lord's account, one can easily visualize the sights and imagine the odors of the crowded conditions associated with supplying an expedition, including food, bedding, tents, wagons, hundreds of animals—surprisingly even dogs—in addition to horses and mules, and people crammed on deck. To pass the long hours and tolerate the hot temperatures on the several day trips between stations, passengers routinely engaged in target practice from the decks, shooting at wildlife along the banks. Interestingly, Lord was not the only one among army personnel who complained of the unpleasant conditions of steamboat transportation of the era—in this case, that experienced on the *Fontenelle*. In his official report on the Northern Boundary Survey Commission, captain of engineers and chief astronomer William J. Twining wrote of the rough, primitively designed, loudly thumping, exhaust-spewing engines with leaky cylinders and the resulting hundreds of holes burned into the upper decks from the clouds of sparks continuously flying. Twining went on to sarcastically opine that he had no recollection of hearing of a single accident by explosion or fire, attributing such to "special providences" as opposed to builders or owners of whom he was sure that "no thought of anything so worthless as human life entered into their calculation."[72]

More important than simply describing the discomforts of steamboat travel, the two letters provide some insight into George Lord's aspirations and emotions apart from his purely military goals and demeanor. Little Big Horn historian C. Lee Noyes astutely observed in his examination of the letters that Lord was engaged in intimate correspondence with a young lady. The letters addressed her as "Cousin Annie." Noyes saw a more serious relationship and suggested that "the reader should draw his or her own conclusions."[73] Since the publication of Noyes's article, other information has come to light that adds insight into the identity of Annie Hooper. In his letters, Lord indicated that Annie and her family lived in Biddeford, Maine, "by the sea-side." Other clues, some hinted at by Lord, some per demographics, helped unmask his lady friend. A search through the U.S. Census records for 1850, 1860, and 1870 for Biddeford and the Biddeford City Directories for 1872–75 reveal there were three families with the last name of Hooper in that city. Only two had daughters with a variation of the name Ann.

Edward H. C. Hooper, a life insurance agent and dry goods mercantile owner, lived in town by the Saco River and seashore (Atlantic Ocean) with his wife, housekeeper, and four children, including Annie Maude F. Hooper. There was also Tristam Hooper, a farmer who resided with his wife and three children, including Annah Hooper, and a boarding farm worker. Their farm was not in Biddeford proper but in the outlying countryside. Official records consistently show that Annah Hooper never used the name Annie or was referred to as such, while the first woman in consideration was always known by that first name. Another consideration is that Annie Hooper was three years younger than George Lord, while Annah Hooper was ten years his senior. Although a larger age-gap courtship is certainly possible, the opposite seems more likely. Additionally, nearby Limerick, where George was staying with his parents, is only twenty-four miles from Biddeford. Also, although George was not adopted until sometime before 1860, the Hooper and Lord families would have likely known of each other since Reverend Lord served as pastor at the Congregational church there in the early 1850s. Lastly, Old Orchard Beach, which Lord indicated in his second surviving letter of October 1874 to Annie that he intended on visiting after his army medical examination was finished, is less than five miles from Biddeford. In that the Old Orchard Beach community has always been an ocean-side beach resort even well before the 1870s, the beach and park areas would have been a logical destination for George and Annie to spend outings in early 1874, which he proposed doing after his return from the Northern Boundary assignment. Regrettably, no letters from Annie Hooper to George have survived. After reviewing all the available clues, it seems reasonable to conclude that the identity of the young lady of George Lord's affection is likely Annie M. F. Hooper of Biddeford, Maine.

There is further evidence that Lord and Annie had a long-established relationship beginning prior to 1872, which also indicates his disappointment from other intimate relationships with women. In his letter to "Cousin Annie" in June of that year while serving at Fort Randall, Lord shared with her that "no maiden . . . in this region has 'bewitched' me," but also that he had been "engaged three times, three times jilted."[74] Although he provided no further information about his failed engagements, from this letter it can be surmised that these relationships likely occurred sometime in his college or medical school years.

The other oddity regarding Annie Hooper is Lord referring to her as "Cousin Annie." Perhaps this was a flirtation or perhaps an attempt at humor. The initial reaction and question raised by this salutation is whether or not there existed a common family lineage. The potential dangers associated with first-cousin marriage have been known since the mid-nineteenth century. Even during the 1870s, many states, although not all, had prohibited cousins from marrying due to the risk of congenital genetic conditions. More recent research has shown some indication that the potential risks are not so dire and, as such, first-cousin marriages are legal in a few states. A search of known family genealogical records has not determined any connection between George and Annie Hooper.[75] It seems reasonable to conclude that this relationship was not between "kissing cousins" but rather between a young couple having developed deep feelings for each other. Alas, for George Lord, his hope for a more permanent relationship was not to be. Perhaps it was Annie who decided she was not suited for or did not desire the life of a military wife at some desolate, western army post. Whatever prompted the decision by either of them, George and Annie went their separate ways by the end of the year and she married another local Biddeford man named Beverly Moore in January 1875, before Lord's examination by the Army Medical Board.[76] Lord would never marry, in contrast to his brother, Thomas, and eventual Little Big Horn medical colleagues, Henry Porter and James DeWolf, who all enjoyed apparently successful marriages.

A month into the survey while at the Quaking Asp camp (in Montana Territory), Lord received his long-awaited invitation to appear before the Army Medical Board as a candidate for an appointment in the medical staff of the army.[77] The army examining board was scheduled to convene in the fall at a date yet to be determined.[78] Army policy limited the top age for men entering service as military physicians to twenty-eight years old.[79] This was borne in the premise that younger candidates were more suited to the rigors of frontier military medicine and service. George was already five months past twenty-eight years old. In his case, the disqualification on that account was removed, likely due to a combination of his previous highly satisfactory service as a contract surgeon and his good reputation and character as evinced in the letters of recommendations from medical school professors and esteemed army colleagues, including Dr. Coues and Dr. Head. Lord had a full summer ahead of him but still made time to prepare for the arduous exam using books from the personal library in his kit. In August, Lord and his contingent of the escort encamped in the Sweet Grass Hills in north-central Montana, where they remained for the rest of that month. The Northern Boundary Survey Commission parties concluded work by early September and the various detachments returned to their assigned winter quarters. Lord reached Bismarck on September 30 and St. Paul on the morning of October 7,[80] taking accommodation at the Merchants Hotel.[81] The following day, after dining with Dr. Head, he traveled to Fort Snelling to visit his brother and sister-in-law but found them away.[82] Major Head informed him that he had been assigned to duty as post surgeon at Fort Ripley, which he reached on October 12. That same day, Lord received word that he had "been requested by the President of the

Army Medical Board, now in session in New York City, to present myself for examination on the sixteenth of November 1874."[83] He petitioned for and was granted a one-month leave of absence to make the trip. Complicating matters, however, Dr. Head, the medical director, informed the Army Medical Board that it had been impossible to relieve Lord from duty in the department until early the following month, which caused a delay in his appearance and resulted in a subsequent rescheduling of his examination date on January 6, 1875.[84] After his contract was annulled on December 3 at his request (once again with appraisal of his character and efficiency being highly satisfactory), Lord journeyed from St. Paul to New York City. He checked in to the Sturtevant House, one of the city's newer upscale hotels located at the corner of Broadway and Twenty-Ninth Street in Manhattan.[85]

The attainment of a regular army medical appointment was a highly coveted and pursued goal by many young physicians. The U.S. Army Medical Department upheld the highest standards in both medical and classical training. The examination process was arduous, and it remains so even today, and George had expressed his apprehension about taking that "fearful examination" to Annie Hooper in his last letter to her from the Merchants Hotel in St. Paul back in October.[86] Perhaps the best description of the exam process during the Victorian era has been provided by Dr. James Kimball,[87] a respected and accomplished army medical physician who penned the following: "The examination lasted a week; there were six candidates and I was the only one that passed! You can imagine it was something of an examination, as we were examined in Latin, Greek, French, and German; Arithmetic, Algebra, Geometry, Trigonometry, and Calculus, Geography, political and physical, Ancient and Modern History and Literature, Mineralogy, Conchology, Botany, and Natural Physics, etc., and then a most exhaustive examination in Medicine and all its branches."[88]

Even for candidates like George Lord, who had received an extensive education in the classical arts and literature in both high school and college, approaching the examination encompassed a sense of dread and anxiety. He was scheduled to appear before the medical board on January 9, 1875. The exam had been reduced to a one-day ordeal as compared to the week-long process during Kimball's day seven years earlier. Still, the exercise made for an extremely tedious experience lasting several hours. Lord's file was already complete with the required endorsements and autobiographical statement. That he was held in high esteem was further confirmed by Major Head's break in protocol entrusting him with hand-delivering the medical director's letter of recommendation to the examining board president, Dr. Joseph B. Brown.[89] Arriving at the Army Medical Building on the corner of Houston and Greene Streets, following introductions at the beginning of the day's exams, Dr. Brown received the following letter:

Dear Doctor,
  This will be handed to you by my young friend Dr. Geo. E. Lord, (late Act. Assist. Surg. U.S.A.) who goes to present himself to the A. Med. B. for examination.
  As to his professional qualifications, the examiners will of course test him.
  To his personal and social fitness for a commission in our Corps—to his zeal, accuracy and efficiency as an Act. Medical Officer—and to the fact that he is "one of the right sort," I can testify most emphatically.
  I depart from the usual practice of leaving letters of introduction unsealed as I do not desire to shock Dr. Lord's modesty.
  Believe me,
  Yrs very truly,
  J. H. Head
  (Surg. US.a.
  Med. Div. D. Dak.-)
  Surg. J. B. Brown, USA Presidt. A.M.B.[90]
  Army Building, corner of Green and Houston Street, South.

Then the inquisition began. Historian John M. Carroll and Edward S. Petersen previously noted a few select questions from Lord's examination before the Army Medical Board:[91]

Physiology

Question: Give the physiology of the Semen, showing where and how it is formed, the constituents essential to it and the role it plays in generation.

Lord's response: The semen is formed in the testes of the male and of material brought by the blood. Its essential constituents are the spermatozoa. The semen supplies to the female ovum the faecundating principle.

Question: What purposes does the bile subserve in digestion?

Lord's response: The true function of the bile is not fully understood by the physiologists. It is believed to aid in the digestion of fatty matters and is said by some to have the power of converting a small amount of starch into sugar. It has been considered an antiseptic. Although its exact use in digestion has not been determined, it is known to be essential to the proper performance of that function, from the fact that animals in whom a biliary fistula has been established soon die from inanition.

Surgery

Question: Describe the antiseptic treatment of wounds, give the results of this treatment as compared with ordinary dressings.

Lord's response: The antiseptic treatment of wounds is based on the theory that certain agents called antiseptics have the power of destroying certain organic germs said to exist in the air and to be injurious to the process of healing—in my opinion it is injurious to freshly granulating surfaces.

Hygiene

Question: Describe the objects of clothing and the means by which they are to be obtained.

Lord's response: . . . woolen goods and furs being poor conductors of heat on account of the air contained in their pores retain the heat of the body and are in consequence used as clothing by those exposed to the severe cold.

Question: Mention the principal places in which specific yellow fever prevails as an endemic; and the conditions necessary for the propagation beyond these localities.

Lord's response: The disease may be developed in other places by the conveyance of the infection through the agency of fomites or in the persons of those afflicted with the disease, and further propagated by the neglect of the hygienic means above mentioned.—these were: foul air from crowds and ill-ventilation, filthy streets, want of care in the removal of excretion.

Candidate Lord physically survived the day and the exam, and then he endured the dreaded interval until learning of the decision. He did not have long to wait. In a letter to the surgeon general immediately after the conclusion of the exams, medical board president Dr. Brown noted the results of the four physicians invited to sit for examination that day. In addition to Lord, the other physicians were Dr. Thomas H. Maghee, Dr. I. J. Reinhart, and Dr. George H. C. Hoffman. Dr. Brown noted that Hoffman and Maghee withdrew at their own requests after being partially examined, Hoffman due to "ill health," and Maghee for an undisclosed reason. The board recommended that Maghee "be afforded an opportunity for re-examination at a future time." Both Reinhart and Lord, meanwhile, were "wholly examined" and Lord was "found qualified for appointment" while Reinhart was not. Dr. Brown added further comment that "it is respectfully recommended, however, that Dr. Lord be directed to denote special attention to Physics, Physiology and Chemistry, on which branches his examination was not wholly satisfactory to the Board."[92] Lord received notice of these results three days later in a letter delivered to him at the Sturtevant House hotel. No doubt relieved and elated at having passed the exam, he was also likely somewhat disappointed in receiving a second letter at the hotel from Assistant Surgeon General Crane shortly thereafter informing him that he would be offered a new civilian contract for service in the Department of Dakota until an opening as an assistant surgeon became available.[93]

Some final comments are appropriate regarding George Lord's medical examination process. Similar to Lord's candidate group, typically nearly three out of every four applicants failed to pass.[94] That statistic does not necessarily indicate that all those physicians were not qualified or competent to serve as army surgeons. There are many examples of physicians who were not passed by the Army Medical Board or chose not to even apply for examination yet were qualified and competent in serving as civilian contract physicians for the army. In the Sioux War story, Charles Petteys, James DeWolf, and Henry Porter are prime examples. All three were highly intelligent gentlemen, excellent physicians with prior medical experience as contract physicians in the army under combat conditions. Petteys served as an acting assistant surgeon in the November 1876 Powder River Expedition, DeWolf served as a hospital attendant and steward from 1865 to 1868 during the Snake Indian War in Washington Territory (present-day Oregon), and Porter had gained his experience serving with then–lieutenant colonel George Crook in the 1872–73 Arizona campaign against the Apache Indians. Although all three had mastered the rigorous education process of their respective medical schools (Georgetown for Petteys and Porter, Harvard for DeWolf), unlike Porter and George Lord, neither Petteys nor DeWolf had formal education in the classical and fine arts curriculums that emphasized history, art, literature, and language studies. The U.S. Army Medical Department was an elite fraternity that sought to select only the most qualified and highly educated physicians in both medical and classical training. The adherence to this standard was, in part, among reasons why some candidates without undergraduate training who applied and were subsequently invited to sit before the army examining board had difficulty. But that process was always subject to some potential personal bias and even differences of opinion regarding various classical academic topics and medical theory among the army physicians on the exam board. In contrast to George Lord and Henry Porter, this lack of a formal classical education likely contributed to Petteys and

DeWolf not passing the exam, although Porter never had an interest in applying as a candidate for an army medical commission.[95]

However, even candidates such as George Lord, who had formal education in the arts, literature, and history, had difficulty in answering some questions in those categories before the Army Medical Board. For example, Lord was unable to answer a few questions such as the mechanism of a watch spring (controls the speed of the wheels of the timepiece, thus the rate of the movement of the hands); who the author of logarithms was (Scottish mathematician John Napier in 1614); the basic themes of Greek poet Homer's *Iliad* (honor, love and friendship, free will, and fate); why the Greek philosopher Socrates was executed (condemned for alleged impiety and corruption of youth regarding disbelief in the official Greek gods); the role of the stop in a microscope (a screw that prevents the stage from elevating too far up and grinding against the lens); and the name of the officer whom British general John Burgoyne surrendered to at the Battle of Saratoga, New York, in October 1777 during the American Revolution (American general Horatio Gates).[96] Nonetheless, despite his minor lapses in memory for these specific questions, Lord's overall response to the other categories in this portion of the exam was deemed satisfactory by the army medical examining officers.

In addition, Dr. Brown's assertion that Lord was somewhat deficient in physiology and chemistry can appropriately be questioned, given that there was no universally accepted medical text among the hundreds of medical schools in existence at the time. Not uncommonly, and similar to the current modern era of medicine, the distinguished physicians who composed the examining boards had differences of opinion as to various medical treatments and theories. In the physiology category, Lord was referring to the renowned doctor Austin Flint's proposed medical theory suggesting a possible connection between the liver and other physiologic processes such as sugar production and possible diabetes and other disease causations. These were outlined in Flint's medical textbook, a recommended text at the Chicago Medical College. Lord studied this book during his time there and continued to use it as an army contract surgeon.[97]

Brown and his board colleagues might well have been either in disagreement with the theory or possibly not even aware of it. Even if the former was the underlying reason, they were perhaps looking for him to expound further on the question. The suggestion that he "brush up" suggests that Lord presented a sufficiency of evidence reflecting well on his intellect and medical knowledge.

Regarding the surgery question, internationally known British surgeon Dr. Joseph Lister's theories for use of antiseptics, which he pioneered in research and practice during the 1860s (specifically carbolic acid dilutions), were controversial and not widely accepted by most physicians and surgeons of the day. Lister's promotion of antiseptics regarding the germ theory of infection encompassed both prevention of such during surgery as well as the treatment of wounds. Criticism focused, in part, on evidence suggesting that antiseptic sprays caused some tissue damage, as alluded to by Lord, although others supported Lister's theory and recommended techniques, including one of Lord's professors in medical school, professor of surgery Dr. Edmund Andrews.[98] Perhaps Lord's examiners preferred he would have expounded on this question as well. Such was the prerogative of the physicians of the Army Board. Yet, Lord's answers were deemed acceptable, and the positive decision was rendered with a mere recommendation for additional personal review.

Not uncommonly, following such an examination, candidates might take the opportunity to spend time with family and friends. Although there was no immediate opening for Lord being commissioned as an assistant surgeon, which would have provided him some additional recreational time, the fact that he had been offered a temporary new contract as a civilian physician by the surgeon general and the fact that his relationship with Annie Hooper had ended likely prompted Lord to accept the temporary contract and to report to Department of Dakota headquarters in St. Paul for assignment.[99] Arriving there on January 22, he was assigned to temporary duty at nearby Fort Snelling and reported on January 25, thereby rejoining his brother, Thomas, who continued as regimental and post quartermaster.[100] Aside from their official duties, the brothers likely spent time socially, with George invited to occasional meals

Fort Snelling, circa 1870s. Photo by Charles A. Zimmerman, St. Paul, Minnesota. (Author's collection.)

with brother and wife, Mary. At this time, Lord also met and began a friendship with the assistant post surgeon, Holmes O. Paulding,[101] who was another rising young army physician. He and Lord would share medical duties at the fort, although only for a short while, as both would soon be assigned to different posts.

A month in to duty at Fort Snelling, Lord was assigned on February 25 to assist in the "relief for grasshopper suffer[er]s in Lacquiparle [Lac qui Parle] & Yellow Medicine Counties, Minnesota."[102] The two adjacent counties in the southwestern corner of the state, some 150 miles from St. Paul, were hit especially hard by the grasshopper plague of 1874. Both Lord and Dr. Paulding were sent with several officers of the Twentieth Infantry and an enlisted man, Corporal Alfred Dale of Company G, Twentieth Infantry, who accompanied Lord at least as far as New Ulm, Minnesota.[103]

Grasshopper plagues ravaged Minnesota for five years from 1873 to 1877. Millions of the pests, a now-extinct species called the Rocky Mountain locust, smothered the plains from the Rocky Mountains eastward. Massive swarms of grasshoppers caused devastation to wheat, barley, oats, corn, and other crops, attacked buildings and people, and even ate clothing. In 1874 alone, Minnesota state officials estimated that the malicious insects destroyed a "considerably larger area than the previous year," accounting for "over half of the cultivated acreage in the twenty-eight counties [sustaining damage], including 38 percent of the wheat crop and half of the oats."[104] The economic devastation was horrendous. With the loss of revenue from destruction of crops, families lost farms and some even died from starvation. County and state officials did what they could to provide supplies and economic assistance to their residents and eventually turned to the federal government for relief. In addition to monetary appropriations, the federal government sent the U.S. Army to counties to help with the distribution of supplies, clothing (largely from military stores),[105] and other care to the families in rural areas suffering the devastation, not unlike the national disaster relief system of the present day.

Lord and the other members of the relief contingent returned to Fort Snelling by March 23. The two physicians and the infantry officers were dispatched on a second humanitarian deployment on April 20, again assisting families affected by the grasshopper crisis.[106] This second mission was also of short duration and they returned by mid-May. Soon after, both Lord and Paulding were transferred to Fort Abraham Lincoln, with Paulding appointed assistant surgeon for the post and Lord reporting for duty with the Black Hills Expedition, then forming at the post.[107] Arriving on May 20 and 21, respectively, they served immediately under Major Charles Christopher Byrne, post surgeon.[108]

As stipulated in the 1868 Fort Laramie Treaty, the Sioux Indians were accorded permanent ownership of their sacred Black Hills. The discovery of measurable amounts of gold during the 1874 Black Hills Expedition triggered a mad rush of prospectors and miners seeking fortune. The 1874 expedition, commanded by Lieutenant Colonel George Custer, was undertaken for the express purpose of finding a suitable location for a military post to oversee the enforcement against white trespass into this sacred land. The worth of the 1874 discovery was disputed, however, and the government authorized a second expedition into the region.¹⁰⁹ This new Black Hills Expedition in 1875 was to further explore and assess this prospect and determine an economic value for possible purchase or lease from the Sioux at some future date.

Lord's and Paulding's special orders transferring them to Fort Abraham Lincoln suggest they were to be a part of the medical staff assigned to the military escort for the expedition.¹¹⁰ For unclear reasons, that did not occur. Army administrators chose to have the escort composed of troops from Fort Laramie under the command of Lieutenant Colonel Richard Irving Dodge, Twenty-Third Infantry.¹¹¹ Meanwhile, at Fort Abraham Lincoln, both young physicians

George E. Lord with Custer hunting party at the Heart River hunting camp site, Dakota Territory, sometime between June 3 and July 9, 1875. Lord is wearing eyeglasses and a blue shirt. Photo by O. S. Goff in 1875. Holmes O. Paulding is sitting front middle. (Courtesy of National Archives and Records Administration, 530885, NWDNS-111-SC-83991.

Dakota Territory and Beyond

Holmes Offley Paulding, MD, assistant surgeon, U.S. Army. (Courtesy of National Library of Medicine, B011248.)

were accepted into the Custer entourage of Seventh Cavalry officers. Lord also appears to have become acquainted with Second Lieutenant Richard E. Thompson of the Sixth Infantry, as Thompson related later how he knew Lord quite well. Not all of Lord's time was spent at the post hospital. Both he and Paulding enjoyed recreational outings, and both are seen among Custer's hunting party in a well-known photograph taken on the Heart River, a favorite established camp located twelve miles west of the fort.[112] This photo is important as it documents Lord's attire, which was likely his outfit at the Little Big Horn. He is seen wearing a blue double buttoned front panel shirt and buff-colored hat.

Lord and Paulding's stay at Fort Abraham Lincoln would not be long. In his fifth week at the post, Lord finally came to the realization of his long-standing goal of becoming a commissioned army medical officer. Receiving notification on June 26 in a letter from the secretary of war that he had been appointed assistant surgeon (entitled to the rank of first lieutenant), Lord promptly sent his acceptance reply along with a signed oath of office to the surgeon general in Washington, D.C.[113] On July 9, he departed the post for Fort Snelling, as ordered, and Paulding left on July 22.[114] They would not see each other again. After a three-month leave visiting family back home, Paulding was assigned as post surgeon at Fort Ellis, Montana Territory, arriving there in late October.[115] At Fort Snelling, likely again enjoying being able to visit with his brother and sister-in-law, Lord learned of his appointment on August 5 as post surgeon at Fort Buford, Dakota Territory,[116] at the confluence of the Yellowstone and Missouri Rivers. Enduring yet another steamboat excursion on the Missouri, he arrived at Fort Buford on August 26 and assumed official duties the following day.[117] He would spend the next nine months at Buford before embarking on what would, unfortunately, become his final assignment.

CHAPTER 3

All in the Line of Duty at Fort Buford

IT WAS FOUND NECESSARY TO ADMINISTER ETHER
IN THE REDUCTION, WHICH WAS EFFECTED
WITH SOME DIFFICULTY, THE MAN HAVING
A POWERFUL MUSCULAR DEVELOPMENT.
*Assistant Surgeon George Lord, Fort Buford, medical log entry
of February 15, 1876, after performing a successful reduction
of an enlisted man's left index finger dislocation*

ALTHOUGH MANY of the western American military posts seemed to be the very definition of "forsaken," suggesting a journey into a forgotten place, certainly Fort Buford was considered by some as the epitome of that description. While it was a regular stop on the trans–Missouri River steamboat route connecting other forts farther west and cities and forts downstream, in looking at its geographic location in the extreme upper northwest portion of the Department of Dakota (present-day North Dakota), Fort Buford had the appearance of being in the middle of nowhere.[1] Dr. Lord was likely entertaining that same thought based on his graphic description of his initial journey on the Missouri River with the Northern Boundary Survey the prior summer. Buford and the surrounding country were certainly nothing like the comfortable, cozy confines of Fort Snelling in Minnesota that he enjoyed while periodically stationed there with his brother, able to enjoy innumerable social outings.

Fort Buford had been in existence nine years when Lord arrived there on August 25, 1876. Built in 1866 at the confluence of the Missouri and Yellowstone Rivers, the location was near the site of the American Fur Company's Fort Union, a fur trading post the army bought and dismantled for use in constructing the new post. The fort quickly proved essential for the protection of traders, miners, and eventual settlers traveling into the Upper Missouri country and the Montana Territory. The region's indigenous Sioux Indians, largely the followers of Sitting Bull, considered the whites as intruders and often attacked the fort during its earliest years. Initially constructed in a conventional form with a stockade and blockhouses, Buford was expanded into a sprawling military compound spanning more than one hundred buildings.[2] It was later the site of Sitting Bull's surrender in 1881.[3]

The extensive country outlying Fort Buford for hundreds of miles encompassed a wide variety of landscapes and wildlife. According to the *1875 Report on Hygiene of the United States Army, with Descriptions of Military Posts*, the Missouri River in the vicinity averaged about "one half mile in width with its flood plain ranging from forty rods to several miles . . . and the surface of the ground is 38 feet above the water." The surrounding "bad lands" were a "succession of barren hills which averaged two to three hundred feet in height, [and] extend back from the plain for five or six miles, beyond which is a rolling prairie."[4] Stratified deposits of sandstone were embedded in the hills, and cottonwood trees were the dominant variety in the area, although there were also ash-leaved maple, red osiers dogwood, and green ash in the vicinity. An abundance of wildlife could be seen, which included the American buffalo, mountain sheep, white-tailed deer, elk, antelope, wolves, coyotes, black bear, red and silver fox, rabbits, and beaver.

The daily routines at many army posts during the Indian Wars era were much the same and usually described as mundane. Yet, a review of the Fort Buford Medical Record, at least during Lord's time, reveals that it was anything but mundane. The medical log (or report) that each post surgeon was required to maintain documented the administrative and financial oversight necessary for every hospital, plus, of course, the description and treatment of various illnesses and deaths suffered by the officers and enlisted men in each garrison. Invariably, these logs were much more than a simple record and account book. The collective pages essentially served as a history of each post, documenting the daily social and military events occurring, the arrival and departure of travelers, army officers, troops, or other important visitors, mail and supply arrivals, construction or renovation of buildings, and the record of meteorological data (weather conditions). Not uncommonly, the log's content was sometimes spiced with rumor, levity, and the personal opinions of the surgeon, which Lord was guilty of doing as much as any army surgeon! The following portion of the Fort Buford Medical Record composed by George Lord during his nine-month tenure as post surgeon is a representative and interesting example of this unique manner of record keeping. Although he did not arrive at the post until late August, as post surgeon, he completed the log for the remainder of that month. The first three months are provided here as a complete transcription to illustrate the flavor of Lord's writing and to give an accurate report of life at the fort and at the hospital. Thereafter, to avoid the mundane of repetition, portions of the log are presented with annotation and commentary on Lord's treatment of the various medical conditions he encountered and a few additional notable events that occurred during the remainder of his tenure at the post.

Fort Buford Medical Log

Record for the Month of August, 1875

1st Headquarters Fort Buford, D.T.
General Orders) August 1st, 1875
No. 44)
Drills and Dress parades at retreats will be resumed to-morrow under the direction of Major O.H. Moore. On Mondays, Wednesdays & Fridays, by Company, and on Tuesdays, Thursdays & Saturdays by Battalion. No one will be excused except the guard, one man in the Hospital, three in Q.M. Dept., three in Subsistence

Dept., one baker and one servant to each family or officer's mess; and these will alternate weekly. The Adjutant is charged with the execution of this order so far as relates to attendance.

General Orders No. 41 from these Headquarters is hereby revoked. The following changes in calls are announced.
Surgeons Call 6 A.M
Drill 1st Call 6.15 A.M
do 2nd " Call 6.30 " "
Recall from Drill 7.30 " "
Fatigue Call 8.00 " "
Recall from fatigue 12 M
Fatigue call 2.00 P.M
Recall from fatigue 6.00 " "
By Order of Col. Hazen[5]
(Signed) S. W. Groesbeck[6]
Lieut, & Adjutant 6th Inf.
Post Adjutant

1st Mule train arrived from Bismarck[7] 6 PM en route to Montana.

2nd Steamer Key West[8] arrived from Carroll[9] en route to Bismarck, with Lieut. Humbert[10] on board. Maj. Smith[11] and Clerk, and the family of Col. Moore[12] left on this boat.

5th Telegraphic instructions received from Fort Lincoln ordering the Adjutant and another officer to proceed to Fort Lincoln to receive and conduct a detachment of recruits to the regiment.

6th Lieuts. Goresbeck and Crowell[13] left post, 10 AM with a corporal and one man en route to Bismarck to receive recruits.

8th Mail arrive from Bismarck.

9th In compliance with previous order A.A. Surg. McKinney[14] examined some Indian women to determine if they had any venereal disease. Two were examined and found free from any such disease—The third refused to submit to any examination and was ordered away from the post.[15]

10th Mail left for Bismarck—Communication received from Gen'l Hazen directing Post Surgeon to furnish him with the records of the date of the earliest frosts here the various seasons since the post has been established.

13th Steamer Benton[16] arrived from Yankton[17] en route to Benton.[18]

14th Headquarters Fort Buford, D.T.
General Orders) August 14th, 1875
No. 51

II Cases of immoral diseases among the men of the Command will at once be reported to these Headquarters by the Post Surgeon with a view that steps be taken for stopping their pay for the period the U.S. is deprived of their services by their voluntary acts.[19]

By Order of Col. W.B. Hazen.
Thomas G. Townsend,[20]
2nd Lieut. 6th Infty.
Post Adjutant

15th Steamer Josephine[21] arrived from Bismarck en route for Carroll with orders to await the Secretary of War.

17th Mail leaves for Bismarck. Gen'l. Hazen and Lieut. Craft[22] leave for the Hay field.

18th Gen. Hazen & Lieut. Craft return.

19th Thermometer registers this morning 41 deg., the coldest night during the month. Steward Richardson's wife confined—child delivered at 3:30 AM.[23]

20th Ambulance returned from Bismarck with the escort of Lieuts. Groesbeck & Crowell.

22nd Mail arrived from Bismarck

23rd High wind storm set in about 3 PM and ended in rain and thunder-storm—Lightning struck chimney on north end of hospital passing down into the store-room and making a large rent in a plastering. The chimney was completely destroyed.

25th Steamer Gen'l. Meade[24] arrived from Benton with Col. Otis[25] on board who is to inspect the post. Steamer Key West arrived with recruits from Bismarck under the charge of Lieuts. Crowell & Groesbeck.

Asst. Surg. Geo. E. Lord arrived in compliance with S.O. No. 156, dated Hdqts. Dept. of Dakota, St. Paul, Minn. August 13, 1875.

Rain began at 11 AM and continued falling incessantly until 7 o'clock the following morning, making the largest rain-fall at the time since the post was established. The amount was two (2) inches.[26]

26th Steamer Key West left. The following Special Order was issued from Post Headquarters.

Headquarters Fort Buford, D.T.
General Orders) August 26th 1875
No. 129
–Extract–
V Assistant Surgeon G.E. Lord, U.S.A. having, in compliance with S.O. No. 145 C.S. Dept. of Dakota and reported at these Headquarters, he is hereby assigned to duty as Post Surgeon and will at once enter upon the performance of his duties.

VI Acting Assistant Surgeon J.A. McKinney, U.S.A. will transfer all the property, money and accounts pertaining to the Hospital Dept. at this post to Assistant Surg. G.E. Lord, U.S.A. who will receive and receipt for the same.

By Order of Colonel W.B. Hazen
(Signed) S.W. Groesbeck,
1st Lieut. 6th Infty; Adjutant

27th Review of troops and inspection of post by Lt. Colonel E.S. Otis, A.A. Inspector Gen'l.

30th Mail arrives from Bismarck.

31st Steamer Key West arrived having on board the Hon. Secretary of War[27] and party including two hours and left on the same boat. The troops were paraded and complimented by the Secretary on their marching and general appearance. Muster and inspection were in quarters on account of rain.

The following *sanitary report* was made by the Post Surgeon. "The health of the command is good and the post in excellent sanitary condition."

Report of Sick & Wounded. Remaining at last report 5; Taken sick 18. Total 23. Returned to duty 20. Remaining 3. No. of patients admitted to Hospital during the month 6. Daily average treated in Hospital 4. Daily average no. treated in quarters 2. Mean strength of command—Officers 10. Enlisted men 187. Total 197. Percentage taken sick 9.13. Daily percentage of sick 3.05.

Meteorological Record.[28] Monthly mean 63.20 76.97, 64.20. Daily Average temperature 68.12. Maximum temperature 92 deg. (Aug. 23rd) Minimum temp. 37° (Aug. 30th). Cloudiness 3.99. No. days rain 11. Rain fall 3.05. Wind S.

Hospital Fund. Balance on hand per last statement 103.86. Savings $16.81. Total Credits $120.67. Disbursements $9.58. Balance on hand 111.09.

Fort Buford, D.T.) Geo. E. Lord,
August 31st, 1875) Asst. Surg., U.S.A.,
Post Surgeon

First Lieutenant George Edwin Lord, MD, assistant surgeon, U.S. Army. Photograph by Charles A. Zimmerman, St. Paul, Minnesota, 1875. (Courtesy of U.S. Army Heritage and Education Center, Carlisle, Pennsylvania.)

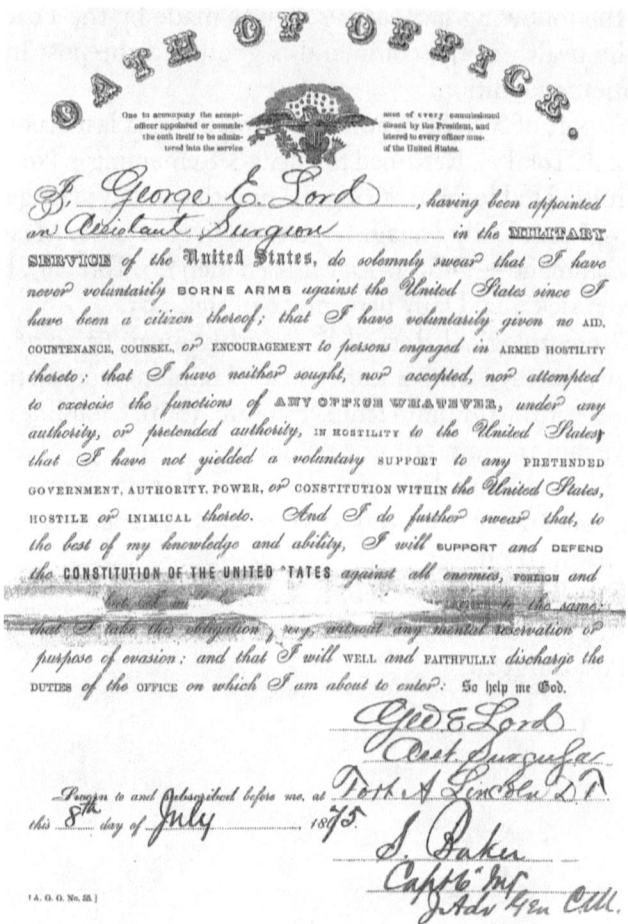

Lord's oath of office as assistant surgeon. (Courtesy of National Archives and Records Administration.)

Record for the Month of September, 1875

Sept. 1st Rain during the night.
" 2nd Rain during & portion of the day. Pvt. Lambourne[29] examined by Post Surgeon for the position of Hospital Steward, U.S.A. The following order issued from Post Headquarters.

Headquarters Ft. Buford, D.T.
September 1st, 1875
General Orders)
No. 56

I In addition to Battalion and company drills, there will at the same hours be squad-drills of the recruits not to exceed four men to a squad. Instructors will be selected from among the non-commissioned Officers to be under the supervision of a Company Officer when there is Company drill and under the supervision of the Officer of the day when there is Battalion drill.

The Officer of the Day will be present at all squad drills, and report any violation of the provisions of the order.

II With a view to facilitate the rendering of his returns, Company Commanders will on or before the 28th day of each month furnish the Acting Commissary of Subsistence Department as Company Savings.

By order of Colonel W.B. Hazen
(Signed) L.W. Groesbeck,
Lieutenant 6th Infantry,
Adjutant

Sept 5th Mail arrive from Bismarck.
" 6th A very bright, warm day.
" 8th In compliance with an order from the War Department the day was made a Holiday for the purpose of paying proper respect to the memory of Ex-President Andrew Johnson.[30] The troops were paraded at 10 AM. Thirteen guns were fired at daybreak, followed by half-hour guns during the day and thirty-seven at Retreat. Flag at half-mast.

A soldier brought the news from the hay camp that the Indians had run off six (6) head of mules belonging to the Government and for which Capt. Penny,[31] Post. Q.M. was responsible. Three scouts were sent out with orders to report to Capt. Penny in charge of the hay party.[32]

9th Str. Key West arrived and tied up for the night. Asst. Surg Paul Brown[33] on board en route to Fort Shaw, M.T.[34]

Colonel William Babcock Hazen. (Courtesy of Library of Congress, Brady-Handy Photograph Collection, Prints and Photographs Division, LC-DIG-cwpbh-03634.)

10th A male child born to Capt & Mrs. Powell,[35] 6th Infty.

12th Indians having been reported to be lurking in the vicinity of the post. Lieut. Jacobs[36] ordered out to investigate, taking with him the scouts and a small detachment. Dr. McKinney accompanies him as Medical Officer. Mail from Bismarck.

14th Lieut. Groesbeck with a party of men left for the "Big Muddy"[37] to cut one hundred (100) tons of hay for the use of officers during the winter. Weather warm and pleasant.

15th Str. Key West passes down.

16th Lieut. Jacobs and Dr. McKinney returned from their scouting expedition. No Indians were seen Weather cool. First frost .Minimum Thermometer—28°.

19th Capt. Penny and Dr. McKinney left for the hay-field.[38] Paymaster Wm. Smith U.S.A. and clerk arrived.

21st Command paid.

22nd Paymaster left for Bismarck (overland) en route to St. Paul, Minn. Lieut. Craft accompanied him as far as Stevenson.[39] The following note received from the Commdg. Officer.

Fort Buford, restored 1870s commandant's house. (Author's photograph.)

Headqrs. Ft. Buford, D.T.
Sept. 22nd 1875
To the Chf Medical Officer
Etc. etc.

I have respectfully to request that you examine the vinegar in the commissary department at this post, furnished for issue to troops, and by the usual chemical tests learn if it is cider vinegar or a weak solution of sulphuric acid, making your written report in due form.

Very respectfully,
(Signed) W. B. Hazen
Col. 6th Inf. Comdg.
Dr. Lord,
U.S.A.

25th Col. Ludlow,[40] Chief Engineer Dept. of Dakota, arrived at the post per Str. Josephine, returning from the exploration of the Yellowstone Country.

26th Mail arrived from Bismarck. Str. Key West passed down Col. Ludlow and party left en route to St. Paul, Minn.

30th Company "F" 6th Infty in command of Lieut. Day[41] arrived at the post from Ft. Rice,[42] D.T. They were about one month on the march having to repair the mounds between Ft. Stevenson & Buford.

Building. Two or three old and dilapidated log buildings in the rear of the Band & Co. E's quarters have been torn down and a store-house for lumber erected—also a shed for the shelter of the cows during the winter. This structure with the corral is too near the barracks for use in the summer.

The following Sanitary Report was made by the Post Surgeon. "The health of the Command is good and the post in excellent sanitary condition. I would respectfully recommend that the bath-house now being built be completed as soon as possible."

Abstract of Sick Report
Remaining at last report - - - - - - - - - - - - - - - - 3
Taken sick or wounded during the month - - - - - - - - - 22
Total sick and wounded - - - - - - - - - - - - - - - - 25
Returned to duty 17
Remaining under treatment 8
No. of patients admitted to Hospital during the month 10
Daily average No. treated in Hospital 3
do do do do do do[43] quarters 1
Mean strength of command—Officers 10, Enlisted Men 210, Total 220
Percentage taken sick .10
Daily percentage of sick 1.82

Abstract of Meteorological Record 7 Am 2 PM 9 PM
Monthly Mean 49.37 66.83 53.00
Daily Mean 56.40
Maximum temperature 86° on the 6th
Minimum " 26° on the night of the 26th
Highest daily mean 70.33° " " 7th
Lowest " " 40° " " 19th
Monthly range 60°
Cloudiness 3.70
No. of days of rain 2
Rain fall .43

Abstract of Hospital Fund

Balance on hand per last statements $111.09
Savings $12.69 Total Credits 123.69
Disbursements 25.76
Balance on hand 97.93
Geo. E. Lord
Fort Buford, D.T.) Asst. Surg., U.S.A.
Sept. 30th 1875) Post Surgeon

Record for the Month of October, 1875

October 2nd Lieut. Craft and Mr. A.C. Leighton[44] and wife arrived on the Steamer Benton

" 3rd Mail arrived from Bismarck. Weather cloudy with slight rain in the evening.

" 4th A cold and cloudy day with slight rain in the morning. A letter was sent to Post HdQrs. requesting that the men on extra duty in the post hospital be excused from attending Reveille roll call.

" 5th The above request returned to Post Surgeon with the following endorsement "Not approved unless the Steward holds a roll call at the same time. In which case it is."

" 6th The paper was returned to the Post Adjutant with this endorsement. "The steward will ascertain who are present at Reveille and report absentees."

" 8th Steamer "Far West"[45] arrived, having on board Capt. Murdock and bride,[46] Lieut. Wagner,[47] assigned to the Reg't. from the Military Academy, and one hundred and three recruits for the 7th Infty. On account of the difficulty of transporting these recruits to their Reg't. This fall, it was ordered by telegraph from Dept. Hdqrs. that they remain here until Spring. They were accordingly assigned to the five companies of the garrison.

" 10th Mail arrived from Bismarck.

" 11th Fatigue party of fifty (50) men in charge of Lieut. Jacob commenced to build a dam across "Garden Coolie"[48] for purposes of irrigation.

" 13th Very high wind.

" 14th Weather mild and pleasant.

" 16th Wild Geese flying south. Strs. Josephine and Western passed Down the river. Weather warm and pleasant.

" 17th Mail arrived from Bismarck., D.T.

" 18th During the last week, the Indians in camp near old Fort Union have left for a buffalo hunt.

" 19th Weather continues delightfully pleasant. Work on the dam at Garden Coolie will probably be completed in three days October 20th Two scouts came in from Fort Lincoln, D.T. bringing a dispatch from Dept. Hdqrs. for Gen'l Hazen. It related to the discharge of some man of Co. F, 6th Inf.

" 22nd Weather cloudy with light rain in the evening.

" 23rd Lieut. Jacob with six recruits for Co. I, 6th Infty and twenty-four men discharged left for Fort Lincoln.[49] Mr. McAllister, Q.M. Clerk accompanied him and will return with the Paymaster.

" 24th Gen'l Hazen and Lieut. Groesbeck left for Bismarck having taken advantage of the leave of absence granted them.[50]

" 25th The first snow of the season—fall very light.

" 26th Snow and rain. The following letter received from Post Headquarters.

Post Surgeon, Headquarters Fort Buford, D.T.
Present October 26th 1875
Sir: I am directed by the Major commanding to say that the operation of par III G.O. No. 51. CS from these Headquarters, requiring you to report cases of venereal diseases among enlisted men of the command, is suspended.
I am Sir,
Very respectfully,
Your Obt. Serv't,
(Signed) Chas. G. Penny
1st Lieut. 6th US Inf.
Adjutant

" 29th Paymaster Major Wm. Smith, U.S.A. arrived, with an escort from Fort Stevenson, under command of Lieut. Gurley,[51] 6th Infty. Mr. McAllister[52] returned with them.

" 30th Scott,[53] who owns a wood-yard a few miles from the post and on the opposite side of the river, came into the post stating that his place had been attacked by four Indians (Sioux) that day and that he had succeeded in killing one of them, whence the others fled. A Sergeant and six men were sent down for the protection of the men at the wood-yard and to move their effects to the vicinity of the post. An escort was also sent out for the mail-wagon.

" 31st Muster at 9 A.M. The following *Sanitary Report* was sent

To the Post Adjutant.
Fort Buford, D.T.
October 31st 1875
To the Post Adjutant
Sir:
In compliance with Circular Orders No. 2 War Department Surgeon General's Office, Washington, D.C. November 25th 1874. I have the honor to submit the following Sanitary Report for the month ending October 31st 1875

It has been noticed during The present month that the barracks have not presented their usual neat appearance—due no doubt to their crowded state and the fact that every available man has been required for constant fatigue duty.

The food of the men has been for the most part very well cooked, and the bills of fare have shown a fair variety, both as to the articles of diet and the manner of cooking[54] In view of the overcrowded state of the men's quarters caused by the attachment to the several companies of the command of one hundred and three recruits of the 7th Infantry, I would respectfully recommend that the set of quarters now unoccupied be used for the accommodations of a portion of the detachment, and that if practicable, some other building at the post be converted into temporary barracks for the remainder. Unless some other arrangements have the present be effected, it is believed that the efficiency of the Command during the coming winter will be materially impaired by reason of the increased number of cases of acute inflammatory affections that will be developed in the foul air of the barrack-room.[55]

Abstract of Sick Report
Remaining at last report - - - - - - - - - - - - - - - - 8
Taken sick or wounded during the month - - - - - - 29
Total sick and wounded - - - - - - - - - - - - - - - - 37
Returned to duty - - - - - - - - - 27   Discharged 1 Total - - - - 28
Remaining under treatment - 9
No. of patients admitted to hospital during the month - - - - - 20
Daily average no. treated in hospital - 7
do do do do do quarters - 2
Mean strength of command—Officers 13, Enlisted Men 372, Total 385
Percentage taken sick .10 Daily percentage of sick 2
Abstract of Meteorological Record 7 Am 2 PM 9 PM
Monthly Mean 37.55 54.45 41.32
Daily Mean 44.44
Maximum temperature 79°
Minimum " 20°
Highest daily mean 58 (October 20th)
Lowest " " 28.33 (" 29th)
Monthly range 59
Cloudiness 5.28
No. of days of rain 2 No. of days snow—1
Rain fall——.45 Wind South.
Abstract of Hospital Fund
Balance on hand per last statements $97.69
Savings 22.51
Total Credits 120.20
Disbursements 36.68
Balance on hand 83.52
Geo. E. Lord
Fort Buford, D.T.) Asst. Surg., U.S.A.
October 31st 1875) Post Surgeon

After two months, Lord had comfortably settled in as post surgeon at Buford. The onset of November signaled that the approach of winter was soon to follow, yet the daily routines at the post

Fort Buford, reconstructed soldiers' barracks. (Author's photograph.)

continued as usual. Lord noted in his log entry of November 2 that after having paid the command, U.S. paymaster Major William Smith[56] had left with Lieutenants Gurley and Wagner for Fort Stevenson. Lieutenant Wagner, "in charge of escort, accompanying them as far as the 'Slide,'"[57] was to eventually escort the mail to the post.[58]

In preparation for the anticipated dull winter months, social events at the post were held for the entertainment of all in the garrison. Lord noted on the twelfth a "ball in the evening given by Co. 'D,' 6th Infty." and on the fifteenth, the day after quite a heavy fall of snow, a "band concert in the evening, the first of a series to be given weekly during the winter."[59] In addition to the weekly Sixth Regimental Band concerts and occasional dance ball provided to the garrison, Lord records the names of the three Fort Buford theatrical groups at the time in the medical log: the Buford Minstrels, the German Theatre Comique, and the New Variety Troupe. Although traveling professional entertainment groups made appearances at some of the military forts on the Missouri, most of the performances at the posts to help alleviate the daily monotony were provided by members of the post garrisons.[60] Lord alluded to one of these initial entertainments evolving into a disappointing experience when he noted, "A Negro Minstrel performance given by men of the Command in the evening was a complete failure owing to the poor quality and inordinate quantity of rum imbibed."[61]

The month appeared to be ending as a relatively quiet one until November 26, when Dr. Lord was confronted with having to handle an explosive incident when one of the enlisted men went berserk. He noted in the medical log:

> Pvt. Mario[62] recruit of the 7th Infty., attached to Co. C 6th Infty., was suddenly seized with a very violent attack of Mania and was taken to the guard-house and placed in hand-cuffs which was done after he had been with difficulty taken to the hospital. His previous history shows him to have been at one time an inmate of an Insane Asylum. The exciting cause of the attack is thought to have been poor whiskey of which he had taken during the afternoon. He is not an habitual drinker.[63]

The following day, Lord noted that "the patient with Mania is less violent but at no time rational—has refused food until this morning." However, three days later, an even more dangerous situation erupted as "The insane although hand-cuffed, drove the attendant out of the Isolation room in which he was kept, took the fire-poker and barricaded the door so that it was impossible to enter the room without breaking down the door which was done with an axe, and the man secured and taken into the vacant ward. He was quieted by means of chloroform inhaled."[64] Private Mario was declared by Dr. Lord as a "fit subject for the Government Insane Asylum at Washington and should be sent there as soon as practicable."[65] However, arrangements were not able to be finalized for his transfer to that facility for further care until almost three months later, and it was not until March 12 that "Lieut. Day with escort left the post in charge of Recruit Edwin Mario 7th Infty" to take him to the Washington, D.C., hospital.[66] In the interim, the patient's hospital care was a challenge for Lord and his staff. On January 4, Mario "escaped from the ward in the evening and was found about two hours later hiding in the engine house" before the post scouts located him and prevented him from freezing to death.[67] Overall, the case of the unfortunate Private Mario is a typical example of the difficulty and challenges faced by physicians in the nineteenth century in attempting to provide care for patients with mental health problems for the safety of both the patient and other persons in contact with them. Unfortunately, this remains a significant challenge even today in modern medicine despite the availability of various psychotropic drugs.

The month of December was a relatively uneventful one at Fort Buford. The daily military routines and theatrical performances continued, although nothing of great significance occurred. Even "Christmas Day was a quiet one. The companies had a very nice dinner and were presented with three gallons each of whiskey by the Post Trader" and, although there was a New Year's Eve ball given by the noncommissioned officers, "a very quiet New Years" day passed, as Lord noted in the medical log.[68]

From December through the first four months of 1876, an average of seven patients were treated daily at the post hospital and a range of nine to seventeen were admitted to the hospital during that period. The records indicate that Dr. Lord and his acting assistant surgeon, Dr. McKinney, treated a variety of illnesses and injuries. As the very cold weather had set in for the winter at Fort Buford after the start of the new year, Lord noted that on January 20 one of the guards walking his post suffered a frozen toe, the "very first frost bite of the winter." The treatment of frostbite remains essentially the same today as was utilized in the 1870s, although there have been some minor changes in the initial treatment guidelines. Gradual rewarming of the affected digit or limb remains the central caveat of treatment. Dr. Lord would have followed the recommendations of the era, which instructed that the exposed part was to be either "slowly rubbed with snow, or bathed with cold water, either in the open air or in a cold room . . . [and] after half an hour, two or three tea-spoons of weak brandy and cold water [were] to be given."[69] Modern-day guidelines recommend immersing the injured tissue in a warm water bath at 104–107.6° F (40–42°C), then lightly wrapping or splinting the injured part to prevent further tissue damage from the ice crystals that have formed; however, rubbing or massage of the involved part is contraindicated.⁷⁰ A remaining standard from Dr. Lord's era is monitoring of the injured part for several days to ascertain nonviable tissue (blackening/necrosis) for determination of either debridement or amputation. Lord does not document any amputations for frostbite in this soldier's case or for any others in the medical record during his time at Fort Buford and, therefore, one can assume these were not as severe as some cases could be.

More serious health cases among two enlisted men were noted as having occurred at the end of the month. Lord described these in more detail than simply noting the afflictions. In the medical log, the following was documented:

> Quite a severe case of Acute Rheumatism was admitted to hospital early in the month and is still under treatment. All of his painful articulations have been in turn affected and the muscles of the thorax and neck have been quite painful. The soreness of his neck and chest have caused the most concern to the patient. He has been unable to Keep in the recumbent posture any length of time owing to dyspnea, but has to be propped up in bed with a pillow. His condition is much improved at this present time. The treatment has been with alkaline and colchicum and morphine at night.
>
> The Case of Diabetes Mellitus presents all the symptoms of the disease in a marked degree. The urine contains an abundance of sugar and the specific gravity ranges from 10.30 to 10.51. The treatment has been Bicarbonate of Soda and Potassa, with Iron Quinoa and Cod Liver oil and Stachina and Carbolic Acid have also been tried [Merlab Metab?—illegible] Equnia [hyingan?—illegible] at night. There is little or no improvement in the patient's condition and the case will probably go on to a fatal termination.⁷¹

In the first case, Lord does not record the name of the soldier; however, he identifies him as "Private Cragen" (probably Craven) in the next month's medical record on February 5 (see n86). The doctor's documentation of the patient's symptoms of acute rheumatism follows exactly those described for the condition in Flint's *Principles and Practice of Medicine*, the well-known medical textbook he studied in medical school back in Chicago. As defined by Dr. Flint, acute rheumatism or acute rheumatic arthritis was an "affection [involving] inflammation of the lining (synovium) of the articulations or joints."[72] Onset was sudden in the majority of cases, with local pain, swelling, erythema (increased redness), and increased warmth. Fever was prevalent but usually fluctuated. The duration of the attack varied but usually lasted anywhere from fifteen to thirty days.[73] Today, rheumatic fever is known to be an inflammatory disease that "occurs as a delayed sequel to pharyngeal infections with group A streptococci" bacteria.[74] It affects the heart, joints, central nervous system, and skin. Even back in the 1870s, just as today, the longer-term danger was known for the tendency to invade the heart, causing endocarditis (inflammation of the heart lining) and valvular disease, particularly the mitral valve, resulting from fibrous or calcific damage to the mitral valve. The latter usually occurs after multiple recurrent episodes of rheumatic fever associated with recurrent streptococcal pharyngeal infections. Although the exact mechanism in which the bacteria triggers the rheumatic disease process remains unknown, it is thought to be an autoimmune mechanism.[75] Pericarditis can also occur, as was noted at the eventual autopsy for Private Abraham Dick, another soldier whom Lord would admit to the post hospital the following month on February 6 with acute rheumatism (see n87). Pericarditis, inflammation of the membrane covering the heart (and/or the other components of rheumatic heart disease) would have contributed to the dyspnea (difficulty breathing) along with inactivity due to the general joint pain experienced by Private Dick, Lord's second patient with this affliction.[76] Although there remains no specific cure for rheumatic fever, and while penicillin is used for the streptococcal pharyngeal infections (and any remaining bacteria once a rheumatic fever episode is diagnosed), treatment in the 1870s was supportive/palliative, as it is today in attempting to alleviate the fever, pain, and joint inflammation. Willey and Scott found 1,056 diagnoses of acute and chronic rheumatism having been recorded in their review of Seventh Cavalry medical records for the Indian Wars period.[77] In the case of Private Craven, Lord's treatment modalities followed standards of the day. Alkaline, such as nitrate of potassa or bicarbonate of soda, given every four hours was used to reduce the acidic condition from lactic acid buildup in the blood and urine from muscle inactivity.

Small doses of colchicum, an anti-inflammatory, and opiates such as morphine or opium were used to relieve the pain and inflammation of joints, although just as today, caution with opiate use was advised due to the potential for intestinal motility decrease (constipation) and drug dependence. Other palliative measures, aside from rest, included application of a cloth soaked in alkaline and opium (or soap and opium) placed on the affected joints for pain relief.[78]

Regarding the second soldier's case, during the 1870s the exact cause of diabetes mellitus was not known, as Dr. Flint noted in his textbook.[79] Today, the metabolic disease, in which carbohydrate breakdown is reduced, is known to be caused by a deficiency of insulin resulting in large amounts of sugar in the blood (hyperglycemia) and urine (glycosuria).[80] However, even during Lord's era, the long-term prognosis was known to be guarded and the resulting chronic complications included degenerative damage to blood vessels, kidneys (nephropathy), the eyes (retinopathy), nerves (neuropathy), and urine changes (uropathy). Increased urination and thirst are common symptoms. There still is no cure, and as such, during Lord's time (and today), the condition was managed. Specific gravity is the ratio of the density of a substance as compared to water. With regard to diabetes, it provides a measurement of concentration of the urine, helpful in indicating if dehydration is present, which is common in the disease due to increased urine elimination. Flint's textbook states the usual range of specific gravity of the urine (in diabetes as 1.030 to 1.074, and Dr. Lord notes the patient's results being exactly within that range).[81] Once again, Lord appears to have followed some of the remedies described in Flint's textbook. The bicarbonate of soda helped decrease the quantity of urine and amount of sugar, as alkalinity of the blood helps in the breakdown of sugar. Strychnia (strychnine), an alkaline, crystalline, very poisonous alkaloid, obtained from the nux vomica plant (sometimes used as a central nervous stimulant, although no longer used in medicine), was "observed to exert a marked effect upon the amount of sugar contained in the urine" as were iodide of potassium, tincture of the chloride of iron, cod-liver oil, quinia (quinine, from cinchona bark), ergot, and opium, the latter three of which also were helpful for pain and muscle spasm. Lord does not name this soldier here, but he identifies him in the next month's medical report as Private Spencer (see n94). Obviously, he was not optimistic about the current prognosis.

With the arrival of February, Dr. Lord was no less busy than he was the previous month in attending to the medical conditions of his current patients and other members of the garrison. On February 2, he recorded that the "Child of Mulligan[82] (Interpreter) died of hemorrhage of the Umbilical cord" and the same day a "Case of Gonorrhoea admitted to hospital."[83] Regarding the latter case, gonorrhea is a nasty venereal disease. Symptoms usually appear within two to seven days. Inflammation of the urethra and penis in men is characterized by a purulent urethral discharge and dysuria (painful urination). Fever, polyarthralgias (multiple painful joints), and pustular skin lesions occur, including on the genitals. Later complications can occur that affect the liver and heart.[84] Lord does not record what treatments he used for the soldier's affliction from this venereal disease. But today, the cause of gonorrhea is known to be the bacteria *Neisseria gonorrhoeae* (discovered in 1879) and is treated with antibiotics. Increased bacterial resistance to antibiotics in recent years has resulted in ceftriaxone replacing penicillin plus azithromycin as the initial recommendation since 2020 (or gentamycin plus azithromycin as an option for cephalosporin allergic persons). However, treatment on the western frontier in the nineteenth century involved palliative measures. Dr. Lord would have used such remedies as rest for the inflamed parts (perhaps a suspension bandage) and a tablespoon of either Dover's powder (a no-longer-used powder of ipecac and opium used as a pain reliever and to promote perspiration) or dried "flaxseed tea containing two drachms of acetate or bicarbonate of potash with belladonna and opium suppository at night" to help alleviate the dysuria (painful urination) and promote perspiration. Dietary measures recommended were avoidance of acidic foods such as meats and liquids such as alcohol and use of rice, nonbuttered bread, and boiled eggs. Penile (urethral) injections were administered 3–4 times per day with a solution of mercury or silver nitrate, although complications could occur, such as gum disease and loose teeth for the former and urethral necrosis for the latter. Indian hemp, *Apocynum cannabinum*, from the perennial herbal plant common in North America ("cannabinum" refers to the flowering plant class, not the psychoactive cannabis) in a dose of 10–15 grains from the powdered root was given three to four times daily to clean out the urethra in passing urine.[85]

On February 5 and 6, Lord noted the "decided improvement in the case of Pvt Cragen[86] sick with Acute Rheumatism" and the admission of his second patient with the same condition, "Pvt. Dick, Co. F."[87] The following day, he admitted Private Gallagher[88] of Company F "with a scald of right arm—mild case." Dr. Lord does not indicate his exact treatment regimen for Private Gallagher. However, there were varied treatments for scalds and burns used, often at the preference of the physician. Aside from the natural healing process, one remedy that was common consisted of a mixture of linseed oil with lime water (another combination added vinegar to this) and gently applied with a lint cloth.[89]

A severe, although somewhat less common specific injury occurred on February 15 to Private Schaffer, Sixth Infantry, Co "G."[90] Lord documented in the log that Schaffer, "while at work on the ice detail sustained a dislocation of the Metacarpal phalangeal articulation of the index finger of the left hand and of the pain and tenderness, it was found necessary to administer Ether in the reduction, which was effected with some difficulty, the man having a powerful muscular development."[91] The metacarpal phalangeal (MP) joints are the articulations of the long bones (metacarpals) of the hand with the first bone (phalanx) of the fingers, which are commonly known as the knuckles.[92] The index finger is the most common digit involved. This injury would have been a subluxation (partial dislocation) rather than a complete dislocation since the latter type requires surgery for reduction due to the volar (bottom) ligament of the joint always being caught between the two bones preventing a closed (nonoperative) reduction. Care must be taken to perform the closed reduction properly to avoid converting the subluxation into a complete dislocation.[93] Fortunately, for this private, Dr. Lord was able to reduce the subluxation, which attests to his skills as a physician.

Another part of the responsibilities of post surgeons was to certify the disabilities of members of the military garrison as such might arise. In addition to being noted in the medical log, these transactions were also recorded in the post returns by the post commanders. Lord noted on February 16 that he signed two certificates "in the cases of Pvt. Spencer[94] Co. 'D,' 6th Infty. and unassigned Recruit Charles McMullin[95] 7th Infty attached to Co. 'D' 6th Infty." that were sent to Post Headquarters. The former was a case of "Diabetes Mellitus" (admitted earlier in the month as discussed above) and the latter one of "Mutual Imbecility." Private McMullin's case is an interesting one. Since early standard intelligence quotient (IQ) tests were not developed until the period between 1904 and 1916, attempts to generally assess human intelligence were essentially done by observing a person's behavior.[96] Thus, one can reasonably assume that Dr. Lord was likely basing McMullin's disability on one of the early medical and moral definitions of an imbecile. One modern source defines those as "an obsolete term for a subclass of mental retardation" or "an obsolete term for a person with pronounced mental defect who has strong criminal propensities little or not at all affected by punishment."[97]

On February 17 and 26, Lord noted "Marked improvement in the condition of Pvt. Dick," his other patient admitted due to acute rheumatism. Writing on the first date, "Pain and swelling of Joints much diminished [the patient] is taking Potass Iodid, & BiCarb. with Palo Xoosi at night." He later commented on the second date that Dick's case of "Acute Rheumatism complicated with Pneumonia. Difficult of breathing much less. The dyspnea in this case has been out of proportion to the affection of the lungs—due probably to the condition of the respiratory muscles which have been the seat of Rheumatism in connection with the joints." The term "muscular rheumatism" was being questioned during this era of medicine. Dr. Flint opined in his textbook that while the various regions of muscular pain symptoms were common in rheumatism, these were not a direct result of an inflammation process. Thus, the affection of so-called muscular rheumatism was probably "allied to neuralgia" (nerve pain associated with muscles) and therefore more "properly called myalgia" (muscle pain). Regardless of the exact medical etiology known at the time, voluntary movements of the various muscle regions were very painful in "so-called muscular rheumatism." In the case of Private Dick, the difficulty in breathing would have been a combination of the actual pneumonia and thoracic muscle pain, likely caused by the forced breathing from the pectoral and intercostal muscles, which were affected due to the pulmonary edema and pericarditis. Lord alludes to this in the medical record, again, essentially following his medical school training involving the use of Flint's textbook.[98]

Aside from attending to the medical and administrative duties of the post hospital, during this time Dr. Lord continued to note various activities and observations throughout the month at Fort Buford. Among these were the general court-martial of First Sergeant Hartford, Co "E,"[99] temperatures, wind direction, and other weather conditions including cold, blowing, snowy days, and a "brilliant Saturn Halo" seen on February 24. The aforementioned band concerts and winter theater group performances continued into the following month, the last performance of the season occurring on March 17 by the Buford Minstrels.

On February 28, "Pvt. Smith [was] admitted to hospital with Tonsillitis."[100] During the 1870s, the cause of tonsillitis (acute inflammation of the tonsils associated with pharyngitis), known as quinsy if a peritonsillar abscess occurred, was often attributed to exposure to cold.[101] However, today the affection is known to be secondary to bacterial infection with group A beta-hemolytic streptococcus pyogenes (the same bacteria involved in rheumatic fever and strep throat when confined to the pharynx, as well as scarlet fever in children).[102] Symptoms include sore throat, swollen tonsils with pyogenic exudate, difficulty in deglutition (swallowing), and fetid breath. If the inflammation progressed from the tonsils and pharynx to the larynx (laryngitis) and involved the vocal cords, it could progress to hoarseness or loss of voice (aphonia), although the latter condition was more commonly due to a virus. Treatment today is with antibiotics, oral penicillin or erythromycin, and surgical removal of tonsils in chronic cases. However, during Lord's era, treatment would have been warm inhaled vapor, poultices (soft moist mass of flower or plant material kept in place with a cloth) to the neck, gargling with chlorate or nitrate of potassa, and possible incision of abscess development on the tonsil.[103] Another enlisted man, Private Jennings (which Lord misspelled as Jenniger in the log),[104] also was "admitted to hospital with *Tonsillitis*" by Dr. Lord the following month.[105] Similar to today, this was not an uncommon disorder. Willey and Scott, in their study of medical history involving the Seventh Cavalry during the Indian Wars era, found that 7 percent of the regiment had been diagnosed with tonsillitis.[106]

Included in Lord's final entry of the month on February 29, he indicated in the medical log that "There have been two cases of quite severe inflammation of the eye healed during the month—one syphilitic Iritis and the other caused by external violence—both are nearly well." This complication of syphilis involving inflammation of the eye and associated with pain, photophobia (eye pain with exposure to light), and blurred vision, occurs in the secondary stage (one to six months post-infection) or late or tertiary stage (several years after infection) of the venereal disease. In about half of the infected persons during this era, the disease went latent after the secondary stage and symptoms resolved; in others, it went on to the more serious end-stage complications involving the musculocutaneous, cardiac, and neuro systems, including the brain and spinal cord. Shortly after the turn of the century, the cause of syphilis was discovered to be from the bacteria *Spirochaeta pallida* (now named *Treponema pallidum*), responsible for the horrible ulcerated chancre sores in the genital areas in the acute stage (usually within three weeks after sexual transmittance from an infected partner) and the later stage complications.[107]

The new month initially started in confidence as Lord sent a letter to the adjutant general in Washington, D.C. (with a copy to the medical director of the Department of Dakota), requesting approval of the estimate for the cost of materials for adding a veranda to the post hospital at Fort Buford during the summer. Presumably to save money, the original hospital building had not been constructed with a veranda. Although fulfilling his duty and

Fort Buford Hospital, 1870s. (Courtesy of National Library of Medicine.)

pledge to improve community health standards at one's assigned post, Dr. Lord was a clever professional and enveloped his request with some flowery language to add some hoped-for enticement for approval. His letter noted that "The addition of a veranda to [the] Post Hospital as provided for in the approved plans and specifications for Post Hospitals would greatly improve the appearance of the building and add much to the comfort of the patients. It would be a protection against the snow and wind in winter and a very agreeable shade in the summer."[108]

Unfortunately, the combined anticipation of an improved hospital building and the upcoming arrival of spring was dimmed by the relapse of symptoms of his rheumatism patient, Private Dick. Although the enlisted man had made some improvement, Lord's log entry of March 6 commented on Dick's rapidly declining condition, noting that his "dyspnea is very great—surface of the body covered with cold sweat. The case will probably soon terminate fatally from the heart complication, the exact nature of which has not been determined." Sadly, but inevitably, and despite Lord's best efforts, Private Dick died the following day at 1:30 A.M. Lord's post mortem report noted, "There were found the usual anatomical characters of Acute Pericarditis viz: exudation of lymph and adhesions: the latter were firm over a portion of the heart, the result probably of two previous attacks of Acute Rheumatism. The sack was almost completely obliterated. The lungs were somewhat congested especially

Fort Buford Medical Log original page, March 1876. (Courtesy of National Archives and Records Administration.)

at the lower Portion—abdominal viscera healthy—brain was not examined."[109]

Pericarditis is inflammation of the pericardium, the membrane covering the heart. Causes include viral, bacterial, and syphilitic infections, as well as tuberculosis, although noninfectious causes are usually associated with other conditions, such as gout, rheumatoid arthritis, scleroderma, mononucleosis, diseases of the kidney, conditions of the blood, myocardial infarctions (heart attacks), and even direct cardiac trauma. In Private Dick's case, this was secondary to his rheumatic condition, as Dr. Lord noted in his medical log entries. Today, direct causes are treated with appropriate medications (antitubercular agents, anti-inflammatory medications, and antibiotics for infections and pericardiocentesis—immediate evacuation/draining of the fluid pressure on the heart) to relieve life-threatening cardiac tamponade (pressure on the heart) causing its inability to pump and resulting in a fatal hypotension. However, in the 1870s, the procedure had not yet been perfected and palliative/supportive measures were utilized for symptoms of any of the causes. In this case and that of Private Craven, the treatment modalities for the various rheumatism symptoms were as Lord recorded.[110] Private Dick was buried at 11 A.M. in the post cemetery on March 8, the "service said by Lieutenant Day." Apparently, he was well liked by many in the garrison as there was "quite a large attendance of the enlisted men."[111]

The cycle of life's realities was seen the next evening as the sad events of Private Dick's death and funeral were somewhat abated by the birth of a son to the wife of First Sergeant Gilneath of Company G, Sixth Infantry.[112] Lord assisted in the delivery. His medical log entry related details of the prolonged process, noting the birth was accomplished "by the aid of forceps after a labor of forty two hours. The tediousness of the labor was due in part to the rigidity of the os and narrowness of the vaginal canal. The case was under the charge of A. A. Surg. [Acting Assistant Surgeon] J. [John] A. McKinney and the forceps were introduced by him."[113]

Little of significance happened for the remainder of the month as the garrison awaited the arrival of spring. Lord's various log entries noted the usual garrison daily routines, signs of water running over the ice in the Missouri River appearing to the point of breaking it up, wild geese seen flying north, milder weather starting to appear, and the arrival and departure of various persons, including some leaving for Fort Peck.[114] Two minor medical incidents occurred, as Private Puck[115] of Company E was admitted to the hospital with "scald of right arm" on March 13 and the aforementioned Private Jennings[116] was admitted with tonsillitis. However, on March 29, one of the unassigned recruits sustained a severe hand injury, which again tested the skills of Dr. Lord. The medical log note from that day related the following detailed description of the trauma injury:

Pvt. Hines,[117] unassigned recruit 7th Infty attached to Co. 6th Infty while working with the fatigue party at the Saw mill slipped and struck his left hand against the circular saw. The little, ring and middle fingers were almost completely severed. The lacerations of the soft part and comminution of the bones were so extensive as to necessitate amputation, which was performed about one hour after the accident. The little and middle fingers were taken off at the articulation of the first and second phalanges and the ring finger just back of the joint. There was considerable injury done to the last phalanx of the index finger involving the bone but the part recovered brought together and retained in place by suture and adhesive straps in the hope of saving his phalanx. There was also a laceration of the hand, but it was uninjured. Sulphine to wash the wound.

Distal fingertip amputations are the most common type of amputations in the upper extremity. Today, while there is no consensus as to which of the several surgical techniques used for treatment are the best, some agreement exists in attempting to maintain as much length as is practical depending on the extent of the injury. If no bone exposure is present, most of these injuries can be treated with nonsurgical management in allowing the natural healing process to occur. Exposed bone, however, needs to be covered with soft tissue, accomplished with suturing of local skin if possible, as Dr. Lord did in this case, and sometimes rongeur (shortening) of the bone to allow that. Today, various skin grafting techniques are used, again depending on the injury and discretion of the orthopedic surgeon. Regardless of surgical or nonsurgical treatment, most fingertip amputations do well, although some cold sensitivity or hypesthesia (decreased sensation of pain, heat, cold, or touch) to the tips remains in about a third of patients regardless of technique used.[118] This soldier appears to have been progressing satisfactorily in the healing progress, as Dr. Lord later recorded in the April medical record. On the eleventh of that month, he noted the "Stumps [were] nearly circular" and that Hinds of the Seventh Infantry was "sent to [company] quarters[,] stumps of amputated fingers healed excepting part small & first."[119] That Private Hinds's hand injury did so well again attests to the fine orthopedic skills of George Lord, a talent that not all frontier army physicians had.

The month of April at Fort Buford was quite uneventful, and this is reflected in Lord's entries in the medical log. Other than noting the variance in the weather as spring was approaching, ranging from mild weather alternating with occasional light snow and rain showers (the maximum and minimum recorded temperatures in Lord's "meteorological register" section were 79° and 11° respectively), more sightings of larger flocks of wild geese heading north and extensive prairie foxes in the vicinity of the post, mail delivery, and daily military drills of the garrison, not much of consequence occurred. The good doctor did mention the arrival of "Major Mitchell[120] the newly appointed Indian Agent for Fort Peck" and "Mr. Joseph Leighton,[121] Trader at Fort Peck Indian Agency" on April 15 and 29, respectively. As listed in the monthly "abstract of sick report" section of the medical log, the number of patients admitted to the hospital dropped to nine patients, about half the number of the previous five months. The afflictions treated were apparently relatively minor, as Lord mentioned only two cases in the log for April, both on the last day. One was an acute inflammation of the middle ear, and for the other he noted, "One quite severe case of piles is still under treatment: the disease has existed for Over twelve years and has been much aggravated by the intemperate, habits of the man."[122]

Piles, another term for hemorrhoids (or a pain in the derriere), is the varicose (swelling) condition of the small veins in the anal canal.[123] Defined as external if located in the mucosal membrane of the anus or internal if underneath it, symptoms include pain and bleeding, and recurrent episodes can occur as in the case of this unfortunate, unidentified soldier's chronic condition. Causes include constipation, hard stool, sedentary habits, and poor hygiene of the area. In the 1870s, conservative treatment remained much the same as today to relieve pain, itching, and swelling, which included both sitz (warm) and cold water baths, diet, various ointment remedies, such as concoctions of opium or belladonna powder mixed with tannins from plants or white oak bark. Incision and drainage (hemorrhoidectomy) of the small blood clots are sometimes necessary for large or recalcitrant occurrences.[124] Exactly what "intemperate habits of the man" were not defined by Lord, although a reasonable guess would be rather poor hygiene or diet causing constipation.

Dr. Lord's tenure as Fort Buford's post surgeon was nearing the end. He would only be at the post for two more weeks as the month of May began. For this brief remaining period, a return to the actual transcription of the medical log is sufficient and appropriate to complete the overview of his time there. The transcription is as follows.

Record for the Month of May, 1876

1st Weather cold and windy in morning back to warm and pleasant in the afternoon

2nd A courier arrived from Fort Peck Indian Agency With a letter stating that the Agent was very sick and requesting Medical aid. Dr. McKinney started in the morning.[125]

3rd Dr. McKinney started for Fort Peck at 5 A.M.

Steamer Carrol[126] arrived at 10 A.M. being the first boat of the season—H. Woodbridge[127] a newly appointed officer was on board en route to join his Co. of the 7th Infantry at Fort Shaw— The boat left about 3 P.M. having taken on board the recruits for the 7th Inft. who were left here last fall and temporarily assigned to the companies of the garrison

Lt. Wagner 6th inf went in command—Steamer "Key West" arrived in the evening with co of 6h Infantry Under command of 2nd Lieut G. B. Walker.

4th Sergt Cummings[128] Co. G 6th Inf was taken sick in the morning with symptoms of acute gastritis and died at 10:30 P.M.— The attack came on suddenly after returning from the store where he had taken two drinks of gin. He had been on an extensive debauch for several days and to this circumstance the cause of the attack is due—a moderate quantity of blood was vomited early in the course of the disease, nothing could be retained on the stomach there was little diarrhea and less pain than usual in the disease.

This case is almost identical with one recorded by Prof Flint in his work on practice in which death occurred a few hours after admission to hospital—the cause was the same in both cases.

5th Sergt. Cummings buried in the Post Cemetery at 6 P.M. Mail arrived from Bismarck.

6th Weather cloudy with slight showers

7th Steamboat supposed to be the Benton passed up during the night without stopping at post

8th Weather warm

9th The wife of Corp Doyle[129] Co "C" was delivered of a female child at 1 P.M. labor rapid and easy.

10th Weather mild—Dress parade in undress in the evening—half hours drill before parade

12th Steamer Durfee[130] arrived, Caps Sanders[131] co "F" and 2nd Lieut Byrne[132] Co "C" reported for duty at the Post = Asst. Surg Hall U.S. A. was on the boat en route to Fort Benton and AASurg Newman[133] the latter is under orders for Fort Shaw. Mr. Jms Leighton returned to the post.

13th Dr McKinney returned from Fort Peck. Steamer "Josephine" at 6 P.M. and will conduct transfer from this post up the Yellowstone. Jas Leighton left for Fort Peck.

14th Companies 6th "D" and "I" left post on the Joseph. with supplies for the Yellowstone. Col. Moore in command. Asst Surg Geo. E. Lord accompanied as Medical Officer.[134] Considerable rain fall at 3 ½ PM.

Thus ended Lord's nearly ten-month tenure as post surgeon at Fort Buford. In summary, the review of this portion of the post's medical log reveals the high competency and talent of George Lord as a nineteenth-century army physician serving in the western frontier. Additionally, the study complements that assessment in the sense of providing an intricate view of the daily atmosphere at such a remote but important military post as Fort Buford. The remainder of the Fort Buford Medical Record for the month of May was then completed by his colleague, Acting Assistant Surgeon McKinney, who had been sharing in those duties and now returned to that position he had served in for the month prior to Lord's arrival in August 1875. Leaving Buford, Lord would serve as medical officer for Major Orlando H. Moore, the officer responsible for oversight

All in the Line of Duty at Fort Buford 95

Colonel Orlando Hurley Moore. (Courtesy of the University of Michigan Bentley Historical Library, BL000032.)

of the large supply depot being established on the Yellowstone River near Glendive Creek. It was being built for the planned U.S. Army campaign that had been developing over the past three months to apprehend Sioux Indian factions who had left the Great Sioux Reservation within the past year and had refused to return. It would also force tradition-bound Lakotas long living in the Powder and Yellowstone River country to move to that reservation.[135] Lord was initially assigned to the depot near the old Stanley Stockade[136] with Moore and other officers from three of Fort Buford's Sixth Infantry companies, C, D, and I.[137] Arriving there on May 18 via the sternwheeler *Josephine*, they would spend the next month guarding the depot and awaiting further directives as the campaign unfolded. This also concludes Lord's personal written record with the exception of one last letter, which would be to the surgeon general relating his arrival at the Yellowstone depot.[138] At this point, the doctor likely gave no thought to the magnitude of danger many of his colleagues and he would face some six weeks later.

CHAPTER 4

To the Little Big Horn

> NOT MUCH, I AM GOING WITH YOU.
> Dr. George Lord to Lieutenant Colonel George Custer
> at the "Divide" before the Little Big Horn Valley,
> 10:00 A.M., July 25, 1876

THE SUCCESSION OF EVENTS occurring during Assistant Surgeon George Lord's brief tenure at Fort Buford and his assignment to the Yellowstone Depot were actually an accumulation of factors over a seven-year period finally reaching a crescendo. Following the signing of the Fort Laramie Treaty of 1868, the Sioux Indians had not fared well. Lack of promised amenities at the various agencies on the Great Sioux Reservation, a dearth of elemental necessities such as food, blankets, and clothing, a reluctance to embrace agriculture, and the widespread mismanagement of agency affairs contributed to a dismal life. Additionally, not all Sioux Indians recognized the treaty. Among them, Sitting Bull of the Hunkpapas and Crazy Horse of the Oglalas had declined to sign the agreement and showed no intent to move to the reservation.[1] By now, too, the threat of the Northern Pacific railroad passing through the northern boundary of the buffalo country further contributed to this discontent.[2] The Northern Pacific had conducted extensive alignment surveys in the Yellowstone River country in 1871, 1872, and 1873, and Indian clashes were frequent, including two fights involving Custer and the Seventh Cavalry in the last year of the survey.[3] At the moment, further westward expansion by the railroad halted at Bismarck in 1873, a result of financial difficulties incurred by the owners of the company coupled with the wicked national economic calamity that came to be known as the Panic of 1873.

Yet perhaps the most dramatic cause of the eventual Great Sioux War of 1876–77 was the massive transgression by whites into the Indians' sacred Black Hills, a direct violation of a major provision of the 1868 treaty. The Black Hills Expedition of 1874, ordered by the government to explore that region for purposes of locating a new military post led by Custer, incidentally discovered gold.[4] This discovery triggered an unauthorized influx of white prospectors, miscreants, and land seekers (all of whom were referred to as Black Hillers) into the region in search of fortune, which further incensed the Indians.

As the invasion of the Black Hills progressed over the summer of 1875, additional bands of Sioux departed from the agencies, joining steadfast non-treaty Sioux and Cheyennes already roaming the unceded Powder and Yellowstone River areas of this region. The government attempted to purchase the Black Hills from the Lakotas in September 1875, but that negotiation ended abysmally.[5] In response to all this, President Ulysses S. Grant called a private meeting at the White House on November 3, 1875, attended by Secretary of the Interior Zachariah Chandler, Secretary of War William W. Belknap, Lieutenant General Philip H. Sheridan, commander of the U.S. Army's Division of the Missouri, and Brigadier General George Crook, commander of the army's Department of the Platte. To "solve" this national conundrum, a course of war was decided on. What emerged was an ultimatum to all the Sioux occupying the unceded areas of Wyoming and Montana to return to the Great Sioux Reservation by January 31, 1876, or be declared hostile and incur a forced return.[6] Thus began this protracted nearly two-year war.[7] Over the next three months, Lieutenant General Sheridan, who was to oversee the campaign because the majority of the operations would occur in his Division of the Missouri, devised a plan to locate and return the roaming bands of Indians to Dakota. The overall strategy was similar to a campaign waged against tribes on the central plains a year earlier: three converging columns acting simultaneously in the unceded areas. Troops from Dakota Territory commanded by Brigadier General Alfred H. Terry and Custer would move westward from Fort Abraham Lincoln, near Bismarck, while a column of troops from western Montana commanded by Colonel John Gibbon started eastward. Brigadier General George Crook, meanwhile, commanded the third column composed of troops from his Department of the Platte in Wyoming Territory and Nebraska, moving northward from Fort Fetterman. While the campaign was intended to start in winter to surprise the Indians in their winter camps, troop assembly and movement were compromised by the weather.[8] At its opening, little went well for Sheridan's Army.

Crook's column deployed in March. Designated the Big Horn Expedition, Crook's force suffered a severe setback to the very start of the campaign. On March 17, troops drawn from the Second and Third Cavalry commanded by Colonel Joseph Reynolds botched an attack at the Powder River on what was thought to be Crazy Horse and his band of Oglala Sioux. It was actually a camp of Northern

Brigadier General Alfred H. Terry. (Courtesy of Brady-Handy Photograph Collection, Library of Congress, Prints and Photographs Division, LG-DIG-cwph-00588.)

Colonel John Gibbon. (Courtesy of National Park Service, Little Bighorn Battlefield National Monument, LIBI_00312_11166, Unknown Photographer, "John Gibbon of the Montana Column in Uniform," 1878.)

Cheyennes led by one of their Old Man Chiefs, Old Bear. Prior to this, the Northern Cheyennes had remained peaceful, but this attack led them to join the Sioux for the course of the war.[9] The Cheyennes prevailed at Powder River and Crook returned with his troops to Fort Fetterman to regroup.

In this late winter season, Post Surgeon Lord had been attending the Fort Buford garrison, overseeing its hospital and the general well-being of the post. Unlike the surviving letters and diary of Acting Assistant Surgeon James DeWolf at Fort Abraham Lincoln, downriver, in which he mentioned news and rumors of outside events occurring at the time, no private correspondence of Lord's exists. He certainly would have been aware, however, of these early war developments from steamboat travelers passing through Fort Buford, or from newspapers or official army correspondence. As the spring progressed, with Crook organizing a second column while the other forces assembled initially, the process was completed, and by May 29 three columns had started on their respective journeys.[10] Gibbon's

Brigadier General George Crook. Photograph by D. S. Mitchell, January 1877, Cheyenne, Wyoming Territory. (Courtesy of Paul L. Hedren.)

troops left Fort Ellis in western Montana on April 3 and would end up being in the field longer than any other summer column.[11]

Over the next two and a half months, Gibbon's troops followed the north bank of the Yellowstone River and eventually met with General Terry in mid-June near the mouth of Rosebud Creek. With General Gibbon was George Lord's friend and colleague, Holmes Paulding. Dr. Paulding's letters to his mother provide compelling personal commentary and behind-the-scenes details on the daily events of their journey,[12] plus descriptions of the scenery and wildlife along the Yellowstone. Paulding was critical of much of the campaign, including Gibbon's slow progress, the general daily monotony, management (or mismanagement) of medical supplies, and lack of action in pursuing what few Indians Gibbon encountered. Although the number of Indian sightings was initially minimal, the column was, in fact, being watched by warriors all along, with both the sightings and numbers of Indians increasing as the expedition pressed eastward. In one episode on May 23, which became known even to the enlisted men in Terry's Dakota Column barely a week later, Paulding noted that a war party had killed and mutilated three men out on an unauthorized hunt. These were the only casualties from Indians suffered by the Montana Column all season long.[13]

In one particularly descriptive portion of a letter to his mother, Paulding summarized the pathetic state of affairs:

> Our C.O.'s excuse [about not attacking a group of about 200 Sioux seen on the south bluffs across the river watching the column at one point] was that he rec'd orders from St. Paul to guard *this* side [north] of the Yellowstone. There's literal obedience for you! This whole trip has been a miserable farce and everything has been as disagreeable as idiotic, pig headed stupidity could make it. We started out with as little as we could make last for 2 months, and here we are at least 22 days hard marching from home even if we started now, but theres no knowing how much longer we may stay out. We have all got into a way of grumbling, it is bad for all of us, taking away interest & causing distrust of everybody and worse than all it tends to make one disagreeable and sour. If it keeps up much longer I am afraid the whole Cavalry outfit will lose all traces of good nature they started with.[14]

In the above excerpt, Paulding was referring to the large body of Indians across the river on the south side that had been watching the burial service for the three soldiers killed by the Sioux war party on May 23. As Gibbon's column slowly and methodically made its way eastward along the north banks of the Yellowstone, scouting parties were routinely dispatched looking for Indians and Indian villages. Lieutenant James Bradley[15] and a detachment discovered evidence of a sizable village on the Tongue River on May 16. Ten days later, he noted a large camp up Rosebud Creek, some eighteen miles south of the Yellowstone, indicating that Indians were continually moving westward.[16] The large group of Indians spotted on May 23 was surmised to be from this constantly moving camp (which, in reality, was true). However, after initially deciding to attack the village, Gibbon rescinded the order, partly owing to difficulties encountered in crossing the river. Dr. Paulding and some of the officers did not take this well. Still, news of this most recent village sighting was relayed to Terry downriver as the two columns continued toward each other.

The Dakota Column had also met with slow progress once eventually starting out on May 17, hampered as it was by varied delays and setbacks while assembling at Fort Abraham Lincoln. Troops assigned to the column from other posts in the Department of Dakota had difficulties arriving due to the unusually harsh winter. The delay was also contributed to by having to await the arrival of Custer, who had been called to Washington to testify in the Clymer-Belknap hearings investigating financial corruption regarding the process of awarding contracts for civilian post traderships at the various military posts.[17] Once their obstacles were resolved, the Dakota Column finally got underway, departing Fort Abraham Lincoln amid great fanfare. Even the Seventh Cavalry band accompanied the contingent.[18] The trail west was difficult, scored by the badlands of the Little Missouri River region and inclement weather, including snow, severe rain, thunder, and hail.[19] As with Gibbon's column, the Dakota Column's daily progress and routine was documented widely, including by Dr. James DeWolf, acting assistant surgeon, who maintained a delightful diary. Additionally, DeWolf's diary was supplemented with letters to his wife, just as Paulding wrote letters to his mother, which were filled with personal commentary and extensive detail on the daily events and interactions between members of the command.[20]

Gibbon would eventually rendezvous with Terry on June 9. The objective of locating Sitting Bull's followers still defying them, Terry's simple plan at this point was to establish and utilize supply bases along the Yellowstone River and scout the lands to the south. An initial base at the mouth of Glendive Creek, known as the Yellowstone Supply Depot, was located about a mile from an older stockade, dating to the days of the Northern Pacific Railroad surveys, known as the Stanley Stockade.[21] This and other depots would be supplied by the steamboats *Far West* and the *Josephine* from the Coulson Packing Company.[22] The use of steamboats proved a novel addition to this great Indian campaign.[23]

Upon reaching the Powder River on June 8, another temporary camp was established.[24] That day, Terry personally led two companies of the Seventh Cavalry to the mouth of the Powder River to meet the *Far West* and hoped especially to receive news on the whereabouts of Gibbon.[25] By this time, Gibbon's column had marched farther east and established camp seventeen miles below the mouth of the Tongue River.[26] The following day, Gibbon and Terry met aboard the *Far West* near Gibbon's camp and exchanged what modest intelligence each had. Having seen and been informed by scouts that no Indians were to be found along the Yellowstone River, but rather somewhere south and west of the Tongue and nearer the Rosebud, Terry decided to send a scouting expedition into the region, to be led by Major Marcus Reno.[27] He also ordered Gibbon to move his column to the mouth of Rosebud Creek, where it would eventually be merged with the Dakota Column.

The Yellowstone Supply Depot, meanwhile, was relocated to the mouth of the Powder River to better accommodate the expedition as the apparent center of operations shifted farther west.[28] During the past month, Dr. Lord had gone about his duties at the Yellowstone Depot while awaiting the anticipated arrival of the several northern columns. The supply depots were necessary components for support of the troops during the 1876 campaign. Various locations were utilized in relocating the depots as the ever-changing operations of the campaign occurred in rapid succession during the initial months of military activities. The first of these locations was on the Yellowstone near the mouth of Glendive Creek, within a mile of the old Stanley Stockade site and crossing. The military guard assigned to protect the depot comprised the officers and three companies of the Sixth Infantry from Fort Buford. Major Orlando H. Moore commanded the initial staff of Captain James W. Powell, Company C; Captain Daniel H. Murdock, Company D; and Second Lieutenant George B. Walker, Company I.[29] Second Lieutenant Bernard A. Byrne, Company C, was appointed acting adjutant quartermaster (in charge of supplies, forage, and ammunition) and acting commissary of subsistence (in charge of food), with George Lord assigned as medical officer overseeing the welfare of the troops.[30] Traveling aboard the *Josephine*, Lord arrived with Major Moore and his command at the planned depot site on May 18. They were unable to set up camp until late that evening owing to heavy rains. The troops worked through the night constructing breastworks for the depot.[31] Being in the vicinity of the old Stanley Stockade, the new location within a cottonwood grove was a familiar one and a good staging point on the river for supplying military operations from the east. The post trader from Fort Buford also arrived with enticing goods for sale to the garrison as they began settling in for the next month.[32]

Little more happened at the depot than the sheer monotony of the daily routine over the next month. One who was there, Private Wilmot Sanford, Sixth Infantry, spoke in his diary of drill, meals, kitchen duty, washing dishes, hunting and fishing, reading newspapers, soldiers getting drunk at night, building a corral for the cattle being brought along by the Dakota Column, and unloading and stocking supplies and commissary goods that were continually delivered by steamboats for the campaign.[33] Several men were afflicted with dysentery, one soldier sustained a cut to his foot, and a drowning involving a small mailboat occurred. Private Sanford mentioned all three events, but did not record any major medical incidents.[34] Why no written record by Lord exists regarding any health issues of the troops or the drowning is unknown. In Lord's last known surviving correspondence, his May 31, 1876, report to the surgeon general from the Yellowstone Depot (Stanley's Crossing), he only related his transfer to that location from Fort Buford "with orders unchanged since [his] last report."[35]

The depot was relocated to the Powder River on June 11.[36] The medical personnel in the field at the time were reorganized for unclear reasons and Lord was assigned to Terry's Dakota Column.[37] The day before, Major Marcus Reno was dispatched on a prolonged scout of the Powder and Tongue River valleys. Terry meanwhile directed Custer and the remainder of the Seventh Cavalry (aside from the regimental band left at the Powder River depot) to move to the mouth of the Rosebud near Gibbon's camp. On June 18, Reno and his troops returned to the Yellowstone and during the next three days, mostly aboard the *Far West*, Terry made the final and fateful arrangements for his column. He met with his officers on June 21 to coordinate operations central to the next few days.

Custer would "proceed up the Rosebud in pursuit of the Indians whose trail was discovered by Major Reno a few days since."[38] That orchestration proved critical and ultimately fatal to George Lord. Also, at this time, unbeknownst to Terry and all his officers, Brigadier General Crook had been stopped in his advance northward on June 17 at the Battle of the Rosebud. Encompassing an enormous battlefield several miles long, Crook's troops were attacked by a large force of Sioux and Northern Cheyenne Indians led by Crazy Horse.[39] Intense fighting occurred continuously over several hours. At the end of the day, Crook chose not to proceed, and the result was neutralization of his portion of the three-pronged movement against the Indians.[40]

After leaving the Yellowstone River camp at noon on June 22, Custer's column, which included all twelve companies of the Seventh Cavalry, systematically made its way up Rosebud Creek and eventually crossed into the Little Big Horn Valley. The morning prior, in the meeting with Terry aboard the *Far West* just below the mouth of the Rosebud, the commander outlined his directives for a presumed final approach of the roaming Indians.[41] Although the exact location of their village was not known, it was understood to be in the vicinity of the Little Big Horn River, west of the Rosebud. This was based on information from Major Reno's recent scout undertaking in the days before and reports from the various Indian scouts employed with the campaign.[42]

Terry's plan ordered Custer to proceed with his regiment up Rosebud Creek toward the Little Big Horn, while Terry and Gibbon would move farther west with the remaining portions of the original Dakota Column and the latter's Montana Column to the confluence of the Big Horn River and Yellowstone.[43] Custer's deployment totaled 647 individuals, including 31 officers and 566 enlisted men of the Seventh Cavalry, 39 Indian scouts including 6 Crows and 25 Arikaras, among the latter his favorite scout Bloody Knife,[44] and 12 civilians including mule packers, guides George Herendeen[45] and Frederick Gerard,[46] and *Bismarck Tribune* correspondent Mark Kellogg.[47] Among these soldiers and auxiliaries, four Custer family members were also present, including George's brother Captain

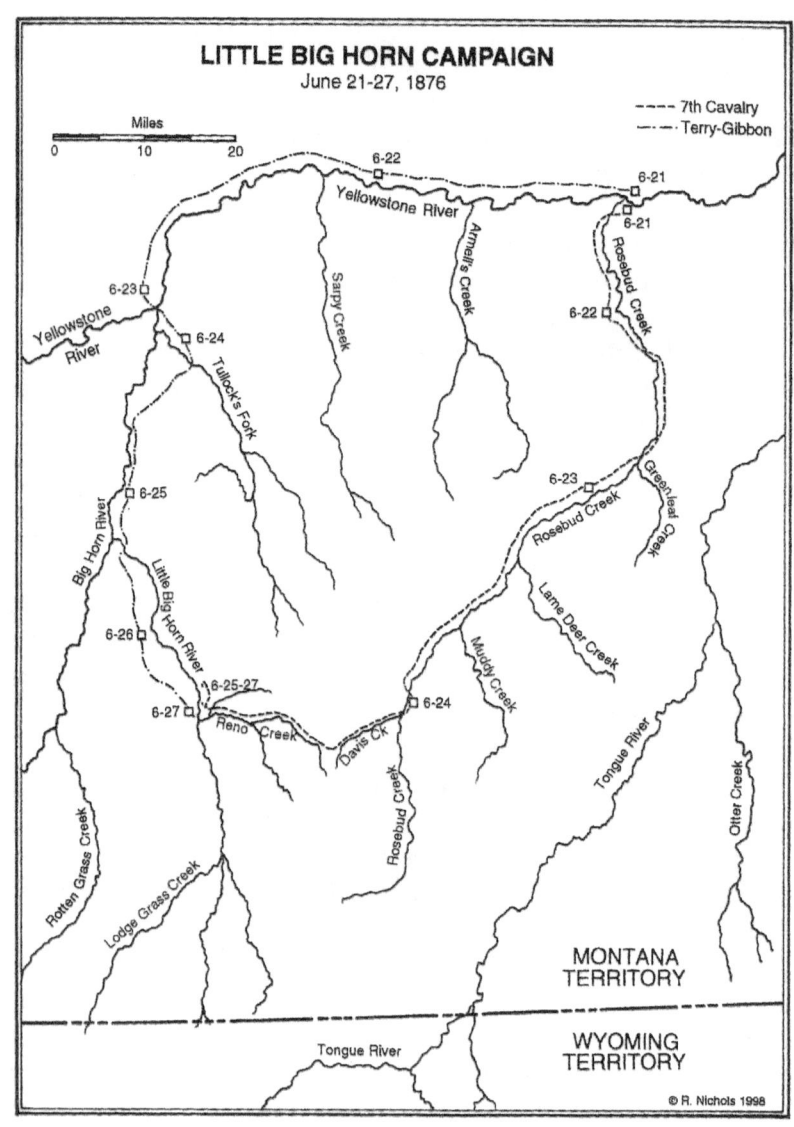

Little Big Horn Campaign. (Courtesy of Ron Nichols and University of Oklahoma Press.)

Henry Rinaldo Porter, MD, acting assistant surgeon. (Courtesy of the National Park Service, Little Bighorn Battlefield National Monument, LIBI_00011_7108. Photograph by D. F. Barry, "[Acting] Assistant Surgeon Henry R. Porter in Civilian Clothes," 1886.)

Tom Custer, brother-in-law Lieutenant James Calhoun, brother Boston Custer, and nephew Harry Armstrong Reed, with Boston serving with the pack train and Harry as an unassigned civilian observer.[48] The medical personnel assigned to Custer were First Lieutenant Lord, designated chief medical officer, and Acting Assistant Surgeons Henry R. Porter[49] and James M. DeWolf.[50] Although Custer was offered the column's Gatling gun detachment, he declined "for the reason that they might hamper [our] movements or march at a critical moment, because of the inferior horses and of the difficult nature of the country."[51]

One intriguing question raised by historians, although only ever minimally discussed, is the reasoning for the medical assignments on Custer's last campaign. Why were George Lord, Henry Porter, and James DeWolf chosen to go with Custer in his fateful search for the Indian village? The official orders and regimental returns are perfectly straightforward. In his chapter on "Medical Service and the Wounded" in *Centennial Campaign*, historian and medical doctor John Gray details the assignments of the physicians and enlisted men serving as hospital stewards and attendants, as documented in the regimental returns and orders.[52] When the depot was moved

James Madison DeWolf, MD, acting assistant surgeon. (Courtesy of the National Park Service, Little Bighorn Battlefield National Monument, LIBI_000312_11138. Unknown photographer, "Dr. James DeWolf in a Civilian Suit and Tie," circa 1875.)

to the Powder River, Gray notes simply that Lord was assigned to General Terry and the Dakota Column. Little Big Horn historian C. Lee Noyes noted that while documentation exists explaining why Corporal John Callahan of the Seventh Cavalry was assigned as the hospital steward for Lord, no specific information in "the General Orders, Special Orders and Special Field orders . . . nor the regimental order book" explains Lord's placement with Custer.[53] Company C, Sixth Infantry records note that Private Leslie Haven was Lord's acting hospital steward at the Yellowstone Depot, but no attendant was identified.[54] Callahan was made Lord's acting hospital steward on June 13 under Lord when the depot was moved to Powder River.[55] We know small things about lesser people, but how do we explain Lord?

Among the four contract surgeons originally appointed to the Dakota Column, Isaiah Ashton[56] and Lord's medical school classmate Elbert Clark were left behind at the new Powder River Depot, where a field hospital was also established for the ill soldiers and noncombatant injuries sustained on the hard journeys en route.[57] Ashton was assigned to the depot likely because it was known that

Custer did not like him, apparently largely due to his not having any military experience. Dr. DeWolf made personal comments about this in one of his letters to his wife.[58] Although Clark, Lord's former medical school classmate, had earlier served at the Cheyenne River Indian Agency, he was probably less well or barely known to Custer. Dr. Porter was likely chosen because Custer knew him from Fort Lincoln and also because of Porter's extensive military experience with Crook in the Arizona Indian conflicts a few years earlier. As for DeWolf, he was likely chosen owing to his military experience in the Civil War as an artillerist and later a hospital steward before graduating from medical school. He probably earned a strong recommendation from Porter as well, as the two physicians had become fast friends after meeting at Camp Hancock and Fort Lincoln before the Dakota Column embarked.

The remaining physicians for consideration, Dr. John W. Williams,[59] Dr. Holmes Paulding, and Dr. George Lord, were each commissioned army medical officers. Although Custer knew Dr. Williams from his experience with him during the 1874 Black Hills Expedition, General Terry likely preferred retaining him as the chief medical officer of the combined columns since he was senior to all and had the most field experience. As for Paulding, the probability is high that Colonel Gibbon preferred retaining him with the Montana Column. Until the columns united, he was the only medical officer with Gibbon's troops and also he had served as Gibbon's post surgeon at Fort Ellis for six months prior to the start of the 1876 campaign. That left Lord for the final consideration. With Custer, he would be the lone commissioned medical officer present. As well, Custer knew him and his capabilities from the time spent together at Fort Lincoln. Although this thinking is speculative since no documentation is known on the matter, these assumptions seem reasonable based on what is known about each of these physicians and their prior relationships with the officers in command.

Leaving at noon on June 22, Custer's regiment traveled twelve miles along the west bank of Rosebud Creek and halted at 4 P.M.[60] There was no mention of encountering any previous Indian camps.

After dinner at about dusk, Custer summoned his officers and "requested [them] to make to him any suggestions they thought fit." He also told them that subsequent "marches would be twenty-five to thirty miles a day."[61]

The march on June 23 began at 5 A.M. and covered thirty-three miles over "completely barren" land, in "very hot" weather, and was halted at 3 P.M.[62] Along the way, it followed portions of the previous Reno scout trail and encountered several large deserted Indian camps—three were noted by Lieutenant Godfrey in his diary. It was here that Captain Frederick Benteen noted a keen observation concerning Dr. Lord,[63] which both Custer and Dr. Porter also commented on. After setting up camp, eating a late afternoon meal, and settling in for the night, Benteen recorded the following:

> Well, after the 2nd day's march, and I had seen to the bivouacking of my troop, I got out my seine for purpose of seeing the kinds of fish the Rosebud could set up for supper. The attempt however resulted mostly of "water-hauls," and being ravenously hungry, "S.O.B. and trimmings," had to serve for a bill of fare. Dr. Lord not putting in an appearance at the meal, however, after I had crawled under a bullberry bush for sweet repose, the Dr. came into camp, telling me that he had halted alone some miles back, being completely tired out, broken down, so much so that he had given up all hopes of getting to camp. He declined tea, and wanted nothing to eat or drink. I state this to show what must have been the physical condition of the Doctor on June 25th, on going into the fight, after an almost continuous march of 84 miles.[64]

Author Joan Nabseth Stevenson, in her biography of Dr. Porter, opined that Lord's affliction was a result of "trail colic," also known as "summer cholera," likely from the "acrid-tasting water runoff of salts from the soils."[65] This was a form of dysentery, a disease resulting from inflammation of the mucus membranes of the colon causing diarrhea "often with blood and mucus, and characterized clinically by pain, abdominal cramping, fever, and dehydration."[66] Depression and malaise often accompanied the aforementioned symptoms. In Flint's *Treatise on the Principles and Practice of a Medicine*, a standard text in Lord's day, diarrhea is described as being "the morbid frequency of the dejections of the bowels" of which, if "mucus be abundant, denotes dysentery," and being common "among, especially in campaigns during the summer season, or in warm climates . . . and attributable to irregular habits as regards diet, conjoined with the exposure and fatigue incident to active service."[67] That the doctor suffered from "trail colic" is certainly a plausible conclusion. However, as there is no concurrent mention or any reference to diarrhea by either Benteen or Lord in existing accounts (and neither Dr. DeWolf nor Dr. Porter mentioned anything about the health or condition of their medical colleague), other considerations for potential causes of Lord's condition could reasonably include dehydration, early heat exhaustion, a viral cause, or simply physical fatigue.[68] Captain Benteen's documentation that Lord had stated he was "completely tired out, broken down . . . and wanted nothing to eat or drink" confirms the presence of fatigue, dehydration symptoms, and some depression, thereby suggesting the possibility of these other potential diagnoses. Regardless of the cause, without question, Dr. Lord was not in the best physical condition as he and his colleagues were approaching what would soon and unknowingly be the end of their campaign.

After what likely seemed a short night, Custer's column again was on the move at 5 A.M. This third day's march on June 24 would end up uncovering some significant revelations by the end of the day and into the wee early hours of the next morning.[69] About two and a half hours in to that day's march, the site of a large, recently deserted village was "estimated as consisting of three or four hundred lodges."[70] Few appreciated then that this was the unifying Sitting Bull Sun Dance camp. At mid-evening of that day, the column halted to camp in the area at the western edge of present-day Busby, Montana.[71] Information from the Crow scouts indicated that the Sioux Indian village was nearby, apparently on the lower course of the Little Big Horn River. After having received this report, Custer dispatched Second Lieutenant Charles Varnum,[72] his officer in charge of the Indian scouts, ahead of the halted regiment to determine the location of the village. Leaving at about 9:20 P.M., Varnum and his scouts, including interpreter Mitch Boyer,[73] guide Charley Reynolds,[74] six Arikaras, and five Crows, proceeded to a prominence known ever after as the Crow's Nest. This was a high prominence within the Wolf Mountains in the divide between the Rosebud and Little Big Horn valleys. From there the Crows said they could see for miles in the direction of the Little Big Horn. Having made their observations as dawn was cracking, about 3:30 A.M. on June 25, Varnum sent word to Custer via Boyer and the Crow and Arikara scouts suggesting that the village in the distance was "immense." The size of the pony herd supported the idea that the village was of a tremendous size, according to the Crow scouts. Varnum later stated the Crow scouts said that "there was an immense pony herd out grazing and [they] told me to look for worms crawling on the grass & I could make out the herd; but I could not see worms or ponies either."[75] Custer returned with the scouts to the Crow's Nest to see for himself. For whatever reason, however, be it fatigue, poor eyesight, the distance, or simply the early morning haze (most likely, a combination of all of these aspects), Custer insisted that he could just not see ponies or the village, even with binoculars.[76] Major Reno later confirmed the latter statement. "He [Custer] said the Indian scouts had reported there was a large Indian village in view from the top of the mountain [i.e., the Crow's Nest]. He did not believe such himself as he had looked with his glass."[77]

The column by then had advanced for another three miles to the "Divide," the area between Rosebud Creek and the Little Big Horn River. Custer gave his last battalion orders just after noon "about one-third of a mile beyond the divide." He was some twelve miles from the Little Big Horn.[78] He divided his command, and each group would go its assigned way in search of the Indian village. Of the three battalions, Custer led Companies C, E, F, I, and L; Major Reno led Companies A, G, and M; and Captain Benteen led his own Company H, as well as D and K. Of the medical personnel, Dr. DeWolf and Dr. Porter were assigned to Reno's command, while Dr. Lord accompanied Custer. Lord, who had not been feeling well that day, declined an offer by Custer to exchange assignments with Porter (who was agreeable to doing so), a decision, of course, which saved Porter's life.[79] Years later, in an 1897 interview appearing in the *Minneapolis Tribune*, Dr. Porter recounted the exact words of the conversation between the three and that fateful decision made by Lord:

> In a short time the scouts reported that we had been seen by the Indians. Custer then decided to divide the command. He sent Colonel Benteen with three companies to the left, Major Reno with three companies in the center and he took three [actually five] companies, and was to go to the right, his idea being to surround the Indian camp. It was about 10 A.M. when they were ready to start. Custer came to me and said, "Doctor, I would like to have you go with me, as you are younger and a better rider than Dr. Lord, The Chief Surgeon." I replied: "All right. I would much prefer going with you." Custer then said: "I will see Dr. Lord and ask him to consent." We rode over to where Dr. Lord was, and Custer spoke to him about the contemplated arrangement. The doctor replied: "Not much, I am going with you." The poor fellow in those few words saved my life and sealed his own doom.[80]

Why Custer did not assign a physician to accompany Benteen's battalion remains a mystery, as no information has surfaced to date answering that intriguing question.[81] Nor did DeWolf or Porter

Lieutenant Colonel George Armstrong Custer, circa 1875. (Courtesy of U.S. Army Heritage and Education Center, Carlisle, Pennsylvania.)

Captain Frederick W. Benteen. (Courtesy of the National Park Service, Little Bighorn Battlefield National Monument, LIBI_00011_07096. Photographed by D. F. Barry "Captain Benteen, Bust Studio Portrait in Full-Dress Uniform," circa 1874.)

make any comments regarding it. Benteen had been ordered to move to the left (meaning southwest) over a series of two or three bluffs and "sweep everything before him."[82] His assignment, at least in part, was meant to explore whether there were other Indian camps in that direction, and if not he would be well placed to prevent Indians escaping in that direction. He and his men soon disappeared over the bluffs and Reno would not see him again until much later that afternoon. The remainder of the command then moved several miles farther west down the creek (today's Reno Creek) leading to the Little Big Horn Valley. Reno's three companies rode the left bank paralleling Custer's five companies traveling the right bank. The columns soon came to a lone tepee containing the body of a dead warrior (killed unbeknownst to them at the Rosebud battle with Crook's troops on June 17). Reno was called over by Custer to join him on his side of the creek. As the columns advanced, Indians were seen by Lieutenant Varnum and his scouts fleeing from just beyond this lone tepee area.[83]

The two columns then continued on a parallel course for nearly four more miles from the lone tepee to a flat near the terminus of

Major Marcus A. Reno. (Courtesy of the National Park Service, Little Bighorn Battlefield National Monument, LIBI_00011_07109. D. F. Barry, photographer, "Major Marcus Reno in Small Oval View," date unknown.)

this tributary valley and also one of the fords of the Little Big Horn River. There other Sioux warriors were seen by the Crow scouts and Frederick Gerard.[84] These sightings, and those near the lone tepee and one near the Crow's Nest, where soldiers actually fired at Indians seen opening a box of hard crackers that had fallen from a pack mule, led Custer to assume that his prospects for a concealed advance on the Indians had been lost. Custer ordered Reno to commence the attack on the village once it came into sight, which was presumed to be about two miles distant, according to the scouts.[85] Adjutant Cooke carried the order. Reno was to "move forward at as rapid a gait as prudent and to charge afterward, and [he] would be supported by the entire outfit."[86] Reno led his companies slightly northwest over subsequent ridges and finally he could peer into the vast valley. Immediately below, the village partly came into view. In truth, it was only a portion, the rest obscured by trees in the distant view. Varnum noted that "owning [sic] to the lay of the land, that is the bends of the stream and the timber around on the left bank, it was impossible unless you get out on the plain to see much of the village. I could see some of the tepees but it was impossible to see the whole extent of it."[87]

After pausing to quickly water the horses, Reno ordered his column forward and commenced his attack just after 3:00 p.m.[88] In charging the village, Reno encountered and chased "with great ease" some Indians who were in the outlying edges. But then a most terrifying scene rapidly came into view. According to Reno, "The very earth seemed to grow Indians, and they were running toward me in swarms, and from all directions."[89] Sensing that he was "being drawn into some trap," Reno halted his mounted attack and formed a skirmish line. From that position, intense firing continued for half an hour, but then the situation turned. Reno sensed that the Indians were attempting to outflank and surround his command.[90] He ordered his men to head for the timber alongside the river, where they remained and fought for another twenty minutes. It was there that Bloody Knife, Custer's favorite scout and friend, was killed at Reno's side.[91] Confusion reigned during the timber fight and Reno abandoned the area hastily, intent on getting to a more defensible position on high ground across the river.[92] As he explained at his Court of Inquiry three years later, "It was plain to me that the Indians were using the woods as much as I was myself, in sheltering themselves and creeping up on me. . . . After going down to the river there and seeing the facilities they had, I knew I could not stay there unless I stayed forever."[93]

When Reno's order was given to abandon the timber area, the mass confusion continued in the rush to cross the Little Big Horn and ascend the bluffs on the opposite side, with Indians rapidly closing in behind at every step of the way. This scene was later characterized by Dr. Porter: "Every man seemed to be looking out for himself, trying to get across as soon as possible."[94] During the retreat, several officers and staff were killed, including Dr. DeWolf and Second Lieutenant Benjamin Hodgson.[95]

Once reaching the bluff top, a defensive perimeter was established on what would forever be known as Reno–Benteen Hill. Benteen,

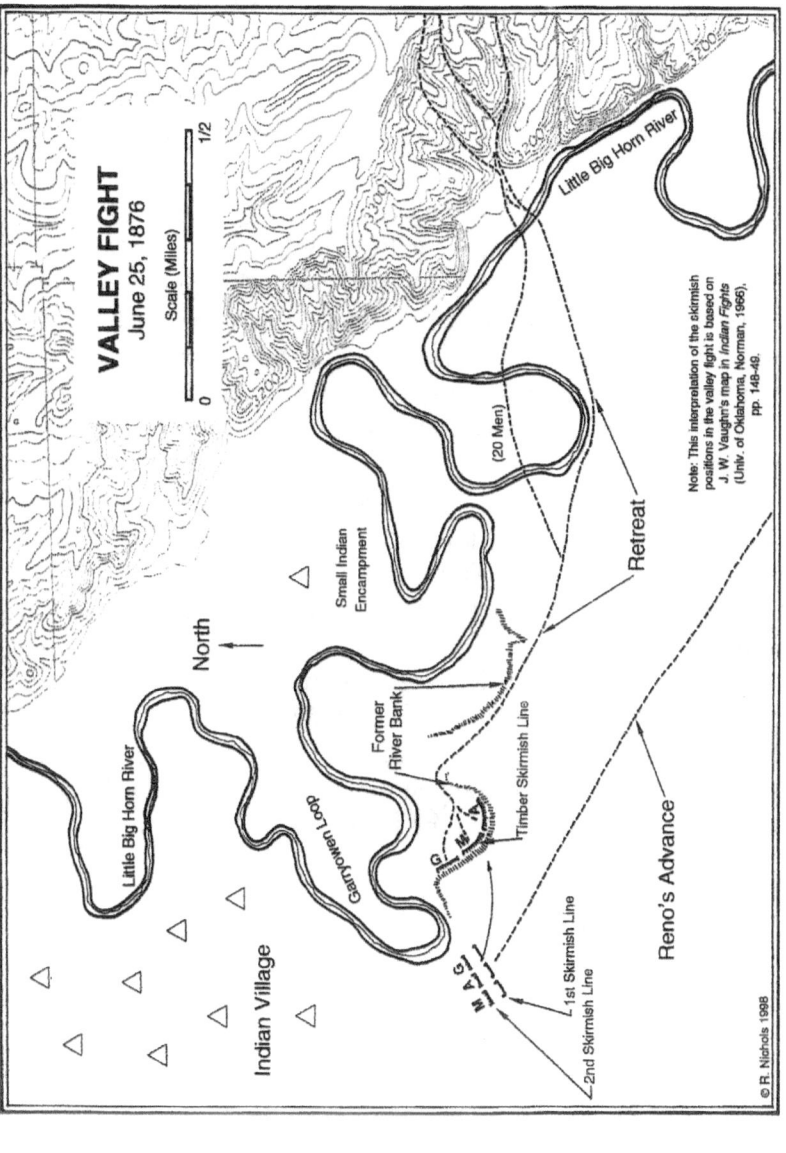

The Valley Fight at the Little Big Horn. (Courtesy of Ron Nichols and University of Oklahoma Press.)

meanwhile, had received Custer's last message written by Adjutant Cooke urgently observing and ordering action: "Come on. Big village. Be quick, Bring packs." Benteen and his column arrived at Reno's position shortly after the major did.[96] Immediately thrown into the ongoing confusion as the Indians continued attacking, Benteen chose to stay and reinforce Reno's troops. They remained in the entrenchment for the next day and a half, during periods of intense fighting.[97]

During this time, Custer and his column had proceeded along the bluff on the east side of the Little Big Horn after separating from Reno. He paused and witnessed Reno's initial charge in the valley. Thereafter, the chronology of events involving Custer and his command have been the subject of conjecture and intense debate that continues to this day. There are discrepancies even in the Indian accounts of the day, and of course, with no military survivors, there are no white accounts of this phase of the battle. But more than a few details can be assembled, including observations of the field immediately in the battle's aftermath and modern archaeological investigations that help explain what happened to Custer and his five companies. What is basically known is that Custer and his column continued on the high bluff until reaching Medicine Tail Coulee, a broad drainage leading to a crossing of the Little Big Horn. Indian accounts insist that Custer never reached the river and was attacked in the coulee, pushing him in a northeasterly direction "step-by-step" toward a distant summit, which ultimately became his last position on the field. The landmark was ever after known as Last Stand Hill (sometimes Custer Hill).[98] Soldiers in Custer's command fought and were killed on a succession of ridges behind him, mostly dismounted. An attempt was made by some to reach Custer's position. Around him were remnants of his company and elements of the five companies that followed him into battle. A few at the last made a dash for the river attempting to escape their dreadful fate.[99]

So where was George Lord during this closing sequence of events? Inasmuch as he was attached to the regimental staff, he would have stayed with Custer, Adjutant Cooke, and other members of the

To the Little Big Horn

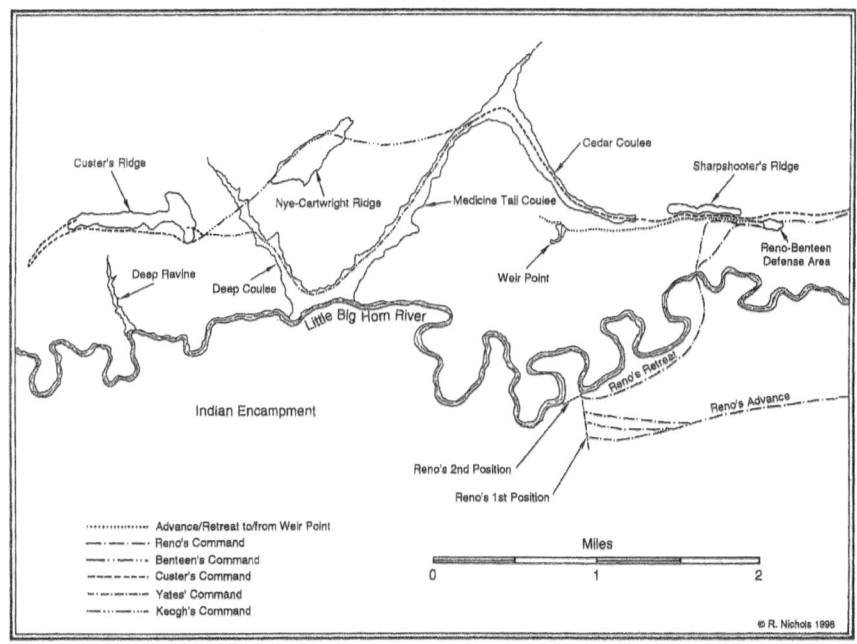

Seventh Cavalry Movements at the Little Big Horn, June 25, 1876. (Courtesy of Ron Nichols and University of Oklahoma Press.)

staff who fought with Custer to the end too, as confirmed by the discovery of their bodies on Last Stand Hill.[100] Unlike Dr. Porter and Dr. DeWolf, whose actions with Reno's battalion are known, there are no primary documents describing Lord's actions during these final desperate minutes. While Porter and likely DeWolf were able to attend to the wounded troopers during Reno's initial attack, and Porter subsequently established a hospital on Reno–Benteen Hill, it is less likely that Lord would have had much time to minister to wounded troopers during the Custer fight.[101] True to his calling as a physician, he may have rendered treatment, but the desperation and hopelessness of the close almost assuredly suggests that Lord was consumed by enveloping catastrophe. In all likelihood, he utilized his own revolver, not a tourniquet, in the end. While civilian surgeon Porter had declined the offer of a revolver,

DeWolf for certain had one in the fight. Lord, a commissioned officer, almost certainly would also have had a weapon. Anything less seems illogical.[102] For George Lord, the end came quickly that Sunday afternoon as the soldiers were overrun by massed Lakota and Cheyenne warriors.

On Reno–Benteen Hill three miles away, an ill-fated attempt by Captain Thomas Weir[103] to reach Custer was thwarted by a massive wave of warriors who had just wiped out Custer. Only the heroic efforts of Lieutenant Godfrey, who covered Weir's retreat, saved that command from disaster.[104] For the next thirty-six hours, Reno, Benteen, and their surviving soldiers endured extreme heat, a shortage of water, constant Indian sniper fire, and occasional Indian advances, while Dr. Porter attended to fifty-four wounded soldiers in the field hospital established in the middle of the defense compound.[105] Three miles to the north, the battle on Last Stand Hill, which took the life of Custer along with the lives of the five companies under his direct command, including George Lord, was over.

CHAPTER 5

Aftermath

> My brother's service was brief, but,
> as I understand, faithful & acceptable.
> At least he gave his life in the service.
> Lieutenant Thomas Lord to the surgeon general,
> U.S. Army, November 28, 1887

While June 25 and 26 were horrific days beyond imagination for the Seventh Cavalry survivors on Reno–Benteen Hill, the third day was even more of a shock as the extent of what had occurred began to unfold. On the morning of June 27, a strange quiet descended on the Little Big Horn Valley. Sioux and Cheyenne warriors and their families had simply abandoned their sprawling camp at the sight of distant dust raised by other soldiers approaching from the north. It was Terry and Gibbon's combined force ascending the river. Not believing Crow scouts who had informed the two senior officers the day before that Custer had met a terrible disaster, two scouting parties were sent in advance of the main column. One group proceeded to the right (southwest) and eventually discovered the site of the once sprawling village; the other, led by Gibbon's chief of scouts, Lieutenant Bradley, set off to the left (southeast) in the direction of the bluffs east of the camp. Both parties encountered the ghastly scenes of the aftermath of a horrific battle.

Lord's old friend Dr. Holmes Paulding, who rode on the right, described the shocking scenes in a letter to his mother:

When we got there we found ourselves on the site of an immense village that had covered the valley for at least 8 miles up & 2 or 3 miles across. It had been hastily abandoned the night before from appearances. Where each tepee had been were left piles of undressed robes, hatchets, axes, tin cups, camp and equipage such as used by soldiers, Indian & cavalry saddles, spurs, hobbles, cut up blue clothing, dead ponies & a good many wounded cavalry horses looking around. Two lodges had been left up and were filled with 16 dead Indians. . . . Some bodies of white men were also found and also heads (which had been cut off and dragged around by throngs [sic]). Feeling sick at heart we went on caring little how soon we shared the same fate. I rode on one flank and picked up a part of a buckskin jacket marked "Porter" [First Lieutenant James Porter], a bullet hole under the right shoulder, from which the blood had streamed down told the fate, a pair of gloves marked "Yates 7th Cav.," The underclothing of Lieut. Sturgis & other things. . . . No signs of a fight having occurred *in the village* were to be seen, but Lieut. Bradley in ascending with a scouting party the ridge, across the Little Horn from us, sent over word he had found 200 dead bodies of white men along the crest and in looking with our glasses we could see the remains of about 40 horses & men in a little clump on top of a knoll, where they had made their last stand. Custer was among the party. We found our Indians had told us what they thought the truth.[1]

Bradley was the first officer to discover the remains of those killed on Last Stand Hill and nearby Calhoun Ridge.[2] Thought to have been a grouping of slaughtered buffalo in a sighting the night before, Bradley was quick to investigate the next morning.[3] The bloated and decomposing bodies were later described as appearing from a distance as "white boulders scattered over the field," or so recorded Lieutenant Godfrey when he viewed the carnage.[4] Paulding related that several of the dead initially discovered included dear friends "Custer, Cooke, Keogh, Jack Sturgis, Porter, Yates, Tom and Boss Custer . . . among them too was my old friend Dr. Geo. Lord."[5] His old friend and medical colleague's body was found on Last Stand Hill near where Custer lay.

Several initial accounts listed Lord as among the missing officers whose bodies were not positively identified. These included Lieutenants Sturgis, Henry Harrington, and James Porter. A careful review of the evidence, however, does not support this and instead clearly shows that Lord's body was identified among the group on Custer Hill. While most of the officers and other individuals who first put forth this claim, including Godfrey, Benteen, Bradley, Dr. Williams, Dr. Porter, and Dr. Paulding, knew Lord, oddly, none of them witnessed Lord's burial. Dr. Williams and Dr. Paulding were immediately ordered to assist Porter with the wounded on Reno–Benteen Hill five miles away and were consumed with that almost overwhelming task.[6] Paulding's letter confirms these details, naming the deceased with Custer: "Capts. Keogh, Cooke, Smith, Yates & Custer—Boston Custer, Lts. Porter, Sturgis, Riley, Harrington, Crittenden & Calhoun, Dr. Lord—a friend of Gen. Custers, Mr. Reed & the Herald [*Bismarck Tribune*] reporter Mr. Kellogg. I did not see any of these as they were buried where they fell & during the 2 or 3 days we were there I was too busy with the wounded from Reno's party."[7] Even chief medical officer Dr. Williams's official letter to the surgeon general in Washington noted that Lord had been missing since the battle, and "there now appears no reasonable doubt, but that he was among the killed in that battle."[8] Paulding equivocated somewhat: "Among those whose bodies were not *positively* identified were Dr. Lord and Lt. Sturgis."[9]

Despite contradictions, conclusive evidence regarding Lord's fate was provided by two officers who knew him and who asserted that they made positive identification of his remains, Second Lieutenant Richard E. Thompson and Captain Otho E. Michaelis. Both were among the four officers sent by Terry who accompanied Benteen and his company to identify the remains of those killed with Custer on Last Stand Hill. (The other two were Captain Robert P. Hughes of the Third Infantry and Lieutenant Henry J. Nowlan, quartermaster of the Seventh Cavalry and chief ordnance officer on the campaign.)[10] Thompson had known Lord from their time together at Fort Buford and a short stint at Fort Lincoln the year before. He was also with Lord on the *Far West* at the Powder River camp during the final planning stages of the Little Big Horn campaign. In a telling letter to Lord's brother, Thomas, Thompson gave a detailed account to the lieutenant about the identification of his brother's remains, fully debunking the previous "missing in action" status of the assistant surgeon. In his letter, copies of which were sent to both the adjutant general's and surgeon general's offices, Thompson writes the following:

> In examining the field in search of our officers as were missing, I found on the hill where the greatest number had fallen, an officer that I am confident was Dr. Lord. You know how well acquainted we were, and therefore that I am quite competent to judge. The remains were lying near Col. Cook's [Lieutenant Cooke's] somewhat higher, (a few feet) on the hill, and where the final and most desperate fighting was done. The points from which I conclude as to the identity are the shapely hands, the moustache, and general appearance. He had on (sole garment) a fine blue shirt, such as he had worn on the march and was not mutilated or disfigured in any way. The only doubt that exists—and it is very slight—arises from the fact that the blue over-shirt was next [to] his body (though such a trifling change from his custom of wearing undergarments might easily be explained by the circumstances of their terribly hard march previous to the attack.)
> Signed, R. E. Thompson
> A true copy.
> T.W. Lord
> 1st Lt. R.Q. M. 20th Inf.[11]

Forwarding this letter of August 14, 1876, from his quarters at Fort Snelling to the adjutant general, Thomas Lord provided additional information supplementing the account he had received from Thompson. He noted the detail "confirms my hope that the body near Col. Cook's [Lieut. Cooke] was that of my brother, Asst. Surg. Geor. E. Lord, USA, heretofore officially reported 'missing.' My brother had a pair of blue shirts, which he had worn on the Northern Boundary Survey and one of which pair I have found in his trunk."[12]

Captain Michaelis, who also knew Lord from their time together at the Powder River camp, provided additional corroborating evidence in a letter to Thomas Lord the following month. In what he termed as "particulars which enabled him to recognize the remains of your brother," he wrote: "The cut of the beard, the shapely hands, and the blue flannel shirt. The socks on the body were unbleached cotton hose, which [he] recognized as having been purchased from the trader at Powder [River]. Dr. Williams, Chief Medical Officer afterwards informed me that he was with your brother when he purchased three pair of these socks for the trip."[13]

Custer battle historian C. Lee Noyes has astutely pointed out that some critics might question some of the "identical language" in Thompson's and Michaelis's statements.[14] While both statements contain similar details with respect to the description of Lord's hands, beard, and shirt, the reference to witnessing of the purchasing of the socks is distinctly different, and that further supports the identification. This is also consistent with the documented fact that sutler John Smith and his employee, John Coleman, both well known to the Seventh Cavalry, had followed the Dakota Column during the expedition, providing goods, clothing, and other amenities for sale to the troops both at the Powder River and Rosebud Creek camps. Lord was at both locations with the headquarters staff.[15] An additional consideration supporting this identification of Lord is that neither Thompson nor Michaelis ever changed their statements in later years, unlike some officers when queried about various aspects of the battle. That Thompson likewise never changed details in his statement is confirmed in his interview with Walter Camp in 1911, where he said: "Dr. Lord was well identified by me and others. He lay 20 ft. southeast of Custer's body on the side [of the] hill. Lord had on a blue shirt and lay near Custer. Only about 20 ft. from him. I identified Lord's body for sure."[16] As a result of the evidence provided by Thompson and Michaelis, both Thomas Lord and General Terry sent their endorsements for having Assistant Surgeon Lord's status officially changed to "Killed in Action" in letters sent from Department of Dakota Headquarters in St. Paul to the Adjutant General's Office. The change was approved.[17]

At the initial burials, Lieutenant Nowlan had written the name of every officer on slips of paper, which were then rolled into empty

Lord's death site at Last Stand Hill. This July 1877 view by John H. Fouch is the earliest photograph ever taken of the Little Big Horn battlefield. The photo was discovered by Dr. James Brust in 1990. (Courtesy of Dr. James Brust.)

cartridge cases and driven into the tops of wooden stakes (actually small sections of lodgepoles from the Indian village) to mark the gravesite.[18] This would have (or should have) been done for Dr. Lord as well since his remains were recognized on Custer Hill. But the actual location of his final resting place devolved into something of a mystery the following year. In June 1877, Lieutenant Colonel Michael V. Sheridan, brother of Lieutenant General Philip Sheridan, was assigned to collect the remains of the deceased Little Big Horn officers for reburial at Fort Leavenworth, Kansas, or other eventual destinations that were requested by individual families.[19] Colonel Sheridan wrote that the remains of all the officers "were identified by Capt. Nowlan and some of the men of the 7th Cavalry who had assisted in their burial, without difficulty, by a distinct recollection of the ground, and also by a numbered cedar stake that had been driven into the ground at the head of each grave at the time of burial," although, he also noted that the search for the remains of Lieutenants Sturgis, Porter, Harrington, and Dr. Lord "was unsuccessful."[20] Why this happened is unknown. Although Lord's body was identified, the possibility exists that a marked cedar stake was not prepared for him. Or perhaps his remains were inadvertently mixed with other unidentified remains of the enlisted men on Last Stand Hill. Both Sheridan and other officers involved in this first reburial effort noted the effects of the weather on terrain and the burials.[21]

Further confusion was added to Lord's disposition in 1890. That year, Captain Owen J. Sweet of the Twenty-Fifth Infantry and enlisted men of his Company D set 249 marble markers to permanently mark the locations where men had fallen in the battle.[22] These locations had been marked and recorded (and disturbed) by previous reburial parties in 1877, 1879, 1881, and partially in 1889, when remains of the fallen were collected and reinterred beneath the 1881 granite monument on Last Stand Hill.[23] Toward the end of Sweet's undertaking in 1890, there was some difficulty in locating the last few of the previous gravesites owing to natural ground erosion, deterioration of the wooden stakes, and disruption from wild animals, and Sweet placed markers in areas where he found any *evidence* of remains. In doing so, some markers were inadvertently placed in the wrong, duplicate, or questionable locations. Regarding George Lord's marker, Sweet noted his difficulty: "To show an extreme case, one is that of Asst. Sugin [Surgeon] G. E. Lord, U.S.A., whose headstone is set in a group of four near the Big Deep Cut Ravine. I found no mark to indicate where he fell in digging into the remains at this spot I found pieces of clothing, a Staff officer's button or two which Dr. Lord was known to wear, hence his headstone was erected."[24]

This marking is suspect for several reasons. General staff officers, including medical officers, medical cadets, aides-de-camp, quartermasters, and storekeepers were authorized to wear special buttons of "gilt, convex, with spread eagle and stars, and plain borders."[25] While Lord had these distinctive buttons on his regulation officer's coat, there is no evidence that he wore these buttons on the non-regulation blue flannel, front panel shirts that he was known to own and one of which he was wearing at the time of the battle. Moreover, the remains found with these specific buttons were never identified as Lord's, but rather *attributed* to him only on the basis of the buttons. Sweet acknowledged this assumption in his own statement and years later reiterating his reasoning in a letter to Walter Camp: "As to the button or two found among vestiges of clothing and human remains in the grave, group four [near Deep ravine], over which I erected a headstone for Assistant Surgeon Lord, as I remember it, they, or it, was, or were of the kind worn by staff officers in general. The fine texture of the particles of uniform found and the button or two were my only means of identification of Dr. Lord's resting place."[26] The assumption of identity was also confirmed at that time during an interview with Major Samuel Burkhardt Jr. by Walter Camp. Burkhardt assisted in the search for locations of the prior burials and placement of the new markers.[27]

We close this summary of information about Dr. Lord's final denouement with one final observation. His remains were never recovered, and thus almost certainly he is buried in the mass grave atop Last Stand Hill, this in accordance with the wishes of his brother, Thomas. In a letter to Colonel Michael Sheridan during the time of the 1877 reinterments, Thomas wrote: "Had I been consulted, I should have expressed the desire to have my brother buried on the field."[28]

Another aspect regarding George Lord's aftermath is that his surgical cases have been preserved, although there is some question as to the provenance of one of those—his small field pocket surgical case. Just over a month after the battle, in a letter dated August 1, 1876, Fort Peck, Montana Territory, Indian agent Thomas Mitchell stated that an Indian there brought in an army pistol and a surgeon's pocket case, but nearly all the instruments in it were missing.[29] Several years later, this case was deposited in the Army Medical Department Museum. It was purported as having belonged to George Lord after being "contributed by Lieut. T.W. Lord, 20th Infantry" as noted in an April 1, 1885, letter from the surgeon general's office to Major John S. Billings, the surgeon who was the curator of the museum.[30] This letter related the same story of origin from the Indian agent at Fort Peck, and since the case had been donated by Thomas Lord, that combination appears to have been the basis for the provenance of it having been in the possession of the deceased assistant surgeon. Exactly how Thomas came into procession of this specific surgical case of his brother's is not known. Some further confusion was added to this history years later, when both Lieutenant Charles DeRudio and Lieutenant Godfrey stated that Lord's pocket surgical case was found immediately after the battle in the Indian village, Godfrey claiming that it was found by "me and my men in the Indian village opposite and across from the lower end of the battlefield when we were destroying the village."[31] However, regardless of where it was found, this pocket surgical case remains today in the National Museum of Health and Medicine located in Silver Spring, Maryland, one of the museum successors of the former Army Museum after it was razed in 1969.

The identification and provenance of George Lord's other larger surgical case, however, is not in question. Shortly prior to his learning from Lieutenant Thompson of his brother's identification on Last Stand Hill, Lieutenant Thomas Lord received George's effects, including "proceeds from [the] sale of furniture" at Fort Buford on July 29 per his request.[32] Among the personal effects was the second blue flannel blouse (shirt) that Thomas had referred to and that had been a contributing aspect in the confirmation of his brother's identity. Also included was a copy of the letter from Buford's commanding officer, Captain William Sanders of the Sixth Infantry, sent to the Adjutant General's Office noting the return of George Lord's personal effects, but additionally inquiring as to "what disposition should be made of [the] set of instruments issued to [the] deceased by the Med. Dept. now in possession of the Post Quartermaster."[33] This provenanced second surgical kit is documented. After being returned to the medical department in Washington, D.C., it was also sent to the army's medical museum, where it remained until the First World War, after which time it was deaccessioned and disposed of. Remaining in a private collection until 2017, the Army Medical Museum Foundation was informed that the kit (with all of its instruments intact) was being offered for sale. The foundation

Left, George E. Lord's regimental dress coat. *Above, left*, chapeau. *Above, right*, pocket surgical kit. (Photographs courtesy of Alan Hawk, National Museum of Health and Medicine, Silver Spring, Maryland.)

made the purchase and it now resides in the Army Medical Museum at Fort Sam Houston, Texas.[34]

Lord's surgical kit is a fine example of those used by the army in the nineteenth century. The wooden case measures 12 × 7 × 1.5 inches, is covered with leather, and is embossed in gold on the exterior of the lid with this inscription: "U.S. Army. As. Surgeon, Dr. George Edwin Lord, U.S.A." The interior of the case is velvet lined, originally a deep purple. There are multiple inlay sections for various medical instruments, which remain with the case. These are individually marked H. Windler. Windler was a nineteenth-century

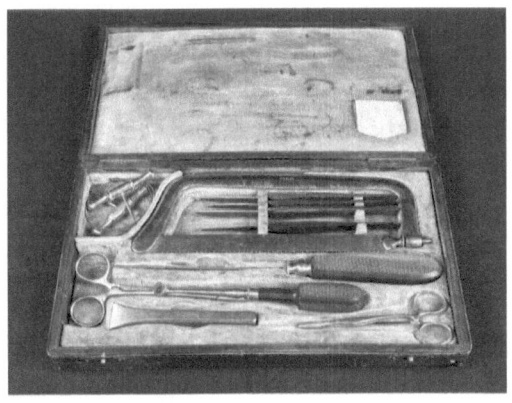

George E. Lord's surgical case. (Courtesy of Robert C. Leeds, AMEDD Museum Foundation, Fort Sam Houston, Texas.)

German surgical instrument maker and the provider of most medical instruments imported by American firms during that time. An interior label in the case reads in part ASTORIA, L.I. and U.S.[35]

Of the three physicians in the Battle of the Little Big Horn, George Lord's surgical case is not the only one that has been preserved. Both of Dr. Henry Porter's surgical instrument cases have survived and are in the collections at the State Historical Society of North Dakota. His pocket field kit used during the battle is displayed at the historical society museum in Bismarck. The location of Dr. James DeWolf's field surgical instrument kit is unknown. The last entry in the account book pages of DeWolf's Little Big Horn diary dated June 22, 1876, notes a memorandum receipt that he turned in "one Medicine Pannier and one Field Case of Surgical Instruments" at the Rosebud Creek camp in Montana.[36] Additionally perplexing is that a surgical pocket case purported to be "among the relics of the Custer massacre . . . and belonging to one of the surgeons killed in that battle" was surrendered to General Crook at the Spotted Tail Agency after the Battle of Slim Buttes in 1877 and was in the possession of Lieutenant Frederick Schwatka at Camp Sheridan near that agency.[37] Just whom either of these two surgical kits belonged to remains a mystery as there were no other surgeons serving in the army killed in the West that year. Of course, it is possible that one of these two surgical kits may have belonged to DeWolf.

That George Lord's surgical cases survive and have been preserved becomes a salient link to the past. History is also indebted to his brother, Thomas Lord, who had the intuition to preserve for posterity the personal effects of his brother. In a heartfelt letter from his then residence at Ebbitt House in Washington, D.C., in November 1887 to the surgeon general of the U.S. Army, Thomas wrote:

> I have in my possession the sword, chapeau, uniform coat, etc. belonging to my brother, the late Assist. Surg. George Edwin Lord, U.S.A. who was killed in the battle of the "Little Big Horn" in June 1876. I have consulted the members of my family most interested & find that it would be gratifying to them as it would be to myself, to have some of the Articles placed for safe-keeping in the Army Medical Museum. My brother's service was brief, but, as I understand, faithful & acceptable. At least he gave his life in the service & I feel very much grateful to learn that a movement is on foot to place a tablet in his memory in the Chapel at Ft. Leavenworth. If the Surgeon General desires to have any or all of the articles mentioned placed in the Museum, I will thank him to notify me & I will give the matter prompt attention.
> Very respt'fly, Your obt Servt.
> T.W. Lord
> 1st Lt. U.S. A. (Retired)[38]

As both his parents, the Reverend Thomas and Mrs. Mary Lord, had by then passed away, in 1884 and 1887 respectively, in Oshkosh, Wisconsin, the mentioned family members were his sisters, Julia and Maria, who lived in the same city. This letter further attests to the warm bond that the Lord brothers and their adopted family had developed during their childhood years. That Thomas was proud of his brother for the profession and personal service he had chosen is plainly evident. George Lord's uniform items were gratefully accepted by the surgeon general, whose reply through Major Charles R. Greenleaf noted that they "will be [a] very acceptable contribution to the Museum."[39] Today, these items remain in the Historical Collections Department of the National Museum of

Aftermath 133

Health and Medicine, J-9, Defense Health Agency, in Silver Spring, Maryland.

One might think that this would conclude the story of Dr. George Edwin Lord and his destiny at the Little Big Horn. Not quite. Two events provide further interest and, perhaps, some additional appreciation of his life. The first of these occurred three years after the Little Big Horn disaster. During the course of the Reno Court of Inquiry in early 1879 at the Palmer House Hotel in Chicago, Illinois, a letter from a person in Bismarck, Dakota, was received by the *Chicago Tribune*. An article in the *Army and Navy Journal* of March 8, 1879, related the sad narrative:

> A Letter from Bismarck, Dakota, to the Chicago Tribune, says: Col. Benteen, of the 7th Cavalry, let the impression in his testimony in the Reno Inquiry that Dr. Lord and Lieut. Sturgis, who were with Custer, and whose bodies were not found, might be still alive and with the Indians. Away down in Maine this ray of hope fell upon the heart of a young lady who is in reality, but not in name, one of the widows of that fatal dash for vindication. There was more in the Colonel's words to her than he intended. For the fifteenth time she wrote to Bismarck pitifully inquiring if there was any possible hope that Benteen's intimation was founded upon fact. Her friend here answered "No." If Dr. Lord was alive and in Sitting Bull's camp the Canadian mounted Police would have found it out long before this. Major Walsh,[40] who is on the best of terms with the hostiles, and is with them a great deal, has made every effort to discover a survivor. He is a great admirer of the dead Custer, and his personal feelings have been heartily enlisted in the vain search. All that he has found has been one of the horses of the white horse company. Dr. Lord may be alive, but it is as improbable as Jules Verne's 80-day trip around the world. The lady in Maine, however, has an intuitive belief that he is still alive and she will yet see him. She reproaches herself for some little thing she did, thinking it sent him off with Custer, and that he was indifferent as to the consequences.[41]

Almost immediately after the battle, rumors surfaced that there may have been one or more survivors who had either escaped or were possibly taken captive by the Indians, in part, since no bodies had been found (or recognized) for some in the regiment. Despite deliberate searches after the battle and later as indicated in the newspaper account, these unsubstantiated stories continued to circulate at times among the public for the next several years and beyond.[42] Some young lady's unrealistic hope that Dr. Lord might have been taken prisoner was a result of her misinterpretation of a portion of Benteen's testimony reported in the newspapers regarding missing officers (Lord, Porter, Harrington, and Sturgis). Asked by the court recorder whether Benteen thought they were killed "or might not some of them been taken there (into the Indian village) wounded," the captain replied, "They may have been wounded, but I can't arrive at that."[43]

Just who this young lady was remains a mystery. Despite careful searches by this author and others, no additional information or any original letters have been found. But a closer review of the *Army and Navy Journal* story and George Lord's two 1874 intimate letters provides clues suggesting that the lady in question may very well have been Annie Hooper. That the writer was from Maine, was not related to Lord in name, and yet apparently had a close, even intimate, relationship with him at some prior time, and the palpable overwhelming guilt for some past action or decision toward him, collectively suggest Hooper. If this, indeed, was Annie Hooper, despite her being a married woman at the time, perhaps her unmentioned reasons for a breakup with Lord and then a subsequent quick marriage to another, which strikingly had occurred at the time of Lord's Army Medical Board examination in January 1875, were causes of this guilt-ridden lament, and a feeling of responsibility for his decision to seek an army assignment in the West, and resulting in his death at the Little Big Horn. Whether this mysterious admirer was Annie Hooper or not, the story is yet another small example of how the Little Big Horn forever affected the lives of those (both Indian and white) who lost friends or family members in that disaster.

Twenty-eight years later, another event concerning the memory of George Lord occurred in his original hometown of Lewiston/Auburn, Maine. The rather bizarre case of "The Romance of Dr. Lord" appeared in the April 3, 1907, edition of the *Lewiston Evening Journal* as a sequel to an article appearing in the *Journal* five days earlier. A man calling himself simply "Montana Harry," purporting to be Custer's last surviving scout, related a supposed "eyewitness" version of the Battle of the Little Big Horn. The newspaper's editors were stunned when he included the "last heroic" actions of Dr. Lord. An excerpt from the story read:

> Then came the tragedy. Yellow Hair [Custer] thought he could catch the Indians in the gap and crush them with the 20 troopers with him and he rushed in. There was where he made his first mistake. His second mistake was in supposing that Reno would come to his aid when he heard the firing. It was only two miles from Reno's camp to where the battle was raging and we could plainly hear the firing. Reno never lifted a hand to help Custer. Dr. Lord, the battalion surgeon, rode up to Reno and asked him what he was going to do. I heard Reno say in reply: "My God; What can I do?" Dr. Lord was enraged by this answer and shouted back, "G__d__you! Give me the authority and I will show you what to do!" Finding that Reno would not form his men and go to the rescue, Dr. Lord rode off alone and joined Custer and was killed with the rest.[44]

The interviewee went on to relate that he witnessed the end of the battle as he lay wounded on Reno Hill "two miles away" (actually five miles), stating he saw "Custer standing and brandishing his sword," but then after having "fallen from exhaustion," he awoke to see that "Custer was down and surrounded with savages."[45]

Almost immediately after the printing of the story and a confirmation that this was indeed the same George Lord who had once lived in the area, local residents inundated the *Journal* office with remembrances and praises of the "clean and bright" character of their former grade school classmate of years ago.[46]

Of course, the entire story is preposterous. At the very least, Dr. Lord was never with Reno at the start of the battle, having gone with Custer and the doomed companies. Moreover, the identity of Montana Harry has never been determined, whether he was a participant in the Reno-Benteen hilltop fight or not. He may have simply been one of those self-obsessed, self-promoting individuals seeking notoriety through blandishment. Nevertheless, setting aside the absurdity and hyperbole of Montana Harry's tale, the story about bravery and the subsequent testaments by local residents as to the fine character and dedication of George Lord in his youth is consistent with other information affirmed in the written record by those who knew him in life. In that spirit, perhaps, the obituary quotation in the brief career summary in Lord's file at Bowdoin College's library archives summarizes that sentiment best: he was a "young man of promise and held in universal esteem."

EPILOGUE

A Note on Thomas Lord at the End of His Life

So ENDS THE TRAGIC NARRATIVE of George Lord. But what happened to his brother, Thomas? Although their lives took different paths, they appear to have remained close. Yet, despite promising careers after being adopted into the same family, they eventually ended in somewhat parallel misfortune.

After inquiries into the fate of his brother's remains and learning that they had likely been interred on Last Stand Hill at the Little Big Horn, Thomas Lord continued serving in his position as regimental quartermaster of the Twentieth Infantry, a position he held until June 30, 1883.[1] He remained at Fort Snelling until December 1877, when his regiment was transferred from the Department of Dakota to the Department of Texas, per General Order No. 10 from the Division of the Missouri.[2] As a member of the Twentieth Regiment's administrative staff, he accompanied its longtime commander, Colonel George Sykes,[3] and other headquarters officers, the regimental band, and Companies B, D, G, I, and K to Fort Brown, Texas.[4] Thomas Lord and his wife, Mary, moved in to quarters at the fort (noted as dwelling No. 1269 by the U.S. Census of 1880), where they resided for the next three years.[5] Unfortunately, Mary died in 1880 at the age of thirty-three. Lord plainly felt the need to continue with his military career and did so for the next eight years. He never remarried. Lord remained with the headquarters staff as quartermaster for the next several years. In late 1881, the regiment was again transferred, this time to the Department of the Missouri, first serving at Fort Leavenworth (Kansas) 1881–83, and then Fort

Supply (Indian Territory) in 1884, where he also served as superintendent of the post school.[6] The Twentieth returned to the Department of Dakota in 1885, with headquarters staff, band, and several companies traveling via railroad and steamers to Fort Assinniboine (Montana Territory).[7] Lord remained stationed at Assinniboine from 1886 to the end of 1887.[8] He retired with the rank of captain in 1888.[9] By this time, both of his parents, Reverend Thomas and Mary Lord, had passed away in Oshkosh, Wisconsin, where they had moved six years earlier to be closer to their married daughters, Julia and Maria, Thomas's adopted sisters.[10] In early March 1889, Lord was appointed as chief of the Assignment Division for the U.S. Patent Office in Washington, D.C., during Grover Cleveland's second term as president. The position entailed a four-year term at a compensation of $2,000 annually.[11]

After completing his four-year stint at the Patent Office, Thomas permanently retired from public service. While continuing to reside in Washington, he became involved in a controversial incident in 1896. Presumably during his time at the Patent Office, he developed a friendship with Anna M. Commagere, a copyist in the same department. A native of Macon, Georgia, she was the widow of Major Frank Young Commagere, a well-known Washington, D.C., journalist and distinguished Civil War veteran who had died in 1892.[12] Anna died on May 23, 1896, after a brief illness and was buried next to her husband in Arlington National Cemetery.[13] Oddly, the day prior to her death, she signed a new will providing the bulk of her estate, valued at $6,000, to her friend Captain Lord "in appreciation of his many acts of kindness since the death of my late husband."[14] Bequeathed smaller monetary portions of her estate, Anna's two sisters, Mrs. H. E. Kibbee and Miss Josette Brown, and other relatives objected to the will and filed suit, alleging that Lord had coerced her into signing the document during the time she was mentally incapacitated owing to her illness. Moreover, they claimed that they had not been notified of their sister's illness by Captain Lord. The attorney for the family presented evidence supporting the claims given by two friends of the deceased. Both confirmed signing the will in person as witnesses. Neither asserted that any romantic relationship between Lord and Anna existed, but rather they claimed that the two were friends. The Washington *Evening Star* chronicled the developments and drama of the trial periodically for several months.[15] Represented by two attorneys, the retired Captain Lord took the stand in his own defense and testified that Mrs. Commagere "had several times told him that she would leave him her property, explaining that her husband would turn in his grave if she left it to her family." Damaging to his case was his own admission that he "locked the body in a room, had her rings at once removed from her hands and took possession of $600 in cash and of the house and contents." He explained that "he did so because as residuary legatee, he believed his duty required him to so do."[16] Lord also admitted that he arranged for the attorney that drew up the will at Mrs. Commagere's request, although he was not present at the signing. The jury found for the plaintiffs, returning their verdict in less than fifteen minutes. Despite the embarrassment, Lord continued to reside in the Washington, D.C., area, surviving on his army pension.

The captain's final tragedy occurred on the evening of December 20, 1901, when he simply disappeared in a dubious sequence of events that remained unsolved for sixteen months. Lord had been living at the boarding house of Susan Magruder at 933 New York Avenue Northwest in Washington, D.C., along with the Magruder family and three other persons.[17] Leaving the residence and bidding a farewell to Mrs. Magruder "asking her pardon for any trouble he might have been to her and her son," he left letters for both her and his friend of several years, Thomas Marshall, a descendant of the family associated with the nearby former colonial plantation house known as Marshall Hall, located across the Potomac River from George Washington's Mount Vernon.[18] Lord's note instructed Marshall to have any debt owed him paid from Lord's will, in the event of anything happening to the captain. He indicated such provisions had been made in that document.

Upon his departure that night, Lord had given the note to Edward Potter, who in turn informed his employer, Marshall, that Captain Lord said that he was going to take a streetcar to the Cabin John Bridge in Georgetown. Immediately suspecting that Lord was contemplating suicide, both from the note and particularly in light of the severe cold weather that evening making a leisurely stroll across the Potomac River not very likely, Marshall notified authorities and posted a $100 reward for information about his friend. Lord, at this point, simply disappeared.

Several false sightings and a couple of misidentifications of local men occurred in the ensuing weeks. Lord's disappearance remained a frustrating, unsolved case, albeit one of suspected suicide. The mystery was finally and unexpectedly solved sixteen months later, on Friday, April 17, 1903, when the Washington *Evening Star* reported the identification of a body found in the water near the Marshall Hall wharf to be that of the unfortunate Captain Thomas W. Lord.[19] The remains were discovered by an employee at Marshall Hall, Anson Neal, who secured the body and informed a riverboat captain, who in turn notified the local police, who arrived on the scene with a police photographer. The newspaper reported the remains as being in "remarkably good condition" despite the "petrified" state and provided further grotesque description relating how the body was devoid of all clothing and flesh. Positive identification of Lord's remains was made at the local morgue based on "the artificial leg and gold teeth" worn by the captain and "on one foot a patent leather shoe . . . known to have been worn by Captain Lord on the day of his disappearance." These aspects were confirmed by local friends of Lord, likely persons from the Magruder boarding house. Relatives were then notified—his adopted sister, Julia Hooper, then of California, and brother-in-law, Theodore H. Eaton Jr. of Detroit.[20] Four days later, on April 21, 1903, Captain Thomas William Lord was buried in Arlington National Cemetery, section 1, site 164, with full military honors.[21] A sizable funeral contingent was assembled, composed of Reverend Dr. Lucien Clark of Hamline Methodist Episcopal Church, a four-black-horse caisson accompanied by soldiers and the artillery band from nearby Fort Myer,[22] pallbearers from Kit Carson Post No. 2 of the Grand Army of the Republic, and several friends from Lord's former department at the U.S. Patent Office. Flowers were provided by his Seventeenth Maine Regiment Association, the G.A.R. post, and the local Loyal Legion post.[23]

Epilogue

Thomas William Lord's headstone at Arlington National Cemetery. (Courtesy of Anne Cady, Colorado.)

On June 8, Thomas W. Lord's last will and testament was executed in a Washington, D.C., probate court. Captain Lord bequeathed to his boarding house proprietor, Susan Magruder, his entire life insurance policy issued in 1894 from New York Metropolitan Life Insurance Company in the amount of $3,000, and most of his personal effects, including his library. The will also stipulated the bequeath (forgiveness) of four promissory notes held by him and due on demand that she owed him totaling $1,530 (individual amounts of $800, $630, and two for $100). The only exceptions among his personal effects were two photos of his late wife and father-in-law, Detroit businessman Thomas Horatio Eaton, Esq., which he instructed be returned to that family, and a $2,000 beneficiary certificate issued by the Grand Lodge of the Order of United Workmen of the State of Michigan, which he provided to his brother-in-law, Thomas Horatio Eaton Jr. as trustee, to be used for his funeral expenses.[24] The will had been composed and signed nine years earlier on January 20, 1894. Somewhat puzzling is that the promissory notes were all executed by Magruder, with the oldest for $800 dating to 1889. All were consummated before Lord became a boarder in 1899 at the personal home of the Magruders. It is possible that Magruder and her husband, a governmental clerk, had needed the loans to help with some personal expenses despite having income from their own boarding house. Whatever the history, the fact that Lord left the bulk of his estate to Susan Magruder suggests a several-year friendship with the family, likely dating from their common employment with the government.

What circumstances led to Thomas Lord's decision to end his life ten days after his fifty-eighth birthday are not known. He had overcome the traumatic experience of losing a leg at Chancellorsville in the Civil War thirty-six years prior. He enjoyed an apparent successful military career thereafter. Reasonable speculation, however, points to several possibilities, one being that he might have suffered from some physical illness. Perhaps he suffered from some haunting mental stress. It does seem strange that he moved to a different residence almost every two years during his time in Washington, from 1888 to his last address at the Magruder home.[25]

Whatever the cause, with this final act, the saga of the Lord brothers can only be seen as a melancholy tale. Both men experienced periodic disappointments in their lives, although such is the human condition. George's is dramatized, of course, his life another intriguing play in the tumultuous and dangerous times of the American West. Unlike his brother and his Little Big Horn medical colleagues, James DeWolf and Henry Porter, George Lord's disappointment in failed relationships, four times, dictated that he was never to enjoy the bliss of married life. Like DeWolf, the promising career of a wonderfully capable, dedicated physician and well-liked gentleman was cut short by his destiny of the ultimate tragic event that was the Little Big Horn.

Notes

Preface

1. Published works on Lauderdale include Robert M. Utley, ed. *An Army Doctor on the Western Frontier: Journals and Letters of John Vance Lauderdale, 1864–1890* (Albuquerque: University of New Mexico Press, 2014); Peter Josyph, ed., *The Wounded River: Civil War Letters of John Vance Lauderdale, M.D.* (East Lansing: Michigan State University Press, 1993); and Jerry Green, ed., *After Wounded Knee: Correspondence of Major and Surgeon John Vance Lauderdale While Serving with the Army Occupying the Pine Ridge Reservation, 1890–1891* (East Lansing: Michigan State University Press, 1996). For Coates, see W. J. D. Kennedy, *On the Plains with Custer and Hancock: The Journal of Isaac Coates, Army Surgeon* (Boulder, Colo.: Johnson Books, 1997).

2. Obituary quotation from the George Lord file in Bowdoin College Library Archives.

3. Noyes, "Tragedy of Dr. George Lord"; Noyes, "Custer's Surgeon, George Lord"; Vaughn, "Dr. George E. Lord, Regimental Surgeon"; Petersen, "Surgeons of the Little Big Horn"; and Carroll, "Surgeon George Lord."

4. See Hutton, *Custer Reader*, 235–36n1, for a brief note regarding the continued controversy over the spelling of the historic name "Little Big Horn" versus "Little Bighorn."

Chapter 1.
From Maine to Chicago

1. *Autobiography* statement of George E. Lord, MD, also noted in his letter of June 3, 1874, at Fort Snelling, Minnesota, to the surgeon general for application for an invitation to appear before the Army Medical Examining Board. George E. Lord, Service File, Adjutant General's Office, Letters Received, National Archives and Records Administration, Washington, D.C., Record Group 94, File 3231, ACP 1875 (hereafter cited Lord ACP).

2. U.S. Census, 1850, Wiscasset, Lincoln County, Maine (for Chandler and Betsey Jackson Dammon [Damon]); Massachusetts, Town and Vital Records, 1620–1988 (for marriage of Robert Lord and Mary Damon, August 12, 1832, and death of Mary Damon Lord, February 24, 1846, at Boston, Massachusetts).

3. U.S. Census, 1850, Biddeford, York County, Maine.

4. *Lewiston* (Maine) *Evening Journal*, April 3, 1907. The article containing three citizen interviews is entitled "The Romance of Dr. Lord . . . Once Lived in Auburn, Me., and Is Well Remembered by Many of Our Older Citizens."

5. A process of elimination, a review of Massachusetts records, and the previously known genealogical family tree of the Reverend Thomas Newman Lord and his wife, Mary, indicated there was only one sibling of the reverend who was a possible candidate for being a parent of Thomas W. Lord—his youngest sister, Sally Newman Lord, born in 1811 in Newburyport, Massachusetts. However, recent information about Sally Newman Lord discovered during the research process for this book does not support that possibility. Sally Newman Lord married Jeremiah Putnam (b. 1802) in 1836. They had two sons, Joseph Porter Putnam (1838–71) and Thomas Lord Putnam (1842–96). Of Reverend Lord's three older sisters, Emily and Sally both died in their childhood years having no children. His oldest sister, Abigail, married Asa Lord (1797–1888) and had five children, of which one son was named Thomas Hodgkins Lord (1829–1916), a trader, who was born and died in Ipswich, Massachusetts. As already noted, the only child of Reverend Lord's youngest brother, Robert Newman Lord, was George Edwin Lord. Thus, the biological parents of Thomas William Lord are currently unknown. Massachusetts Birth, Marriage and Death Records, 1700–1850, including Vital Birth Records of Ipswich, Massachusetts to 1849; Massachusetts Town and Vital Records, 1620–1988, including Newburyport, Essex County, Massachusetts Birth Records to 1850, p. 244 (for Abigail Lord, Robert Newman Lord, Emily Lord, Sally Lord, Robert Lord, and Sally [Sarah] Newman Lord); and Danvers, Essex County, Massachusetts Birth Records to 1850, p. 213; www.ancestry.com Death Register for Peabody, Massachusetts for 1869 from Museum of Old Newbury, Newburyport, Massachusetts; Findagrave.com for Abigail and Asa Lord and family.

6. The only information that can be documented to date, based on U.S. Census records, is that Thomas was adopted sometime before age six when the Lords lived in Biddeford, Maine. George was adopted sometime before age fourteen in 1860, after his biological grandparents died and when Reverend Lord's family lived in West Auburn, Maine, fifty-eight miles north of Biddeford and Portland, Maine. There were only two orphanages in existence in this region of Maine during the 1850s, but both institutions were for female children: the Bangor Female Orphan Asylum in Bangor, Maine, founded in 1835 (now known as the Hilltop School) and the Female Orphan Asylum of Portland, established in 1827. Although Thomas W. Lord is listed in the census records as being born in Massachusetts, no information has been located to date indicating what orphanages, if any, he may have been a resident at. Nor are there any facts on his biological parents, on the circumstances of his adoptions, about whether he was adopted from an orphanage or from relatives, or about his possible relation to Reverend Lord as his nephew. U.S. Census, 1850, Biddeford, Maine; U.S. Census, 1860, Auburn, Maine. Another helpful source is Maineorphans.com,

a website containing historical records and relating the history of orphanages in Maine, maintained by Sylvia Marcotte-Cloutier (accessed February 4, 2020). Sylvia Marcotte-Cloutier, personal communication with author, February 4 and 16, 2020.

7. *Lewiston Evening Journal*, April 3, 1907.

8. Reverend Thomas Newman Lord's parents were Thomas Lord and Sally Newman (b. 1772 in Stamford, Connecticut, to Stephen and Sarah Newman), who were married in Newburyport, Essex County, Massachusetts on April 18, 1801 (some Massachusetts sources say May 3, 1801). Reverend Lord (1807–84) was one of six children, his siblings being Abigail (1801–99), Ester (1805–18), Sally (1803–7), Robert Newman (b. 1809), and Sally (Sarah) Newma+n (1811–69); *Connecticut Town Birth Records pre-1870 (Barbour Collection)*, vol. 1, p. 55 for Sally Newman; Newburyport, Essex County, Massachusetts Compiled Marriages 1633–1850; Massachusetts Town and Vital Records, 1620–1988; Massachusetts Birth Records to 1850; Massachusetts Birth, Marriage, and Death Records, 1700–1850; Massachusetts State Census, 1865, Ipswich, Massachusetts; U.S. City Directories 1822–1955 for Ipswich, Massachusetts, 1897.

9. *Bowdoin College Catalogue, 1864*, 35.

10. U.S. Compiled Marriages for Belfast, Hallowell, and Pittsdon, 1748–1875 (for Thomas N. Lord and Mary E. Tupper).

11. Cleaveland and Packard, *History of Bowdoin College*, 479 (quotation). According to the published obituaries in the *Oshkosh (Wisconsin) Daily Northwestern* for both Lord sisters in the years of their deaths, Julia A. Lord Hooper was born in Gardiner, Maine, in 1836, while Maria Lord Swasey is listed as born on June 9, 1838, but her obituary does not name a town of birth. A Swasey family tree lists Maria as being born in Topsham, Maine, but does not indicate if she was adopted. Gardiner, Maine, is a small city in Kennebec County, about ten miles from the town of Litchfield, Maine, in the same county, the latter town where Reverend Lord and his wife lived in 1836–37. The Lords resided in Topsham, Maine, a small town in Sagadahoc County, from 1837 to 1842. No Maine probate records for either Lord daughter are found in the county or state collections, so which daughter was adopted is unknown.

However, much information is known about the Lord sisters' later lives. Both sisters had moved to Oshkosh, Wisconsin, by 1880. George Lord's older sister, Julia had taught at a school in Washington, D.C., for children of color as a member of the Freedmen's Bureau Society, an organization established by the U.S. Congress. On May 23, 1876, in Limerick, Maine, she married Moses Hooper (1835–1932), a lawyer and native of Lyman, Maine, in a ceremony performed by her father. Moses, who graduated from Amherst College, Bowdoin College, and Yale University, had relocated to Neenah, Wisconsin, in 1857, later moving to Oshkosh. This was the first and only marriage for Julia. It was the second for him, as his first wife, Caroline Bailey, whom he had married in 1858, had died in 1875. The newly wed couple resided back in Oshkosh on Church Street, where Julia became stepmother to his five children from his first marriage. Hooper was a distinguished attorney for the Kimberly-Clark Paper Mills for many years. Unfortunately, the marriage was not a happy one and they divorced in 1897, although Julia retained her married name, Hooper. Except for a short stint in Sacramento, California, in 1903, she resided in Oshkosh for the remainder of her life, mainly by herself. She died in 1919 and her remains were disposed of in Milwaukee, Wisconsin. Her husband, Moses, is buried in Wausau. U.S. Census, 1880, 1900, 1910, and 1920, Oshkosh, Wisconsin; 1903 City Directory for Sacramento, California; 1910–1919 City Directories for Oshkosh, Wisconsin; Wisconsin State Census, 1855–1905, Oshkosh Ward 5; *The Daily Northwestern (Oshkosh, Wisconsin)*, August 17, 1897; obituary for Julia A. Lord Hooper, *Daily Northwestern (Oshkosh, Wisconsin)*, February 17, 1919; obituary for Moses Hooper, *Wausau Daily Herald*, November 14, 1932. Information regarding Julia's teaching position is from the author's personal communication with Sylvia Marcotte-Cloutier, Maineorphans .com, February 19, 2020.

George Lord's younger sister, Maria (also spelled Mariah), married Maine native Fredrick W. Swasey in Auburn, Maine, on October 6, 1862, when she was twenty-four years old. Their only child, Caroline (Carrie) Holmes Swasey, was born in Limerick, Maine, on January 27, 1867, where they lived until moving to Oshkosh, Wisconsin, in 1880 to be closer to Maria's sister. They resided at 477 Algoma Street. Frederick Swasey was employed as a machine hand for the Paine Lumber Company. However, by 1889, he established a "fancy family" grocery business with their daughter, Carrie (1867–1928), specializing in fresh produce. Frederick died in 1913, Maria in 1927, and Carrie in 1928. All three are buried in Riverside Cemetery in Oshkosh. *Oshkosh Daily Northwestern*, January 22, 1927, and July 5, 1928; Findagrave.com; 1870 and U.S. Census, 1880, Limerick, Maine; 1884 and 1889 U.S. City Directories, Oshkosh, Wisconsin; Swasey family tree for Maria Holmes Lord, Ancestry.com.

12. The Reverend Thomas Newman Lord was an 1835 graduate of Bowdoin College in Brunswick, Maine. He studied theology under the Reverend David Thurston, DD, of Winthrop and the Reverend Thomas Shepard, starting his long pastoral career by serving in Litchfield, Maine, in 1836–37. He was pastor in Topsham, Maine, in 1837–42; and served churches in succession from 1842 to 1882 in various Maine towns including Biddeford, 1842–51, West Auburn, 1851–57, 1858–62, Limerick, 1857–58, 1870–74; Woolwich, 1863; North Yarmouth, 1864–67; Parsonsfield, 1867 and 1875; Osipee, New Hampshire, 1867–68; five other towns in Maine, the last at Limerick in 1882. He and his wife moved to Oshkosh, Wisconsin, in 1882 to be near their married daughters Maria Lord Swasey and Julia A. Lord Hooper. Reverend Lord died in 1884, his wife, Mary, died in 1888, and both are buried in Riverside Cemetery in Oshkosh. General Conference of the Congregational Churches in Maine, *Anniversary*, Google Books, e-book, https://books.google.com/books/about/Anniversary .html?id=hsQlmtloVIAC; Findagrave.com.

13. "Book of Records of the First Congregational Society in Auburn," Book 1, Annual Meetings of October 18, 1851, and October 31, 1855. At the latter 1855 meeting, the church committee voted to "refund to Rev. Thos. N. Lord the taxes on the Parsonage-house for the year 1856." Androscoggin Historical Society, Auburn, Maine.

14. Merrill, *History of Androscoggin County*, 44–46.

15. Merrill, *History of Androscoggin County*, 716, 725, 757, and 768 regarding Bakersfield, Poland, and Minot.

16. Coolidge, *History and Description of New England*, 36–38. At the time Reverend Lord and his family resided in Auburn, the population of the town had grown from 2,840 in 1850 to 4,500 by 1860. It became the second-largest community in Maine until the decline of the shoe manufacturing industry by the early 1960s.

17. Merrill, *History of Androscoggin County*, 609.

18. *Lewiston Evening Journal*, April 8, 1884 (quotation), as contained in General Conference of the Congregational Churches in Maine, *Anniversary*; and "West Auburn Congregational Church History," in Merrill, *History of Androscoggin County*, available at genealogytrails.com/maine/androscogginco/andro_history_part_thirty _eight.html.

19. Lord, *Autobiography* statement, Lord ACP.

20. Edward Little (1773–1849) was born in Newburyport, Massachusetts, but raised in New Hampshire. A 1798 graduate of Dartmouth College, he lived in Newburyport, became an attorney before moving to Auburn in 1826, and continued his law practice there. He inherited money and property in Auburn after his father's death in 1830 and became one of the leading citizens of the city. As a philanthropist, he donated significant amounts of money and property to the city and community. He founded the Lewiston Falls Academy in 1834, which eventually was given over to the public school system of Auburn in 1874 and continues in existence today as Edward Little High School. Little is buried in Oakhill Cemetery in Auburn. Merrill, *History of Androscoggin County*, 703–7; U.S. College Student Lists, 1763–1921, for New Hampshire, Dartmouth College 1797, for 1832, p. 10; Findagrave.com.

21. Merrill, *History of Androscoggin County*, 703.

22. Merrill, *History of Androscoggin County*, 704.

23. Merrill, *History of Androscoggin County*, 706.

24. Heitman, *Historical Register (1903)*, 642; Houghton, *Campaigns of the Seventeenth Maine*, 322; *Index to Compiled Service Records of Volunteer Union Soldiers Who Served in Organizations from the State of Maine*, NARA, RG 94, M543, Roll 13, Fold3 .com (accessed February 24, 2020); Merrill, *History of Androscoggin County*, 133. In Merrill's *History*, the enlistment date and company number are correct for Thomas, although the company roster lists his name as George W. Lord. There was a different George W. Lord, age eighteen, who enlisted in Company I of the Eighth Maine Infantry on August 26, 1862. Heitman, NARA, and Houghton's history are all correct as to Thomas's name, enlistment date, and rank. Edwin B. Houghton was from Portland and served during the war with the Seventeenth Maine, and his history of the regiment is a primary source.

25. Merrill, *History of Androscoggin County*, 132–34.

26. There is extensive literature concerning the actions of these battles with multiple scholarly secondary sources published in the last two decades. Primary sources for

both are documented in U.S. War Department, *War of the Rebellion*, series I, vol. XXI, part I, and vol. XIX, part II.

27. Houghton, *Campaigns of the Seventeenth Maine*, 36, 58 (Extract from the Official Report for the Battle of Fredericksburg by Brigadier General Hiram Gregory Berry and Extract from the Official Report for the Battle of Chancellorsville by Brigadier General John Henry Hobart Ward).

28. NARA, RG 94, Carded Medical Records, Volunteers: Mexican and Civil Wars, 1846–65, Entry 534 for Thomas W. Lord.

29. Houghton, *Campaigns of the Seventeenth Maine*, 66.

30. U.S. Army Registers, 1798–1969, for 1876, Twentieth Regiment of Infantry, Thomas W. Lord, Fold3.com, 157; Heitman, *Historical Register (1903)*, 642; NARA, RG 94, Carded Medical Records, records the date of Lord's discharge as September 10 instead of September 6.

31. *Bowdoin College Catalogue, 1863*, 16 and *Bowdoin College Catalogue, 1868*, 35 (quotation). The word "presecute" (prosecute) in Lord's entry is used with the meaning "to pursue until finished."

32. Heitman, *Historical Register (1903)*, 642; Houghton, *Campaigns of the Seventeenth Maine*, 811; U.S. Seventeenth Regiment, Veteran Reserve Corps, National Park Service, U.S. Civil War Soldiers, 1861–65, Ancestry.com; National Park Service, Civil War Soldiers and Sailors Database, Film: M636, roll 23/24, https://www.nps.gov/civilwar/search-soldiers.htm (both accessed February 28, 2020); U.S. Army Registers, 1876, Twentieth Regiment of Infantry, Thomas W. Lord, 157, Fold3.com; a brief description of the Veteran Reserve (Invalid Corps) is in "Veteran Reserve Corps (Originally the Invalid Corps)" in *Massachusetts Soldiers, Sailors, and Marines in the Civil War*, vol. 7 (Norwood, Mass.: Norwood Press, 1933), 122–23, at www.civilwardata.com/vrc_desc.html (accessed February 28, 2020); U.S. War Department, *War of the Rebellion*, series III, vol. V, 543–68. Heitman and the U.S. Army Registers have a minor discrepancy in the date of Thomas Lord's first appointment to the Veteran Reserve Corps—Heitman lists December 8, while the *Register* records it as December 29.

33. Heitman, *Historical Register (1903)*, 642; Houghton, *Campaigns of the Seventeenth Maine*, 811; U.S. Army Registers, 1876, Twentieth Regiment of Infantry, Thomas W. Lord, Fold3.com, 157; U.S. Fifth Regiment, Veteran Reserve Corps, National Park Service, U.S. Civil War Soldiers, 1861–65; and National Park Service, Civil War Soldiers and Sailors Database.

34. Bates College is a private, coeducational liberal arts college in Lewiston, Maine. The college was established in 1855 and named for Benjamin Bates, a Boston textile businessman who made major financial contributions for the founding of the school. The college has always been a coeducational institution. Bowdoin College in Brunswick, Maine, is also a coeducational, private liberal arts college, although women were not admitted until 1971. It was founded in 1794 with sanction by the Massachusetts State Legislature (which had jurisdiction of the region at that time)

and named for former Massachusetts governor James Bowdoin. Bowdoin's medical school, the Medical School of Maine, operated from 1821 to 1921 before closing. Bates College website (Bates history), www.bates.edu; Bowdoin College website (Bowdoin history), www.bowdoin.edu (both accessed February 24, 2020).

35. *Bowdoin College Catalogue, 1863* (also *1864, 1865, 1866*), 17. William Smyth (1797–1868) was a Bowdoin college alum (1822) and professor (1825), and Cicero was a Roman statesman. A bucolic is a pastoral poem, and a georgic is a poem or book dealing with agriculture or rural topics (named from Virgil, the Latin poet, circa 29 B.C.). Sallust was a Roman historian, Xenophon was a Greek historian, and prosody is the pattern of rhythm and sound used in poetry. These requirements for proficiency in classical literature, humanities, and language composition reflected the high academic standards for consideration of admission to small colleges and other universities at the time.

36. *Bowdoin College Catalogue, 1862*, 32; *Bowdoin College Catalogue, 1866*, 32. See also *1864* and *1865*.

37. *Bowdoin College Catalogue, 1863* (also *1864, 1865, 1866*), 16, 12, 10. The catalogs relate that George lived in Room 6 at Appleton Hall for his sophomore and junior years and Room 24 for his senior year in 1866. The building is still in use today.

38. *Bowdoin College Catalogue, 1863*, 21.

39. *Bowdoin College Catalogue, 1866*, 18–20.

40. The surviving academic transcripts from Bowdoin College for Lord include the first and second terms of his freshman year, the third term for his sophomore year, the second term for his junior year, and the third term for his senior year. Each term was usually eleven weeks (one term was ten), with the top potential score on the scale for the weekly recitations being 30. Out of all the students listed in these transcripts, there were only 13 single recorded perfect scores of 30 for recitations in all the weeks of the four years noted. Lord finished in the upper one-third of the class his first two years, and while he slipped slightly in the last two years, he still finished in the top half of the class. Thus, overall, he appeared to score well as compared to most of his classmates. Academic Transcripts for Bowdoin College, Years 1862–1863 for the Class of 1866, Bowdoin College Library Archives.

41. Delta Kappa Epsilon (DKE or Deke) was founded in 1844 at Yale University and is one of the oldest fraternities in North America. The fraternity's mission has been to develop future leaders in society for service to others through education, citizenship, and promoting the character of men as "scholars, gentlemen and jolly good fellows" as noted by one of the organization's mottos. Although prestigious during Lord's years at the college, Bowdoin's DKE chapter is currently inactive as the college discontinued fraternities in 1997. Delta Kappa Epsilon official website, www.dke.org, and Edward Griffin Bartlett, "The Founding of DKE," *Delta Kappa Epsilon Quarterly* 1, no. 1 (January 1883), https://dke.org/founding/.

42. George Sumner enlisted in the Twenty-Sixth Maine Infantry during his freshman year in 1863, was discharged five months later due to an injury, and returned to

Bowdoin. After earning his law degree there in only three years, he later became a federal judge after practicing law. Edwin S. Rogers and Leander O. Merriam both enlisted in the Thirty-First Maine Infantry in the spring of 1864. Rogers was killed in action at Cold Harbor, Virginia, that year. Merriam was also wounded in the war but returned to Bowdoin to graduate with Lord and their classmates. He became a lumberman in Maine and worked for a railroad company in Minnesota. Cross, "Whispering Pines," 2–4.

43. Lord, *Autobiography* statement, Lord ACP.

44. In his *Autobiography* statement, Lord mistakenly wrote the name as South Abington instead of North Abington.

45. Osgood and Murphy, *Abington High School Association*. Photos of a young George Lord and the model bridge are on an unnumbered page near the back of the program booklet. The model depicted one of the bridges built by Roman military leader Julius Caesar across the Rhine River during the Gallic War in 55 B.C. and 53 B.C., based on Caesar's own recorded descriptions of his bridges. The model still exists today and is on display at the Dyer Memorial Library & Archives in Abington, Massachusetts.

46. *Selectmen's Annual Report, 1868*, 58, Dyer Memorial Library & Archives.

47. Heitman, *Historical Register (1903)*, 642; Thomas W. Lord to Brevet Major General G. Thomas, Adjutant General U.S. Army, November 3, 1867, in Letters Received, AGO, Main Series, 1861–70, Fold3.com (accessed February 23, 2020).

48. Heitman, *Historical Register (1903)*, 642.

49. Fort Wayne Post Returns, April 1867–April 1869. Fort Wayne (1842–1948) was named after American Revolutionary War general "Mad" Anthony Wayne. It was built on the Detroit River to serve as a defense of the border between Canada and the United States. During the Civil War and Indian Wars, it was a garrison post for various U.S. Army regiments and was used through World War II. The preserved fort is a historic site today. Barry, "Fort Wayne," 140–43.

50. Mary Montgomery Eaton (1847–80) was the daughter of Theodore Horatio Eaton Sr., and Anne Eliza Gibbs Eaton (1816–79). Theodore Eaton was born in New Brunswick, New Jersey, and became owner of an established drug business in Buffalo, New York, and then Detroit in 1842. He was a leader in the mercantile and philanthropic circles in Detroit. Mary's brother, Theodore Jr., later become a partner with their father. Mary died at Fort Brown, Texas, shortly after her husband Thomas was stationed there. The Eatons are buried in Elmwood Cemetery in Detroit. U.S. Census, 1850 and 1860, Detroit, Michigan; U.S. Census, 1880, Brownsville, Cameron, Texas; Theodore Horatio Eaton Sr., memorial no. 77997956, Findagrave.com.

51. Lord, *Autobiography* statement, Lord ACP. Lord inadvertently misrecorded Dr. Johnson's initials as W. H. instead of the correct first initials of H. A.

52. *Bowdoin College Catalogue, 1868*, 29.

53. *Bowdoin College Catalogue, 1868*, 29–32. The catalog also noted that "all operations in the presence of the Medical Class will be performed *without charge*" and this was "extensively made known to the Public."

Notes to Chapter 1

54. Detroit Medical College (now Wayne State University School of Medicine) was founded in 1868, while the University of Michigan's medical department was founded in 1848 (opened for students in 1850). Stephenson, *Wayne State University School of Medicine*, 52; Bordin, *University of Michigan*, 11.

55. Hosmer A. Johnson, MD (1822–91), a native of New York, spent his high school years in Michigan. He graduated from the University of Michigan in 1849 (later also earned M.A. LL.D degrees). He graduated from Rush Medical College in 1852. After completing a one-year internship (the first ever) at Mercy Hospital in Chicago, he practiced and served as a faculty member at Rush Medial College until 1858. He left Rush to become one of the four cofounders and faculty members of the Chicago Medical College in 1859 and served at that institution until his death. He married Margaret Ann Seward in 1855. Johnson was a respected physician, instructor, and leading advocate for improvement in medical education. He had a general medical practice, subspecialized in pulmonary medicine, and became one of the early leading laryngologists in the country. In addition to his teaching positions at the medical school, he was involved in many local, state, and national medical organizations. "Hosmer Allen Johnson," in *Biographical Sketches of the Leading Men of Chicago*, 229–34; Sperry, *A Group of Distinguished Physicians and Surgeons of Chicago*, 49–53; Freidberg, "Memorable Life of Hosmer A. Johnson," 470–72.

56. *General Catalogue of Bowdoin College and the Medical School of Maine, 1794–1912*, 189.

57. Author's personal correspondence March 18, 2020, with Roberta Schwartz, research services archivist, and George J. Mitchell, Department of Special Collections and Archives, Bowdoin College. It was not until 1871 that actual course work was required for graduate degrees in letters, science, and philosophy at the college. By 1874–75, these graduate studies were deemphasized, although in 1898, a one-year postgraduate course of study with successful passing of a written and oral examination was required for a master of arts degree.

58. *Biographical Sketches of the Leading Men of Chicago*, 232.

59. Friedberg, "Memorable Life of Hosmer A. Johnson," 471.

60. Friedberg, "Memorable Life of Hosmer A. Johnson," 471 (first quotation); *Biographical Sketches of the Leading Men of Chicago*, 234 (second quotation).

61. Chicago Medical Society, *History*, 206; Arey, *Northwestern University Medical School*, 32–34. Edmund Andrews (1824–1904) was a leader in promoting Joseph Lister's antiseptic principles and early anesthesia techniques, and he was also a geologist; Ralph N. Isham (1831–1904) was a specialist in surgery and surgical anatomy; William Heath Byford (1817–90) was a leader in obstetrics and diseases of women in Chicago as was David Rutter (1805–65); Nathan Smith Davis (1817–1904) was instrumental in medical education reforms and the founding of the American Medical Association. The founders of the Chicago Medical College were dissatisfied with the medical education system, including Dr. Daniel Brainard (1812–66) founder and previous president of Rush Medical College, the oldest medical school in Chicago, its first class

having commenced in 1843. Short biographical sketches of each of these physicians are in Chicago Medical Society, *History*, 65–67 for Andrews, 87–88 for Isham, 50–51 for Byford, 27 for Rutter, 48–50 for Davis, and 37–39 for Brainard.

62. Chicago Medical Society, *History*, 207–9, 211; Arey, *Northwestern University Medical School*, 52–53, 58–60; Solberg, *Reforming Medical Education*, 24. Mercy Hospital had been affiliated with the Chicago Medical College since its inception and its facilities (hospital and clinics) provided the venue for the clinical instruction of the medical students by the faculty and practicing physicians of the college.

63. Arey, *Northwestern University Medical School*, 108; Northwestern University Feinberg School of Medicine, www.feinberg.northwestern.edu.

64. Arey, *Northwestern University Medical School*, 31; for histories of medical schools in Chicago during the nineteenth century, see Chicago Medical Society, *History*, 187–232.

65. Chicago Medical Society, *History*, 205; Arey, *Northwestern University Medical School*, 9; Stephenson, *Wayne State University School of Medicine*, 56.

66. Chicago Medical Society, *History*, 191; Arey, *Northwestern University Medical School*, 23–24, 42; *Bowdoin College Catalogue, 1863*, 28 (quotation).

67. *Chicago Medical College Catalogue, 1870–71*, 8.

68. *Bowdoin College Catalogue, 1868*, 30 (first quotation); *Chicago Medical College Catalogue, 1869–70*, 11; Arey, *Northwestern University Medical School*, 130 (second quotation).

69. Chicago Medical Society, *History*, 205–6; Stephenson, *Wayne State University School of Medicine*, 59.

70. Arey, *Northwestern University Medical School*, 62–65, 86, 92, 109–10, 116.

71. Harburn, *A Surgeon with Custer*, 20; Jack Eckert and Andra Langoussis, *A Broad Foundation*, chap. 7, page 2, para. 5, Harvard Medical Library, Harvard University, https://collections.countway.harvard.edu/onview/exhibits (accessed January 14, 2022); Stephenson, *Wayne State University School of Medicine*, 59. The University of Pennsylvania and Syracuse University would not implement these changes to a three-year graded curriculum until 1877, the University of Michigan not until 1880.

72. Arey, *Northwestern University Medical School*, 65, 153. Comparatively, the Medical School of Maine at Bowdoin College had 90 medical students enrolled in 1869 and 96 students the following year, 1870; *Bowdoin College Catalogue, 1869 and 1870*, 32.

73. *Chicago Medical College Catalogue, 1869–70*, 6. *Bowdoin College Catalogue, 1869*, 29 shows most of these same courses, however, divided into two terms annually.

74. *Chicago Medical College Catalogue, 1869–70*, 6, 10.

75. *Chicago Medical College Catalogue, 1869–70*, 11; *Bowdoin College Catalogue, 1869*, 29.

76. *Chicago Medical College Catalogue, 1869–70*, 12.

77. *Chicago Medical College Catalogue, 1869–70*, 12. Austin Flint, MD (1812–66) was an internal medicine physician, graduate of Harvard Medical School, a founder and faculty member of Bellevue Medical College in New York City; Henry Gray, MD

(1827–61), a physician in London, England, first published his anatomy textbook in 1858; Samuel D. Gross, MD, a graduate of the University of Pennsylvania Medical School, was a trauma surgeon and faculty member at Jefferson Medical College in Philadelphia, his two volume textbook published in 1862; Rudolf Virchow, MD (1821–1902) was a German physician and politician born in Prussia, and is considered the founder of the field of cellular pathology; George Bacon Wood, MD (1797–1874), a physician from New Jersey, graduate of the University of Pennsylvania Medical School, taught at the Philadelphia College of Pharmacy, had his treatise published in 1856; John Call Dalton, MD (1825–89), from Massachusetts and a Harvard Medical School graduate, was a professor of physiology at Columbia University of Physician and Surgeons in New York City whose textbook was published in 1869; see n61 for William H. Byford, MD.

78. Harburn, *A Surgeon with Custer*, 193n95. C. A. Theodor Billroth, MD (1829–94), an Austrian abdominal surgeon, practiced and taught at the Universities of Zurich and Vienna, his classic textbook published in 1863; Thomas H. Huxley (1825–95) was a leading English biologist and anthropologist in the nineteenth century. This textbook was published in 1872.

79. Arey, *Northwestern University Medical School*, 77; Chicago Medical Society, *History*, 207.

80. *Chicago Medical College Catalogue, 1870–71*, 9.

81. *Chicago Medical College Catalogue, 1869–70*, 13.

82. Harburn, *A Surgeon with Custer*, 197n93. *Chicago Medical College Catalogue, 1871*; U.S. Census, 1860, 1880, 1890, 1900, and 1910, Rockford/Winnebago, Illinois; *Dictionary of Deceased American Physicians, 1804–1929*; *Ohio Deaths, 1908–1932, 1930–2007*; S.F.O. No. 5, Brig. Gen. Terry, May 14, 1876, AGO, DeWolf Collection, WSL/LIBI.

83. *Chicago Medical College Catalogue, 1870–71*, 11.

84. Noyes, "Custer's Surgeon, George Lord," 15.

85. S.O. No. 240, Headquarters, Department of Dakota, Saint Paul, Minn., October 30, 1871, NARA, RG 94, 4666, ACP 1871.

86. George E. Lord to J. F. Head, January 2, 1871, Chicago, Ill., Lord ACP.

87. Agnew, *Medicine in the Old West*, 32; Gillett, *Army Medical Department*, 16; Ashburn, *History of the Medical Department of the United States Army*, 89.

88. War Office, *Revised U.S. Army Regulations*, article XLI/no. 135, p. 314 and appendix B. Medical Department, no. 71, p. 518.

89. H. A. Johnson, MD, letter of recommendation, December 30, 1870, Lord ACP.

90. Edmund Andrews, MD, letter of recommendation, December 30, 1870, Lord ACP.

91. N. S. Davis, MD, and W. H. Buford, MD, letters of recommendation, December 28, 1870, Lord ACP.

92. George E. Lord, Chicago, Ill., to the Surgeon General, Washington, D.C., April 6, 1871, and Contract with a Private Physician, U.S. Army, Form 50, April 27, 1871, both in Lord ACP; *Register of Officers and Agents, Civil, Military, and Naval in the Service of the United States, 1863–1959*, for 1871, vol. 1, 231.

93. Charles Knickerbacker Winne (1838–1919), born in New York, served as assistant surgeon for the Union Army in the Civil War and during the Indian Wars era. He was a post surgeon at Fort Ripley and then at Fort Snelling into the 1890s. In 1874, he married Caroline Elizabeth Frey (1841–1922). Promoted to lieutenant colonel, Department of Surgeon General, in 1901, he retired the following year. He and his wife are buried in Albany Rural Cemetery, Menands, New York. Heitman, *Historical Register (1903)*, 1050.

94. Fort Ripley Post Returns, April 1871.

CHAPTER 2.
DAKOTA TERRITORY AND BEYOND

1. Fort Ripley (1848–77) was built by the U.S. Army to keep the peace between the Winnebago (Ho-Chunk) and the Dakota and Chippewa (Ojibwe) tribes. Today nothing remains of the fort except ruins of the powder magazine, located and preserved on the active training grounds of the Minnesota National Guard at Camp Ripley along with the Minnesota Military Museum. Baker, *Muster Roll*, and Billings, *Report on the Hygiene*, 425–27.

2. Billings, *Report on Barracks and Hospitals*, 426.

3. A history of Old Crow Wing village and site is found in Coleman, LaBud, and Humphrey, *Old Crow Wing*.

4. John Addison Manley (1837–90) was born in Mansfield, New York. He served in the Sixty-Fourth New York Infantry during the Civil War in 1861, being promoted through the ranks to captain in 1863. He joined the Eighteenth U.S. Infantry in 1867 and became first lieutenant before being assigned to the Twentieth Infantry in 1870. He served at various posts, was promoted to captain in 1887, and died at Fort Assinniboine, Montana, on July 15, 1890. He is interred at the Custer National Cemetery, Big Horn, Montana. Heitman, *Historical Register (1903)*, 687; Findagrave.com.

5. Fort Ripley, Post Returns, May 1871.

6. Whetstone Indian Agency Post Returns, July 1871 (through May 1872); *Register of Officer and Agents, Civil, Military, and Naval Service, 1863–1959*, for 1871, vol. 1, 231.

7. A full transcript of the 1868 treaty can be reviewed in Lazarus, *Black Hills/White Justice*, 435–96. Gray, *Centennial Campaign*, 308–20, provides an in-depth analysis of the various Sioux bands and the agencies serving them during the Indian Wars period.

8. Clow, "Whetstone Indian Agency," 292, 294; Greene, *Fort Randall on the Missouri*, 99–100.

9. Clow, "Whetstone Indian Agency," 298, 300–01, 303.

10. Whetstone Indian Agency Post Returns, July 1871 (through May 1872). There were three commissioned officers and fifty-three to fifty-four enlisted men of the Twenty-Second Infantry at the agency post.

11. Clow, "Whetstone Indian Agency," 296–301.

12. Clow, "Whetstone Indian Agency," 306–7.
13. Fort Randall Post Returns, May and June 1872.
14. Greene, *Fort Randall on the Missouri*; Billings, *Report on the Hygiene*, 417–21.
15. Billings, *Report on the Hygiene*, 417.
16. Billings, *Report on the Hygiene*, 420.
17. Elwell Stephen Otis (1838–1909) was born in Frederick, Maryland, and graduated from the University of Rochester (New York) and then from Harvard Law School in 1861. During the Civil War, he served in the 140th New York Infantry. He became lieutenant colonel in the Twenty-Second Infantry during the Indian Wars and was commandant at Fort Randall for several years. Later he was appointed colonel in the Twentieth Infantry in 1880, then to major general in 1900, and he retired in 1902. He is buried in Arlington National Cemetery. Heitman, *Historical Register (1903)*, 762.
18. Elliott Coues (1842–99). Born in Portsmouth, New Hampshire, he received both his undergraduate and medical degrees from Columbian College in Washington, D.C. (now George Washington University) in 1863. After being a medical cadet in that city for a year, he became an assistant surgeon and was assigned to Fort Whipple, Arizona. He served with the Northern Boundary Survey Commission in 1873–76. Aside from his medical duties, he was a scientist/naturalist and historian, authoring several publications in ornithology relating observations from his various army medical assignments and later taught at his alma mater medical school as a professor of anatomy. He was a believer in Theosophy and Spiritualism. Coues died in Baltimore and is buried in Arlington National Cemetery. Heitman, *Historical Register (1903)*, 329; Cutright and Brodhead, *Elliott Coues*.
19. James Foulke Weeds (1832–75). A native of Norfolk, England, his parents moved to the United States when he was two years old. Weeds graduated from the University of Michigan Medical School in 1857. He became an assistant surgeon in the army in 1861, and served in Tennessee, Florida, and New Mexico during the Civil War. He was promoted to major in 1868. During the Indian Wars period, most of his medical duties were in Nashville, although he served at Fort Randall in 1873. He returned to Nashville, where he died due to chronic dysentery, and he is buried in the Nashville National Cemetery. *American Medical Association*, 28/635–36; Heitman, *Historical Register (1903)*, 1014.
20. Captain John Hartley (1838–83), Twenty-Second Infantry, was commanding Company B at Fort Randall during Lord and Coues's time there. Born in Maine, Hartley served in the Eighth Minnesota Infantry during the Civil War, receiving promotion to captain (later brevet major). He became a captain in the Twenty-Second Infantry in 1866. He served in that position during the Indian Wars until he resigned in 1882 after working for Major Robert N. Scott in Washington, D.C., in publishing the Official Records of the Rebellion (Civil War). He is buried in Oakland Cemetery, St. Paul, Minnesota. Heitman, *Historical Register (1903)*, 507; *Army and Navy Journal* 28 no. 5 (September 2, 1882): 96; Findagrave.com.

21. Cutright and Brodhead, *Elliott Coues*, 143; Brodhead, "Natural History along the Parallel," 271.

22. Brodhead, "Natural History along the Parallel," 271; also cited in Greene, *Fort Randall on the Missouri*, 113.

23. T. W. Lord to J. F. Head, Medical Director, Dept. of Dakota, St. Paul, August 22, 1872, Lord ACP.

24. Charles H. Crane, Assistant Surgeon General, reply to J. F. Head, August 26, 1872, Lord ACP.

25. C. H. Crane to Geo. E. Lord, Fort Randall, March 13, 1873, Lord ACP.

26. Cutright and Brodhead, *Elliott Coues*, 139–40.

27. Elliott Coues to William Baird, October 28, 1872, cited in Cutright and Brodhead, *Elliott Coues*, 139. Baird was the assistant secretary of the Smithsonian Institute in Washington, D.C., and mentor and friend to Coues.

28. Billings, *Report on the Hygiene*, 421.

29. James H. Head, St. Paul, Department of Dakota, to SGO, November 14, 1873, Lord ACP.

30. Geo. E. Lord to Assistant Surgeon General, May 18, 1874 (Lord's acknowledgment of receipt of the contract), and Contract with a Private Physician, C. H. Crane, Asst. Surg. Gen., U.S.A, to George E. Lord, Limerick, Maine, May 22, 1874, Lord ACP.

31. J. K. B. (Joseph K. Barnes), Surgeon General, Washington, D.C., to Geo. E. Lord, Limerick, Maine, May 22, 1874, Lord ACP.

32. George E. Lord to Secretary of War through Surgeon General, U.S.A., Fort Snelling, Minn., June 3, 1874; Charles H. Crane, SGO, to Geo. E. Lord, June 9, 1874, Lord ACP.

33. History of Military Services performed by George E. Lord, War Department, SGO, Washington, D.C., Lord ACP.

34. *Reports upon the Survey of the Boundary between the Territory of the United States and the Possessions of Great Britain from the Lake of the Woods to the Summit of the Rocky Mountains*, North American Boundary Commission (1872–1876) (hereafter cited as *Reports . . . Northern Boundary Commission*). This extensive publication contains the final reports and summary of the U.S. commissioner and U.S. Boundary Commission army engineers to the U.S. Congress of the three years involved in completing the boundary survey.

35. *Reports . . . Northern Boundary Commission*, 19.

36. For the United States, its Northern Boundary Commission was formed with input from Secretary of State Hamilton Fish; Secretary of War William Belknap; the chief of U.S. Army Engineers, Brigadier General Andrew A. Humphreys; and the president. Also Archibald Campbell of Washington, D.C., was appointed as commissioner, with engineers Captain/Brevet Lieutenant Colonel Francis U. Farquhar as chief astronomer, assisted by engineers Captain/Brevet Major William J. Twining, Captain (then Lieutenant) James F. Gregory, and Lieutenant Francis V.

Notes to Chapter 2 157

Greene. Their British counterparts were commissioner Captain Donald R. Cameron, Royal Artillery, and British chief astronomer Captain S. Anderson, Royal Engineers, *Reports... Northern Boundary Commission*, 20–21.

37. *Reports... Northern Boundary Commission*, 20. In subsequent years, Congress would increase the appropriation to $125,000 to cover the costs of supplies, wagons, mules, and payment to civil assistants hired for these expeditions.

38. Captain Abram A. Harbach (1841–1933) commanded Company K, Twentieth Infantry, stationed at Fort Totten. He was born in Pittsburgh, Pennsylvania, and served in the Eleventh Iowa Infantry during the Civil War. He transferred to the Twentieth Infantry in 1866. He founded Fort Pembina, North Dakota, in 1874, along with Captain Loyd Wheaton of the same regiment. Harbach later was lieutenant colonel in the Third U.S. Infantry, served in Minnesota in the 1890s, and assisted in the aftermath of the Battle of Sugar Point with the Ojibwe Indians at Leech Lake, Minnesota. He married Lilian Otis in July 1895. He was promoted to brigadier general in 1902, shortly before his retirement. He died in Santa Barbara, California, but is buried in Arlington National Cemetery. Heitman, *Historical Register (1903)*, 499; Fort Totten Post Returns, 1869–1877; Matsen, "The Battle of Sugar Point," 274; California Death Index, 1905–1939; Findagrave.com.

39. Fort Pembina (1870–95) was a U.S. Army post established on the Red River in Dakota Territory (present-day North Dakota) near the forty-ninth parallel and the international border with the Province of Manitoba, Canada. A previous U.S. fort had been built on the site in 1863 for protection of local settlers from potential hostile Sioux Indians following the 1862 Dakota Sioux Uprising, although that post was abandoned the following year. The 1870 fort was built under the direction of Captains Loyd Wheaton and Abram Harbach of the Twentieth Infantry. A fire destroyed most of the fort buildings in 1895 and the post was abandoned. The lands were sold at public auction in 1902. The Pembina area was previously the location of British NorthWest Company and Hudson Bay Company trading posts from 1797 to the late 1820s. Today, all the fort sites are marked with historical monuments. Billings, *Report on the Hygiene*, 412–17; see also State Historical Society of North Dakota, Pembina State Museum, www.history.nd.gov (accessed July 08, 2020).

40. *Reports... Northern Boundary Commission*, 20–21; Twentieth Infantry Returns, June 1873.

41. Fort Abercrombie (1858–77) was constructed on the Red River in northeastern present-day North Dakota to protect the "Gateway to the Dakotas" for settlers and merchants proceeding west and north into Fort Garry at present-day Winnipeg, Manitoba. It was attacked during the Dakota Sioux Uprising of 1862 and was later used in railroad laborers and sending troops during the 1870s Indian Wars campaigns. A partial reconstruction and original guardhouse are maintained at the state historic site. Billings, *Report on the Hygiene*, 389–91; Frazer, *Forts of the West*, 109.

42. *Reports... Northern Boundary Commission*, 24.

43. *Reports... Northern Boundary Commission*, 69. This was Fort Dufferin. See n48.

44. *Reports... Northern Boundary Commission*, 59. Engineer and chief astronomer Captain/Brevet Major Twining's report provides detailed descriptions of the terrain of all these areas. Regarding the end point of the 1873 field operations, he described Turtle Mountain as "an irregular mass of drift, rising at the highest point to not more than 500 feet above the general level. The eastern slope is gentle, while the western escarpment is quite sharp. It is covered by a continuous forest of birch, aspen, and oak, interlaced with briers and wild pea vines, forming an almost impenetrable thicket.... The width of the mountain, from east to west, was found to be thirty-four miles."

45. *Reports... Northern Boundary Commission*, 69.

46. Fort Snelling Post Returns, June 1873; Twentieth Infantry Returns, June 1873 noting Special Orders No. 106, Department of Dakota; *Reports... Northern Boundary Commission*, 69–70. Companies D and K left Fort Snelling at St. Paul, Minnesota, on June 3 for Fort Pembina. Major Reno left St. Paul on June 5 via train and eventually arrived at Fort Pembina on June 22. He proceeded to Turtle Mountain, where a supply depot was established. Harbaugh and Company K left Fort Pembina on June 10, 1873, marched seventy-one miles to join the survey parties that had already moved westward from the post, and eventually joined the main body of the escort troops by mid-July.

47. *Reports... Northern Boundary Commission*, 24, 71 (quotation).

48. Brodhead, "Natural History along the Parallel," 277. Fort Dufferin was built by the Canadian government in 1872 on the west bank of the Red River in Manitoba, about three kilometers north of Pembina and the Canadian/United States border. Named for then–Canada governor General Lord Dufferin, it was used as the base for the British commissioners of the North American Boundary Commission and later as an immigration post for the North-West Mounted Police from 1874 until its abandonment in 1879. Now a Canadian National Historic Site, several original buildings remain and are in the process of being preserved by the Canadian government and local historic groups. "Dufferin: Then and Now," in *Manitoba History*, Historic Resources Branch, Province of Manitoba, 23 (Spring 1992), www.mhs.mb.ca/docs/mb_history/23/dufferin.shtml (accessed July 17, 2020).

49. Lubetkin, *Custer and the 1873 Yellowstone Survey*, 247–55 provides a detailed narrative of the formal battle encountered during the railroad's expedition on August 11, 1873. Stanley's *Report on the Yellowstone Expedition of 1873* provides the official report of the expedition.

50. "Raid on the English Party of the Northwest Boundary Survey," *Chicago Tribune*, June 30, 1873, p. 2. The letter received from the American party reported that two of the Englishmen were captured while the remaining members of the party were driven back out of the mountain, and the American party was to move forward.

51. U.S. Sixth Infantry Returns, June 1874.

52. *Reports... Northern Boundary Commission*, 24, 29.

53. Francis Orlando Nash (1841–1922) was a native of Columbia, Maine. His mother, Phebe Coffin Nash Hill (1811–94), married Obadiah Hill (1786–1860) in

1851 in Machias, Maine. Francis and his three adopted sisters attended the Machias Common School and Machias Academy. He registered for the U.S. Civil War Draft at age twenty-one in 1863 but never served. He attended Amherst (Massachusetts) College from 1863 to 1865, although he did not graduate, as he enrolled in the Medical School of Maine at Bowdoin College, graduating there in 1868. After being dismissed as a civilian contract physician for the army during the 1873 Northern Boundary Survey, resulting from a rift with Major Marcus A. Reno, he relocated to Hollister, California, in 1874, where he was a private physician for many years. He and his wife, Ida, were married in 1880, although they were divorced by 1900. He died in Hollister. U.S. Census, 1850, Columbia, Maine; U.S. Census, 1860, Machias, Maine; *Bowdoin College Catalogue*, 1867, p. 7; U.S. Civil War Draft Registration Records, 1863–65, RG 110, July 1, 1863, NARA; U.S. College Student Lists, 1763–1924, Amherst College, 1883, p. 136; U.S. Census, 1880 and 1900, Hollister, California; Directory of Deceased American Physicians, 1804–1929; Findagrave.com for Phebe Coffin Nash Hill and Obadiah Hill.

54. The local newspaper noted that two days prior to the departure, camp fixtures and other supplies were being brought up from Fort Snelling and loaded on the railroad cars. *Minneapolis Daily Tribune*, June 3, 1873, p. 4.

55. Reno to Assistant Adjutant General, O. D. Greene, Department of Dakota, June 29, 1873, Francis O. Nash personal file, NARA, cited in Nichols, *In Custer's Shadow*, 126.

56. *Minneapolis Daily Tribune*, June 6, 1873, p. 4.

57. Marcus A. Reno to Major O. D. Greene, Department of Dakota, June 29, 1873 (three quotations), cited in Carroll, "Surgeon George Lord," 8.

58. Marcus A. Reno to Major O. D. Greene, June 29, 1873 (both quotations).

59. Brodhead, "Natural History along the Parallel," 272.

60. Nichols, *In Custer's Shadow*, 126–27. Nichols relates in more detail the sequence of events in this nearly three-month feud between Reno and Nash. Nash was initially reinstated by Major Oliver D. Greene, Department of Dakota's assistant adjutant general (telegraph from Greene to Reno, July 23, 1873, copy in Nash's personal file, RG 94, NARA).

61. Cutright and Brodhead, *Elliott Coues*, 161–62. Coues received a reprimand from his superiors in the Office of the Surgeon General; Brodhead, "Natural History along the Parallel," 274.

62. The *Fontenelle* was a sternwheeler built in Brownsville, Pennsylvania, in 1870. One of the larger steamboats, it was 205 feet in length and 33 feet wide with a capacity of 297 tons. It was majorly rebuilt twice, the first time in 1868 after hitting a snag and sinking in the Missouri River and then in 1873 after being damaged by a fire in New Orleans. Putz, "Missouri Riverboat Wreckage," 536; Stepenoff, *Working the Mississippi*, 12; Lass, *Steamboating on the Upper Missouri River*, 94.

63. George Lord to Annie Hooper, June 7, 1874, in Noyes, "Tragedy of Dr. George E. Lord," 4–6 (quotation); also, transcribed copy of the original letter is

in the Lord file, Seventh Cavalry Collection, White Swan Library, Little Bighorn Battlefield National Monument (hereafter, WSL/LIBI). As acting assistant surgeon, Lord was concerned with the personal hygiene of military personnel. Comments regarding the cook also reveal some personal levity. His observation is consistent with an opinion that would soon be expressed by Dr. John S. Billings, author of an 1875 report on hygiene in the army and its military posts for the Office of the Surgeon General. Billings noted that "cooks could spoil not only the appeal to the palate but the healthfulness of any food, and some items beyond redemption." As opined by Lord, this was in more ways than one! Gillett, *Army Medical Department*, 47.

64. George Lord to Annie Hooper, June 7, 1874.

65. George Lord to Annie Hooper, June 7, 1874 (both quotations).

66. The Sixth Infantry Returns, June 1874. These record orders, dates, distances marched, and locations of the major encampments for each company during the 1874 Northern Boundary Survey Commission.

67. The Quaking Asp River was also known as the Poplar River, which is its current name today. The river is a tributary of the Missouri River, originating from several forks in southern Saskatchewan, and joins the Missouri in eastern Montana. From this established base camp, where Lord remained the first month, three of the Sixth Infantry companies escorted the topographical parties up the river to the northern boundary line about seventy miles north. *Reports . . . Northern Boundary Commission*, 76; Lord Memorandum of Military Service, Lord ACP, documents his duty stations during the expedition; Sixth Infantry Returns, June 1874 for the 135-mile march.

68. Sweet Grass Hills was also known as the Three Buttes. which comprised three elevations. The central elevation was about 7,000 feet in height. Archibald Campbell of the Northern Boundary Survey Commission wrote that "from the summit of these peaks on a clear day a fine view of the crest of the Rocky Mountains" could be seen. Also, "delicious, cold, spring water was found there, a great luxury." Captain Twining noted that the "slopes consist of a mass of blocks of broken stone of small size" and the area leading to the slopes of the buttes being "the center of the feeding-ground of the great northern herd of buffaloes." *Reports . . . Northern Boundary Commission*, 26 (first and second quotations), 63 (third and fourth quotations).

69. Formed by its north and south forks at the northern border of Montana and the Canadian province of Alberta, the river extends from there toward eastern Montana just northeast of the present-day Fort Peck Dam. Described by Northern Boundary Survey Commission chief astronomer Captain William J. Twining as "sluggish in their flow, with a more or less alkaline tendency" the Milk River derives its name from the South Fork "noticeable for the milky color of its waters." *Reports . . . Northern Boundary Commission*, 64.

70. Brodhead, "Natural History along the Parallel," 278–80, 282.

71. George Lord to "Cousin Annie," October 6, 1874, in Noyes, "Tragedy of Dr. George E. Lord," 6 (all quotations); a quotation from this letter is also cited in Noyes, "Custer's Surgeon, George Lord," 15; transcribed copy in Lord file, WSL/LIBI.

Notes to Chapter 2

72. *Reports . . . Northern Boundary Commission,* 75.

73. Noyes, "Tragedy of Dr. George E. Lord," 4.

74. George Lord to "Cousin Annie," June 7, 1872, cited in Noyes, "Custer's Surgeon, George Lord," 15.

75. Research has not uncovered any evidence of blood relation between George Lord and Annie Hooper. Even if they had been cousins to any extent, this would not have necessarily been a social taboo in some regions of the country, although after the Civil War, many states had prohibited such unions. Eleanor Cummins, "Go Ahead, Marry Your Cousin—It's Not That Bad for Your Future Kids," *Health,* March 8, 2018, https://www.popsci.com/marrying-cousins-genetics/ (accessed August 12, 2018).

76. Maine, Marriage Records, 1713–1922, Beverly Moore and Annie M. F. Hooper, January 5, 1875.

77. Assistant Surgeon General Charles H. Crane to Medical Director, Dept. of Dakota, St. Paul, Minnesota, July 25, 1874, and George E. Lord, Army Medical Board catalog card, Lord ACP.

78. George Edwin Lord to Surgeon General, Washington, D.C., October 12, 1874, Fort Ripley, Lord ACP.

79. War Office, *Revised U.S. Army Regulations,* Art. XLIV/no. 1317, p. 315.

80. George E. Lord, Memorandum of Military Service, Lord ACP. Although his file lists the date of arrival to St. Paul as October 7, Lord must have arrived and registered at the hotel the evening before since his second letter to Annie Hooper is dated October 6 from the Merchants Hotel.

81. Merchants Hotel was associated with the oldest hotel in St. Paul. The St. Paul House was built in 1849 and renovated several times before the new construction of a large Italianate-style structure on the same site in 1871, which was renamed the Merchants Hotel. Located at 159 East Third Street (now Kellogg Boulevard), it was four stories with a fifth added in later years. The hotel went out of business and was torn down in 1923. Millett, *Lost Twin Cities,* 62–63, 311; Warner et al., *History of Ramsey County,* 439.

82. George Lord to Annie Hooper, October 14, 1874, in Noyes, "Tragedy of Dr. George E. Lord," 4–5, transcribed copy in WSL/LIBI.

83. George Lord, Fort Ripley, Minnesota, to Surgeon General, U.S. Army, Washington, D.C., October 12, 1874; also in Lord, Memorandum of Military Service, Lord ACP.

84. J. F. Head to Recorder of Army Medical Board, New York, December 5, 1874, Lord ACP.

85. The Sturtevant House opened in 1871 and operated for the next three decades, closing in 1903. Typical of such upscale establishments, the hotel had luxurious accommodations and a restaurant featuring an exquisite menu. "A Thanksgiving Dinner Menu from 1899," Ephemeral New York, November 17, 2010, www.ephemeralnewyork.wordpress.com/tag/sturtevant-house-hotel/ (accessed May 11, 2020).

86. George Lord to Annie Hooper, October 7, 1874, in Noyes, "Tragedy of Dr. George E. Lord," 6, transcribed copy in WSL/LIBI.

87. James Pelog Kimball (1840–1902) was born in Berkshire, New York, and graduated from Hamilton College, then Albany Medical College in 1864, both in New York State. He served as surgeon in the 121st New York Volunteers in the Civil War. Passing the army medical exam in 1867, he had a well-respected military career, served at various western posts, in administrative duties toward the end of his career in the Department of the Surgeon General. Promoted to colonel in 1902, he died three months later. Kimball, *Soldier-Doctor of Our Army*; Heitman, *Historical Register (1903)*, 598.

88. Kimball, *Soldier-Doctor of Our Army*, 30.

89. Joseph Bullock Brown (1822–91) twice served as president of the army's Medical Examining Board in New York. Born in Albany, New York, he graduated from Albany Medical College and was in private practice before being commissioned assistant surgeon in the army in 1850. Brown served at several western posts, including Fort Dalles, Oregon, during the Yakama Indian war before becoming the medical director of the Army of the Potomac Fourth Corps during the Civil War. After his first tenure for the examining board, he was medical director for the Department of the Platte. Retiring in 1886, Brown died in Albion, New York, and is buried with his wife and two daughters in the Mt. Albion Cemetery. Heitman, *Historical Register (1903)*, 252; also www.fortdallesmuseum.org (accessed November 4, 2020).

90. Letter, undated, J. F. Head, MD, Medical Director, Dakota Territory to J. B. Brown, MD, President, Army Medical Board, Lord ACP.

91. Carroll, "Surgeon George Lord," 8–9; Petersen, "George Edwin Lord," 5–6.

92. Joseph B. Brown, Surgeon, U.S.A., President, Army Medical Board, to Surgeon General, January 9, 1875, Lord ACP.

93. C. H. Crane to George E. Lord, Sturtevant House, January 14, 1875, Lord ACP.

94. In 1877, there were 185 physicians invited to sit before the board for examination, with only 21 passing. Hedren, "Dr. Charles V. Petteys," 35.

95. Charles V. Petteys (1845–1933) was born in New York. Despite twice failing to pass the Army Medical Board examination, he was considered an excellent and well-liked surgeon. He served as a contract surgeon in the army for fourteen years, including in General Crook's November 1876 Powder River Expedition. His biographer Paul Hedren has noted that "Petteys's difficulty may have centered on his minimal classical training," as he had no undergraduate degree, although he graduated from the Georgetown Medical School in Washington, D.C. Hedren, "Dr. Charles V. Petteys"; Hedren, *Great Sioux War Orders*, 86, 144. Like Petteys, DeWolf also did not have an undergraduate degree. For Porter's education, see Walker, *Dr. Henry R. Porter*, 5–7.

96. Examining Board Report for George E. Lord, NARA, RG 112, Army Medical Board, New York City, N.Y., 1874–1875–1876, Entry 323, No. 26, 128–29.

97. The exact paragraph to which Lord was referring to in Flint's medical textbook notes the following: "The great discovery by Bernard of the production of sugar

within the liver suggests the inquiry whether important disorders may not relate to this function. A deficient production of sugar may be among the proximate morbid effects of disorganizing hepatic lesions, and of function inactivity for the organ due to anaemia and defective innervation. But of this we have, as yet, no positive knowledge. The question whether an excessive production of sugar be not involved in the affection know as diabetes mellitus will come up in treating of the pathological character of that affection." Flint, *Principles and Practice of Medicine*, 563.

98. Quine, "Edmund Andrews," 826.

99. Jno M. Cuyler, Medical Director, Division of the Atlantic, New York to the Surgeon General, January 18, 1875; Lord's army "Contract with a Private Physician," January 18, 1875; Memorandum of the Military Service of Dr. Geo. E. Lord, all in Lord ACP.

100. S.O. 13, Headquarters Department of Dakota, January 25, 1875; Fort Snelling Post Returns, January 1875.

101. Holmes Offley Paulding (1852–83) was born in Washington, D.C., to a distinguished family. His father, Leonard Paulding, was a prominent naval officer and his mother, Helen Jane Offley Paulding, was from the area's well-known Offley family. He graduated from the National Medical College of Columbian University (now George Washington University) in Washington, D.C., in 1874, soon passed the Army Medical Board examination, and was assigned to Fort Snelling in Dakota Territory. He later served at Forts Abraham Lincoln, Ellis in Montana Territory for several years, Fort McHenry in Baltimore, and Fort Sidney, Nebraska. In 1889, he married Mary E. French in Alexandria, Virginia. He was the lone army medical officer with Colonel Gibbon's Montana column. Paulding's surviving journal and letters to his mother provide some interesting "behind the scenes" observations of that campaign. He died due to underlying heart and rheumatic conditions at Fort Sidney, Nebraska. He is buried in St. Paul's Cemetery in Alexandria, Virginia. Fort Snelling Post Returns, December 1874–July 1875; U.S. School Catalogs, 1765–1935, National Medical College of Columbian University, 1875, pp. 14–15; Virginia Select Marriages, 1785–1940; U.S. Registers of Deaths in the Regular Army, 1860–89, NARA, RG 94, 134–35; Findagrave.com; *Army and Navy Gazette*, May 1883.

102. Memorandum of Military Service of Geo. E. Lord, Lord ACP; Fort Snelling Post Returns, February 1875.

103. Twentieth Infantry Returns, February 1875, Fort Snelling Post Returns, February 1875. The officers were Joseph S. Stafford and John Bannister, both first lieutenants in the Twentieth Infantry. Bannister was born in New York and served in the Civil War with New York units, initially the Twenty-Seventh Infantry. After the war, he served in the Forty-Third Infantry, then ten years in the Twentieth Infantry until his retirement in 1879. Heitman, *Historical Register* (1903), 189. Stafford, born in Pennsylvania, served in the Third Pennsylvania Artillery during the Civil War. He served as a lieutenant in the U.S. Thirteenth Infantry before the Twentieth Infantry. He died of gastric hemorrhage at the fort and is buried in the Fort Snelling National

Cemetery. Heitman, *Historical Register* (103), 914; U.S. Registers of Deaths in the Regular Army, 1860–89, NARA, RG 94, 208–09; U.S., Burial Registers of Military Posts and National Cemeteries, 1862–1960, NARA, RG 92 (Fort Snelling), 23.

Alfred W. Dale (unknown–1847) was born in Pennsylvania and enlisted in the Twentieth Infantry at Fort Snelling at age twenty-five in 1872. His previous occupation was a clerk, and he was described as having hazel eyes, black hair, and a height of five feet, six and a half inches. He was appointed as a hospital steward at Fort Snelling and served in that position during the Little Big Horn campaign with the Dakota Column on the *Far West* under the chief medical officer John Williams. Gray, *Centennial Campaign*, 274. He continued to serve as a hospital steward, reenlisted in 1877, and was discharged in 1882 at Fort Hale, Dakota Territory. Fort Snelling Post Returns, February 1875, U.S. Army Register of Enlistments, 1798–1914, 1872, p. 35; 1877, p. 92.

104. Atkins, *Harvest of Grief*, 22 (both quotations).

105. Atkins, *Harvest of Grief*, 116.

106. S.O. 65, Department of Dakota, Fort Snelling Post Returns, April 1875.

107. Fort Abraham Lincoln Post Returns, May 1875 for Paulding; S.O. No. 87, Headquarters, Dept. of Dakota 1875 and S.O. No. 88, Headquarters, Fort Abraham Lincoln, both in Fort Abraham Lincoln Post Returns, May 1875 for Lord.

108. Major Charles Christopher Byrne (1837–1921), born in Pikeville, Maryland, was an 1859 graduate of the University of Maryland Medical School and an army assistant surgeon during the Civil War. He served at various Dakota Territory forts as post surgeon and retired as a colonel in 1901. He and his wife, Henrietta Colt Byrne (1847–1914), are buried in Arlington National Cemetery. Heitman, *Historical Register (1903)*, 271; U.S. Select Military Registers, 1862–1988 (Army 1921), 1186; Findagrave.com.

109. Kime, *Black Hills Journals*, 5–6. Kime edited the journals of the military escort commander Lieutenant Colonel Richard Irving Dodge, the originals of which are in the collections of the Newberry Library, Chicago, Illinois.

110. Another civilian contract physician, E. W. Du Bose, who had been post surgeon at Fort Cross (Seward) in Dakota Territory since 1872, was also transferred to Fort Abraham Lincoln for the Black Hills Expedition on June 11. However, like Lord, he was placed on temporary duty at the post and never sent with the expedition. S.O. No. 83, Headquarters, Department of Dakota, S.O. No. 115, Headquarters, Fort Abraham Lincoln Post Returns, June 1875.

111. Kime, *Black Hills Journals*, 6–7.

112. The Heart River camp site had been used for expeditions leading out of Fort Abraham Lincoln. It encompassed approximately 1,000 acres of level ground, surrounded by cottonwood trees, plenty of firewood, and good drinking water. Perhaps the only drawback was the infestation of rattlesnakes, of which the troops routinely disposed in a systematic "skirmish line" manner before setting up camp. The site was described as a "delightful spot for a camp" by *Bismarck Tribune* correspondent

Mark Kellogg during the Little Big Horn campaign in 1876. Chorne, *Following the Custer Trail*, 18–23; Barnard, *I Go with Custer*, 170.

113. George Edwin Lord to the Surgeon General, July 8, 1875, Lord ACP.
114. Fort Abraham Lincoln Post Returns, July 1875.
115. Fort Ellis Post Returns, October 1875.
116. S.O. No. 145, July 31, 1875, Department of Dakota, received, August 5, 1875, Headquarters, Fort Snelling, Minnesota, Fort Snelling Post Returns, August 1875.
117. S.O. 129, Fort Buford Post Returns, August 1875.

CHAPTER 3.
ALL IN THE LINE OF DUTY AT FORT BUFORD

1. In two examples referring to this perception, noted during Secretary of War William Belknap's spring 1876 impeachment trial in the post tradership scandal, Fort Buford was referred to as being a place of "exile" and devoid civilization as well as the "artic." Kroeker, *Great Plains Command*, 148, 150.

2. Fort Buford (1866–95), near present-day Williston, North Dakota, was named in honor of Major General John Buford of Gettysburg fame. A primary source on the fort compound is Billings, *Report on the Hygiene*, 399–402. The fort today is a North Dakota State Historic Site featuring the original 1871 commanding officer's quarters, 1872 powder magazine, and a reconstruction of the barracks.

3. Hedren's "Sitting Bull's Surrender" provides an excellent account of the incident. See also Utley, *Sitting Bull*, 230–33.

4. Billings, *Report on the Hygiene*, 399–400 (both quotations).

5. William Babcock Hazen (1830–87) was post commander of Fort Buford, serving from 1872 to 1880. He was a native of Vermont but was raised in Ohio, and during his childhood he became a lifelong friend of future president James A. Garfield. He graduated from the U.S. Military Academy in 1855, served with distinction as a Union commander in the Civil War, and was promoted to brevet major general of the volunteers. Thereafter, he served in the Sixth Infantry in the Indian Wars period, during which his career was marked by controversies with various army colleagues and government officials. He became brigadier general and head of the U.S. Signal Corps in 1880. Hazen is buried in Arlington National Cemetery. Kroeker, *Great Plains Command*; Innis, *Sagas of the Smoky-Water*, 288–98; Heitman, *Historical Register (1903)*, 518.

6. Stephen Walley Groesbeck (1840–1904) was born in Albany, New York, and his family later moved to Illinois. He served in the Fourth Iowa Cavalry during the Civil War. After rejoining the army, he transferred to the Sixth U.S. Infantry for the remainder of his career. At Buford, he was post adjutant. He retired in 1903 and received promotion to brigadier general. Groesbeck died of typhoid fever in St. Louis, Missouri, and is buried in the Jefferson Barracks National Cemetery. Heitman, *Historical Register* (1903), 481; U.S. Census, 1850 and 1880, LeRoy, Illinois, and

Fort Buford; U.S. Civil War Soldier Records and Profiles, 1861–65; Sixth Infantry Returns, 1879–88; Missouri Death Records, 1850–1931, St. Louis, 1896–1904; all per Ancestry.com; Findagrave.com.

7. Bismarck had become a major stopover on the Upper Missouri River for the steamboat companies for shipping, mail, and passenger service. The town was founded in 1872 by settlers and Northern Pacific Railroad personnel. The Mandan Indians had occupied the area from the late 1500s. The U.S. Army built Camp Hancock and nearby Forts McKeen and Abraham Lincoln to protect railroad workers and settlers when the railroad reached there in 1873. Dr. James DeWolf described the town as a "squalid dunghill sort of place," Harburn, *A Surgeon with Custer*, 71–72; see also Barnard, *I Go with Custer*, 77–82.

8. The *Key West* was a steamboat operating on the Missouri and Yellowstone Rivers in the 1870s. Built in 1871 in Pittsburgh, Pennsylvania, it was 200 feet long by 33 feet wide and weighed 422 tons. Owned by the Coulson Line, headed by Sanford B. Coulson, it was later was sold in 1882 and operated under a different name until the late 1880s. "Upper Missouri River Steamboat Companies & Independent Operators," PDF, p. 28, Richard C. Frajola's Philatelist's Site, www.rfrajola.com/ks/ks1.pdf (accessed March 26, 2020, and January 13, 2022); Lass, *Steamboating on the Upper Missouri, River*, 108; Lass, *Navigating the Missouri*, 335.

9. Carroll, a town with an associated stockade, was a steamboat landing and trading post established in 1874 by the freighting company Diamond R and named for one of the company's owners, Matt Carroll. The fort was built by two companies of the U.S. Seventh Infantry and a company of the Second Cavalry and garrisoned in the summers of 1874 and 1875. The town and fort were then abandoned as business was not as profitable as initially envisioned. Oscar Mueller, "Old Carroll Trail—George Berry Tells of Town's Founding on Missouri River," *Great Falls Tribune*, May 22, 1932, https://mtmemory.recollectcms.com/nodes/view/3929 (accessed March 26, 2020). See also Lass, *Steamboating on the Upper Missouri River*, 130–31.

10. James Humbert (1839–83), a native of Uniontown, Pennsylvania, served in the Fourteenth U.S. Infantry during the Civil War and the U.S. Eighth Infantry as a lieutenant from 1867 to 1868. He married Virginia Gibbon in 1868. Assigned to the Seventeenth Infantry in 1870, he served at various western posts, Fort Rice, 1871–76, Camp Hancock at Bismarck 1872–74, Abraham Lincoln 1874 and 1877–78, and the Standing Rock Indian Agency 1878. Promoted to captain in 1882, he died the following year and is buried in Oak Grove Cemetery in Uniontown, Pennsylvania. Heitman, *Historical Register (1903)*, 554; Post Returns for above-named forts; U.S., Civil War Pension Index: General Index to Pension Files, 1861–1934, NARA, Records of the Department of Veterans Affairs, 1773–2007; Pennsylvania, Veterans Burial Cards, 1777–2012 all per Ancestry.com; Findagrave.com.

11. Major William Smith was the paymaster in the Department of Dakota for posts on the Missouri River from his base at Sioux City, Iowa. (Forts Rice and Abraham Lincoln, Camp Hancock, Stevenson, and Buford). Originally from

Vermont, he served in the volunteer forces from Minnesota as assistant paymaster during the Civil War. Thereafter, Smith joined the regular army, appointed as paymaster and major. Promoted to brigadier general and paymaster general in 1890, he retired in 1895. Heitman, *Historical Register (1903)*, 904; *Army and Navy Journal*, July 12, 1873, p. 760.

12. Orlando Hurley Moore (1827–90) was born in Wilkes-Barre, Pennsylvania, although he grew up in Schoolcraft and Kalamazoo, Michigan. He married Sarah Abigail Haynes in 1855 and served in the U.S. Sixth Infantry. During the Civil War, he had a distinguished career as colonel with the Twenty-Fifth Michigan Infantry. Thereafter, the majority of his career was with the U.S. Sixth Infantry, and he was promoted to major in 1874. He commanded detachments guarding the supply depots during the Little Big Horn campaign. He served at various posts, including Buford, Stevenson, Abraham Lincoln, and Yates, retiring in 1884. He died in Detroit, Michigan, although he and his wife are buried in Tulare, California. Heitman, *Historical Register (1903)*, 723; Hedren, *Great Sioux War Orders*, 61, 90–92, 118, 122; Michigan, County Marriage Records, 1822–1940; Post Returns for the above-named forts; *Bismarck Tribune*, January 18, 1884, p. 2; Findagrave.com.

13. William Henry Harrison Crowell (1841–1913) was born in Geneva, Ohio. He served in three different Ohio Volunteer Artillery units during the Civil War, the last as a captain in the Second Ohio Volunteer Artillery. After the war, he entered the Seventeenth U.S. Infantry until assigned to the Sixth U.S. Infantry in 1870. Promoted to captain in 1893, he retired in 1900. Crowell died in New York City and is buried in Arlington National Cemetery. Heitman, *Historical Register (1903)*, 341; Arlington National Cemetery Unofficial Website, www.arlingtoncemetery.net (accessed March 27, 2020); also Arlington National Cemetery official website, www.arlingtoncemetery.mil.

14. John Alexander McKinney, MD (1848–87) was born in Perche, Missouri. An 1873 medical graduate of the University of the City of New York in 1873, he served as a house staff intern at Charity Hospital his last year. McKinney then became a contract surgeon for the army, serving at Forts Abercrombie (1873), Stevenson (1873–74), Buford (1874–76), Garland, Colorado (1879–80). He married Susan Elizabeth Radcliff (1858–1918). Both are buried in Elmwood Cemetery, Kansas City, Missouri. U.S. Census, 1860, Perche, Missouri; U.S. Census, 1880, Fort Garland, Colorado; *Society of the Alumni of City (Charity) Hospital: Report for 1904* (New York: Society of City Hospital, 1904), 13–19, 135, 218; Post Returns for above-named forts; Findagrave.com.

15. Aside from encounters with infected prostitutes at brothels, interaction with infected Indian women at some posts was a cause of venereal disease. This had been the situation at Fort Buford previously, a reason for the examination of the Indian women. Willey and Scott, *Health of the Seventh Cavalry*, 209.

16. The steamboat *Benton* was built in 1875 in Pittsburgh, Pennsylvania, and originally owned jointly by two mercantile companies based in Fort Benton, Isaac G. Baker & Company and Thomas C. Powers & Bros. The *Benton*'s dimensions were

197 feet long by 33 feet wide. It was destroyed in 1897 when it struck ice and ran into a drawbridge near Sioux City, South Dakota. Lepley, "Old Reliable," 44, 51.

17. Yankton had become a major riverboat port on the Missouri River. It was founded in 1861 as the initial territorial capital of the new Dakota Territory about two years after the region was opened to settlement following the signing of a treaty with the Yankton Sioux Indians. Lass, *Navigating the Missouri*, 181–82.

18. Fort Benton and the surrounding town became one of the other major riverboat ports at the western end of the Missouri River. An American Fur Company trading post among the Blackfeet Indians, it was rebuilt about 1849. The fort was leased by the U.S. Army in 1869 and garrisoned with troops. The army abandoned the post in 1881. Today, following archaeological excavations, the fort has been reconstructed on the original site. Billings, *Report on the Hygiene*, 397; Frazer, *Forts of the West*, 79.

19. The threat of venereal disease was always present in the West, and the U.S. Army recorded 2,626 cases in the year 1875. Today, the "diseases of immorality" syphilis and gonorrhea are treated with antibiotics. During the 1870s, as no cure was known, treatment was palliative. Mercury was used for both in a variety of distributions including ointments on the chancre sores, oral intake, and direct penile urethral injections; Agnew, *Medicine in the Old West*, 83, 91. However, due to concerns of mercury poisoning, which included bleeding gums and loss of teeth, some physicians recommended against its use in gonorrhea for the painful penile discharges. Instead, injections "of a weak solution of some astringent, . . . grains of the sulphate, or acetate, of zinc to the ounce of water" were recommended; U.S. Sanitary Commission, *Report of a Committee*, 4.

20. This was Second Lieutenant Thomas Gerry Townsend (1849–1902). He was born in Washington, D.C., and he graduated from the U.S. Military Academy in 1871, serving in the Sixth Infantry at Forts Douglas (Utah), Omaha, and Sheridan (Illinois). He was eventually promoted to captain and retired in 1896. He and his wife, Clara Pell Townsend (1855–1937), are buried in Arlington National Cemetery. Heitman, *Historical Register (1903)*, 968; U.S., Returns of Military Posts, 1800–1916, above mentioned forts; Findagrave.com.

21. The steamboat *Josephine* was built at Pittsburgh in 1873, originally owned by the Coulson Line. Its dimensions were 178 feet long by 83 feet wide and its carrying capacity was 300.51 tons. It was used in the Yellowstone expedition of 1873 to evaluate the potential for steamboat travel on the Missouri River by the army. The boat sank after striking ice in 1907. Lass, *Navigating the Missouri*. 302, 310,326, 338, 375; Lass, *Steamboating on the Upper Missouri River*, 108.

22. David Lucius Craft (unknown–1890), a native of Pennsylvania, served in the Eighth Pennsylvania Reserves and later the Signal Corps during the Civil War. Thereafter, he served in the U.S. Sixth Infantry and was promoted to lieutenant in October 1876. He is buried in Arlington National Cemetery. Heitman, *Historical Register (1903)*, 332; Findagrave.com.

23. William Richardson, Sixth Infantry, hospital steward, had been appointed to the position March 19, 1874. He enlisted April 11, 1872, and was discharged April 11, 1877, at Fort Buford. He died on December 19, 1880, at Fort Sill, Indian Territory, due to "paralysis of the heart." Fort Buford Post Returns, April 1874–April 1877; U.S. Army Register of Enlistments, 1798–1914 (1854–99 for Hospital Stewards), 226, Ancestry.com.

24. The steamer *General Meade* was owned by the Kountz Line, later the Coulson Line. Built in 1875 in Pittsburgh, it operated primarily on the lower Missouri, Osage, and Mississippi River routes, although it was also used on the Upper Missouri and Yellowstone Rivers. The boat was 193 feet long by 30'6" wide. It sank near Pelican Bend, Missouri, on the Mississippi River in 1888. Lass, *Steamboating on the Upper Missouri River*, 108; Lass, *Navigating the Missouri*, 335, 367.

25. Elwell Stephen Otis (1838–1909). Born in Frederick, Maryland, Otis served as a lieutenant colonel with the 140th New York Infantry during the Civil War. Wounded at Peebles Farm, he was regulated to administrative duties for the remainder of his life. He served as lieutenant colonel in the Twenty-Second Infantry. As a major general, he oversaw commands in the Philippine-American War 1898–99. He is buried in Arlington National Cemetery. Heitman, *Historical Register* (1903), 762; U.S. Civil War Soldier Records and Profiles, 1861–65; Twenty-Second Regimental Returns; Findagrave.com.

26. This amount of rainfall in a day was substantial. Post commander William B. Hazen had previously opined about the lack of rainfall in an article he wrote during his controversial war of words with the Northern Pacific Railroad, the government, and Lieutenant Colonel George Custer over the viability of lands for agriculture in the Fort Buford region that was being promoted for homesteaders. In comparison to more recent data compiled from 1981 to 2010 by the National Oceanic and Atmospheric Administration (NOAA), formerly the National Climatic Data Center, the average August rainfall for North Dakota in the Williston area (where Fort Buford was located) was only 1.45 inches total with an average of 8.2 days of rainfall. For the controversy involving Buford, see Kroeker, *Great Plains Command*, 120–42; State Historical Society of North Dakota, Digital Horizons excerpt from Hazen, "The Great Middle Region of the United States," www.digitalhorizonsonline.org/digital/collection/uw-ndshs/id/5128 (accessed April 9, 2020) and Innis, *Sagas of the Smoky-Water*, 296–98. NOAA, U.S. Climate Normals Quick Access, North Dakota, Williston Sloulin International Airport, page 2 of PDF download at https://www.ncei.noaa.gov/access/us-climate-normals/#dataset=normals-monthly&timeframe=81&location=ND&station=USW00094014 (accessed March 5, 2022).

27. This was Secretary of War William Worth Belknap (1829–90), former Union Army brevet brigadier general, who was on his way back to Washington, D.C., from a two-week tour of Yellowstone National Park. Belknap had requested the expedition and chose Lieutenant Gustavus Cheyney Doane (1840–92), an explorer and U.S. Second Cavalry officer stationed at Fort Ellis, Montana, to lead it. Doane

had been involved in the 1870 expedition, after which Yellowstone was established as the nation's first national park in 1872. Bartlett, *Yellowstone: A Wilderness Besieged*, 31; Scott, *Yellowstone Denied*, 105.

28. The chief surgeon at each post was required to record meteorological data of the conditions and temperatures, although those activities began to be taken over by the U.S. Signal Corps in the 1870s. The Smithsonian Institution was also involved in compiling information in years prior. The U.S. Signal Corps did not begin operation at Fort Buford until 1879. Dr. Lord recorded the daily average temperature for August to be 68.12° with a high of 84° and low of 37°; the average daily high and low temperatures for September, October, and November were recorded as highs of 70°, 58°, 48° and lows of 40°, 28°, 19.33°. Interestingly and in contrast, the average daily temperature for Williston, North Dakota, as recorded 1981–2010 by the NOAA for these same four months were 84°/54°, 71°/42°, 56°/30°, and 38°/16° respectively. Studies on weather parameters for some historic forts in the Dakotas during this era have been published in recent years, although none for Fort Buford. War Office, *Regulations for the Medical Department of the Army, 1863*, no. 25, p. 9; Raines, *Getting the Message Through*, 46–73; NOAA Data Tools: 1981–2010 Normals, Monthly, North Dakota, Williston Sloulin Field, https://www.ncdc.noaa.gov/cdo-web/datatools/normals (accessed March 5, 2022).

29. This was Private Thomas Lambourne, Company C, Sixth Infantry. Born in Buckingham, England, he enlisted in the Sixth Infantry on September 5, 1871, at age 23. Accepted for the position, he was transferred to Fort Stephenson, where he reported for duty on November 5, 1875. He served there until discharged on September 5, 1876. U.S. Army Register of Enlistments, 1798–1914, Sixth Infantry (1871–77); Post Returns for Forts Buford and Stevenson 1875. Only one hospital steward was allowed for each post; War Office, *Regulations for the Medical Department of the Army, 1863*, no. 58, p. 16. Since Private William Richardson was the long-standing hospital steward at Fort Buford, Lambourne was assigned to Fort Stevenson.

30. The former president of the United States had recently died from a series of strokes on July 31, 1875. Johnson, the seventeenth president, had been elected to the U.S. Senate from his home state of Tennessee earlier that year.

31. Charles George Penny (1844–1926). Born in Newark, Ohio, he attended Kenyon College in Ohio. During the Civil War, he served in the Seventy-Sixth Ohio Infantry and the Fifty-First U.S. Infantry. Afterward, as an officer in the army, he was assigned to the Sixth Infantry in 1870 and served in quartermaster duties much of the time. He became a brigadier general in 1903 at his retirement. He and his wife then moved to Ojai, California, and are buried there in Nordhoff Cemetery. U.S. Select Military Registers, 1862–1985 (for 1918), 977; Heitman, *Historical Register (1903)*, 782; Findagrave.com.

32. During Lord's time at Fort Buford, the post returns document six to seven scouts in garrison. The Army Reorganization Act of 1866 authorized enlistment of Indians as scouts for the army in the territories. The scouts were to receive the same pay and allowances as cavalry soldiers. Plante, "Lead the Way" 1.

33. Brown replaced Assistant Surgeon John D. Hall at Fort Shaw in Montana Territory. U.S. Returns for Military Posts, 1806–1916, Fort Shaw, September–October 1875; Sixth Infantry Returns, Fort Shaw, September 1875. Heitman, *Historical Register (1903)*, 253 and 489.

34. Fort Shaw (1867–91) was located near present-day Great Falls, Montana, on the Sun River. The fort was named for Colonel Robert Gould Shaw, the commander of the Fifty-Fourth Massachusetts Infantry killed at Fort Wagner, South Carolina, in 1863 during the Civil War. In 1876, fort commander Colonel John Gibbon led troops from the fort comprising part of the "Montana Column" to the Little Big Horn. The fort was abandoned in 1892, became an Indian school until 1910, later a high school, and German POW camp during World War II. A National Register Historic Site today and overseen by the Sun Valley Historical Society, only six original buildings remain, including the commanding officer's quarters. Billings, *Report on the Hygiene*, 430–34; Frazer, *Forts of the West*, 83–84; Traci Rosenbaum, "Fort Shaw Celebrates 150 Years with a Day of Fun and History," *Great Falls Tribune*, July 8, 2017, https://www.greatfallstribune.com/story/entertainment/2017/08/07/fort-shaw-celebrates-150-years-day-fun-and-history/545074001/ (accessed April 2, 2020).

35. James William Powell Jr. (1840–1907). Powell and his wife, Angeline (1845–1931), named their son Leighton (1875–1938), the second of their eventual three children. Born in New York, the captain served in the Civil War with the Seventy-First New York Infantry. Promoted to major in the Sixth Infantry in 1891, he finished his army career as a colonel in the Seventeenth Infantry, retiring in 1899. He and his wife are buried in Arlington National Cemetery. Heitman, *Historical Register (1903)*, 803; Findagrave.com.

36. Richard Taylor Jacob Jr. (1848–1923). Born in Louisville, Kentucky, he served with the U.S. Sixth Infantry as second lieutenant beginning October 1867. He was at Camp Supply and Fort Arbuckle in Oklahoma Territory, Fort Hays and Dodge in Kansas, then Fort Buford. Promoted to first lieutenant in 1879, he left the army in 1881, although he served as a captain in the U.S. Volunteer Infantry during the Spanish-American War in 1898–99. He lived his last years in a veterans' home and is buried in Oklahoma City. Heitman, *Historical Register* (1903), 569, Post Returns for above-named forts; Sixth Infantry Returns, March 1871, NARA; U.S. National Homes for Disabled Volunteer Soldiers, 1866–1938, 26161; obituary in *Daily Oklahoman*, December 25, 1923, all available on Ancestry.com; Findagrave.com.

37. Big Muddy Creek, a tributary of the Missouri River from Saskatchewan, Canada, to Northern Montana, about forty-four miles from Fort Buford.

38. Post commander Colonel Hazen's Sixth Infantry Return of the month lists the names, company, and dates of the soldiers who went out on hay-cutting parties. Sixth Infantry Returns, 1869–78, September 1875.

39. Fort Stevenson (1867–83) was founded as Fort Berthold in north-central Dakota Territory and later renamed for Brigadier General Thomas G. Stevenson, who was killed in the 1864 Civil War Battle of Spotsylvania. The fort was built to protect

peaceful Indian Arikara, Mandan, and Hidatsa tribes from the Sioux Indians and to protect people traveling west from Minnesota. It was built of adobe brick walls and cottonwood. The original fort site now lies under the water of man-made Lake Sakakawea due to the 1950s damming of the Missouri River. A reproduction of the post's main uniquely designed guardhouse has been built two miles from the original site overlooking the lake. The building hosts a museum and is maintained by the Fort Stevenson Foundation and state of North Dakota. Billings, *Report on the Hygiene*, 438–41; Frazer, *Forts of the West*, 114; De Trobriand, *Journal of Philippe Regis de Trobriand*.

40. William Ludlow (1843–1901) was a career army engineer. Born in New York, he was an 1864 U.S. Military Academy graduate and served as first lieutenant in the engineers during the Civil War. During the Indian Wars period, he oversaw engineering projects in Dakota Territory, the Great Lakes, Washington, D.C., New York, and Philadelphia. He was brigadier general of the volunteers in the Spanish-American War. He is buried in Arlington National Cemetery. Heitman, *Historical Register (1903)*, 646; Findagrave.com.

41. Russell Hannibal Day (1844–82). Born in Buffalo, New York, Day served in the Sixteenth New York Artillery during the Civil War and in the U.S. Sixth Infantry as a first lieutenant during the Indian Wars period at various western posts. He died of "Acute Dysentery" at Fort Thornburgh, Utah, in 1882 and is buried in the Fort Douglas Cemetery in Salt Lake City, Utah. Heitman, *Historical Register (1903)*, 362; U.S. Register of Deaths in the Regular Army, 1860–89; Findagrave.com.

42. Fort Rice (1864–78) in Dakota Territory was built on the Missouri River for the expedition against the Sioux in 1864. It served as the command base for the three Yellowstone expeditions of the 1870s and was home to four companies of the Seventh Cavalry. Nothing remains of the fort today other than markings of building foundations, although there are interpretive signs and markers. Billings, *Report on the Hygiene*, 422–24; Frazer, *Forts of the West*, 113.

43. The abbreviation "do" and symbol " stand for "ditto" or "same as above." In this case, the line refers to the daily average number of men treated in their quarters.

44. Alvin C. Leighton was awarded the post trader license for Fort Buford in 1871. With his brother James Leighton and Walter B. Jordan, their firm conducted business as a general store for both the garrison and citizens. He was appointed U.S. Postmaster at the fort in February 1876. In 1879, George Hedderich joined them. "Report of the Committee of Indian Affairs to the House of Representatives," First Session of the Forty-Fourth Congress, Volume 285, 341–44; U.S. Appointments of U.S. Postmasters, 1832–1971, Dakota Territory, 1876, p. 818; Innis, *Sagas of the Smoky-Water*, 236–38; Delo, *Peddlers and Post Traders*, 179–80.

45. The *Far West* is probably the most famous steamboat in Missouri and Yellowstone River transportation history. Built at Pittsburgh, Pennsylvania, in 1870 for the Coulson Packet Line's Missouri River business, it measured 190 feet by 33 feet and had a loading capacity of 397.81 tons. The *Far West*, captained by Grant Marsh,

transported the wounded survivors from the Battle of the Little Big Horn to Fort Abraham Lincoln. Lass, *Navigating the Missouri*, 293, 304–5.

46. Daniel Hamilton Murdock (1842–86) and his bride, Emily Megrath Murdock (1838–1911), had recently been married in Milwaukee, Wisconsin, on August 11, 1875. Born in Green County, Pennsylvania, he served in the Civil War in the Third Iowa Cavalry and the 122nd U.S. Colored Infantry. He then served in the U.S. Sixth Infantry, being promoted to captain in 1874. After Buford, he and his company were assigned to guard supplies at the Powder River Depot during the Battle of the Little Big Horn. In 1880, at Davis Island, New York, their only child, Adelade, was born. Murdock accidentally drowned in June 1886 near Montezuma Creek, Utah, and is buried at Fort Douglas Cemetery in Salt Lake City, Utah. Milwaukee, Wisconsin, Marriages, 1838–1911; Heitman, *Historical Register (1903)*, 736; U.S. Civil War Records and Profiles, 1861–65; U.S. Register of Deaths in the Regular Army, 1866–89, 47; Findagrave.com.

47. This was Arthur Lockwood Wagner (1853–1905). Born in Illinois, he was an 1875 U.S. Military Academy graduate. He served with the Sixth Infantry as a second lieutenant with gradual promotions to adjutant general; later in the Philippines. He died of tuberculosis in Asheville, North Carolina, and is buried in Arlington National Cemetery. Heitman, *Historical Register (1903)*, 992; Fort Buford Post Returns, 1875–76; Findagrave.com.

48. The Garden Coulee is the site of a Hidatsa Indian settlement of the 1870s and 1880s adjacent to the grounds of the abandoned Fort Union Trading Post (1828–67) of the American Fur Company, a couple miles west of Fort Buford. See "19th Century Archeology at the Garden Coulee Site," Fort Union Trading Post National Historic Site, last updated March 26, 2020, https://www.nps.gov/articles/garden-coulee-site.htm. An interesting note is that the earthen dam across Garden Coulee still exists today, an unexplained oddity on the border of the Fort Union site.

49. The names of these twenty-four men (discharged and transferred) can be found on the Return for the Sixth Infantry, Fort Buford, September 1875.

50. Hazen was granted a leave of absence from his command of Fort Buford for the next nine months, initially due to health as his 1859 side wound from battling Comanche Indians early in his career had flared up. While away, he testified at the Clymer/Belknap hearings as to Secretary of War Belknap's corruption in appointments of post traders. Groesbeck's leave was for six months. Fort Buford Post Returns, October 1875; Kroeker, *Great Plains Command*, 33–36, 143–52.

51. Charley Lawrence Gurley (1849–1916). A native of Indiana, he entered the army in 1872 as a second lieutenant in the Sixth Infantry. After Fort Buford, he served at Forts Thornburgh and Douglas in Utah. Promoted to first lieutenant in 1882, he resigned a year later and worked as an army clerk in Washington, D.C., until his death in 1916. He is buried in Glenwood Cemetery in Washington, D.C. Heitman, *Historical Register (1903)*, 484; Fort Douglas Post Return, December 1882; U.S. Register of Civil, Military and Naval Service, 1863–1959 for 1905, p. 301; Findagrave.com.

52. Charles McAllister (unknown–1876) was a clerk in the Quartermaster Department for Major William Smith. He committed suicide by shooting himself in the heart on the morning of January 29, 1876, at Fort Buford. Assistant Post Surgeon J. A. McKinney recorded his death as being "an imaginary disease of brain, producing hypochondriac Melancholy." Lord did not mention the death in the medical log. Burial Registers of Military Posts, Camps, and Stations, 1768–1821, Record Book of Interments, Post Cemetery, Fort Buford, Records of the Quartermaster General, RG 92, NARA, 123; Innis, *Interments at Fort Buford*, 21.

53. Steve Scott was a homesteader and eventual cattle rancher whose log cabin was a couple of miles west of the fort. He came to the area in 1867 as a squatter; however, he unhappily left the area with his wife and children in 1887 because the Great Northern Railroad survey placed the tracks within twenty yards of his home. Innis, *Sagas of the Smoky-Water*, 248, 347–48.

54. Private Wilmot P. Sanford, Company D, Sixth Infantry, left a diary for 1874–75 (and 1876–77) during his time serving at Fort Buford. Many of his entries provide an interesting description of the meals for enlisted men and his thoughts about the dietary composition and post gardens. His original diary is in the archive collections at Yale University, although it was published by the State Historical Society of North Dakota in *North Dakota History* in 1966 and 1985.

55. Army surgeons of the era were also responsible for implementing evolving general guidelines regarding preventative and community health. Here, Lord noted his concern regarding potential health problems posed by the enormous number of recruits that would be staying at Fort Buford that winter. Army medical regulations stipulated the medical officer was to "promote heath and prevent contagion, by ventilated and not crowded rooms, scrupulous cleanliness, frequent changes of bedding, linen, &c." War Office, *Regulations for the Medical Department of the Army, 1863*, no. 15, p. 7.

56. Lord's monthly record notes that paymaster Major Smith and his clerk, Mr. McAllister, returned every other month to Fort Buford. Troops were to be paid in a time frame not to exceed two months. War Office, *Revised U.S. Army Regulations, 1863*, Art. XLV, no. 1338, p. 351.

57. There were many geographic areas on the Missouri Rivers that contained extremely high sloping banks from which natural landslides occurred, making travel of military expeditions extremely difficult and dangerous. However, "The Slide" was a specifically named area near Shell Creek, a small tributary of the Missouri River, which was about 103 miles east of Fort Buford on the route toward Fort Stevenson. "Annual Report of Lieutenant Edward Maguire, Corps of Engineers, . . . *Third Session of the Forty-Fifth Congress*," U.S. War Department, Annual Reports of the War Department, 1673.

58. Fort Buford Medical Log, entry for November 2, 1875.

59. Fort Buford Medical Log, entries for November 12, 14, and 15, 1875.

60. Mattison, "Army Post on the Northern Plains," 37; Chambers, *Fort Abraham Lincoln*, 120.

61. Lord was commenting here on an example of the occasional drunkenness among the enlisted troops at Fort Buford. Also, such a theatrical performance would likely be considered a racially overtoned event today.

62. Edwin Mario (b. 1853), born in Boston, Massachusetts, was among the recruits for the Seventh Infantry brought to Fort Buford in 1875. Mario enlisted at age twenty-two, and his previous occupation was a painter. He had blue eyes, light brown hair, light complexion, and a height of five feet, six and three-fourths inches. Assigned for training with Company C of the Sixth Infantry, his service in the regiment never stated due to his mental health behavioral problems. It was also discovered that he enlisted under the name of Frank Civeken, who was discharged in the same regiment in 1873. His exact mental diagnosis was not known, although Lord noted he had a history of prior admission to a mental asylum. Mario was transferred to the Government Asylum for the Insane in Washington, D.C., on June 2, 1876. U.S. Army Register of Enlistments, 1798–1914, for 1875, p. 94; Sixth Infantry Returns, October 1876; Fort Buford Medical Log, entries for November and December 1875, January and February 1876.

63. Fort Buford Medical Log, entry for November 26, 1875.

64. Fort Buford Medical Log, entry for November 27, 1875 (first quotation); entry for November 30, 1875 (second quotation).

Chloroform (Trichloromethane), a colorless, sweet-smelling liquid made from the interaction of chlorine and alcohol, was commonly used as a sedative and for anesthesia during the mid to late nineteenth century. Similar to ether, administration was performed by use of a cloth dosed in the liquid, although the dosage was essentially a judgment of the individual physician. Both had to be used with caution as either could cause respiratory depression and death of the patient, and chloroform could cause cardiac arrhythmias. However, chloroform was nonflammable and acted quicker than ether, whereas ether could explode if exposed to flame. Stedman, *Stedman's Medical Dictionary*, 265; Agnew, *Medicine in the Old West*, 141–42; Miller, *Domestic Medical Practice*, 1090. Richardson, *Health and Longevity*, 923.

65. Fort Buford Medical Log, entry for December 1, 1875.

66. Fort Buford Medical Log, entries for February 25, 1876, and March 12, 1876.

67. Fort Buford Medical Log, entry for January 4, 1876.

68. Fort Buford Medical Log, entries for December 25 and 31, 1875, and January 1, 1876.

69. Billroth, *General Surgical Pathology*, 251: Chase, *Dr. Chase's Recipes*, 228–29 (quotation); Miller, *Domestic Medical Practice*, 831.

70. Golant et al., "Cold Exposure Injuries"; DeLee et al., *Orthopaedic Sports Medicine* I:547–49.

71. Fort Buford Medical Log, entry for January 31, 1876.

72. Flint, *Principles and Practice of Medicine*, 949; for modern era discussion of rheumatic arthritis, see Jameson et al., *Harrison's Principles of Medicine*, 2527–40.

73. Flint, *Principles and Practice of Medicine*, 949–65 for acute rheumatism.

74. Jameson et al., *Harrison's Principles of Internal Medicine*, 2542–45.

75. Jameson et al., *Harrison's Principles of Internal Medicine*, including for mitral stenosis in rheumatic heart disease, 245, 1814.
76. Jameson et al., *Harrison's Principles of Internal Medicine*, 1841–45, for pericarditis.
77. Willey and Scott, *Health of the Seventh Cavalry*, 165.
78. Flint, *Principles and Practice of Medicine*, 956–58, 962.
79. Flint, *Principles and Practice of Medicine*, 786. Discussion of signs, symptoms, pathogenesis, diagnosis, and treatment of diabetic disease as known in the 1870s is on pp. 785–95 of that book, and in the modern medical text Jameson et al., *Harrison's Principles of Medicine*, 2850–79.
80. Stedman, *Stedman's Medical Dictionary*, 385.
81. Flint, *Principles and Practice of Medicine*, 786.
82. George P. Mulligan was the civilian interpreter hired at Fort Buford at a salary of fifty dollars per month. Fort Buford Post Returns, August 1875; his child's death also noted in U.S. Military Burial Registers, 1768–1921, Fort Buford, Dakota Territory, 123.
83. Fort Buford Medical Log, entry for February 2, 1876.
84. Jameson et al., *Harrison's Principles of Internal Medicine*, 1122–28.
85. Early gonorrhea treatments are noted in Richardson, *Health and Longevity*, 578 (flaxseed tea quotation), 936; Agnew, *Medicine in the West*, 88–92; and Willey and Scott, *Health of the Seventh Cavalry*, 214–15.
86. This patient admitted the month prior was likely Private John Craven, recruit of the Seventh Infantry assigned to Company D. Lord does not indicate a first name. Craven enlisted on August 10, 1875, at Indianapolis, Indiana. A native of Ross, Ohio, his former occupation was listed as a farmer. He had hazel eyes, brown hair, ruddy complexion, and a height of five feet, seven inches. He was discharged for disability at Camp Baker in September 1877. There was a James Corgan who enlisted in the Seventh Infantry, assigned to the same company, on June 2, 1875, in St. Louis, Missouri. However, as John Craven enlisted with the other Seventh Infantry recruits sent to Fort Buford as well as his discharge for disability within two years, supports the documented medical condition of rheumatism. U.S. Army Register of Enlistments, 1875, A–G, 310, 311.
87. Private Abraham Dick (1853–76) Company F, Sixth Infantry was from Alton, Illinois, and enlisted on August 25, 1873, at Fort Buford. His previous occupation was as a barber, and he had black eyes and black hair. He spent the next three years at the post until his death on March 7, 1876. Lord's entries in the medical log detail his symptoms, treatment, and his burial. U.S. Army Register of Enlistments, 1873, p. 42; Fort Buford Post Returns August 1875; U.S. Military Burial Registers, Fort Buford.
88. Private James Gallagher, Company F, Sixth Infantry (b. 1845). Born in Limerick, Ireland, he enlisted at Toledo, Ohio, in the Sixth Infantry at age twenty-six. His former occupation was a laborer, and he had gray eyes, brown hair, fair complexion, and a height of five feet, five inches. He was at Fort Buford September 1873–May 1876 and served at the Yellowstone Supply Depot that month. He was discharged

from the army due to expiration of service in September 1876. U.S. Army Register of Enlistments, 1871–77, for 1871, A–G, 241; Sixth Infantry Returns, September 1873, May and September 1876.

89. Chase, *Dr. Chase's Recipes*, 192; Richardson, *Health and Longevity*, 999.

90. Lord spelled the soldier's last name as Schaffer of Company G, but he does not record the first name. In an extensive review of the Fort Buford Post returns from August 1875–May 1876, Sixth Infantry Regimental Returns, and U.S. Army Register of Enlistments 1871–77, the injured soldier was probably Private Eugene Schaefer, Sixth Infantry, Company G, who had enlisted in the regiment at age twenty-two on April 8, 1872, in Brooklyn, New York. He was from Germany and was described as having black eyes and a height of six feet and one-half inches. He was discharged on April 8, 1877, at Fort Buford for expiration of service, with his character described as good. U.S. Army Register of Enlistments, 1871–77, P–Z, 207. There was a Private Edward A. Shaffer, Company G, Sixth Infantry at Fort Buford; however, he is not recorded as enlisting as a recruit assigned to Company G of the Sixth Infantry until May 8, 1878, in Chicago, Illinois, and thus is not the injured soldier. Incidentally, this Shaffer was murdered two years later on December 13, 1878, at Fort Buford. U.S. Army Register of Enlistments, P–Z, 207; Fort Buford Post Returns, June and September 1876 for Eugene Schaefer; U.S. Army Register of Enlistments, P–Z, 297; Innis, *Interments at Fort Buford*, 25; and U.S. Military Post Burials, Fort Buford, 123 for Edward A. Shaffer.

91. Fort Buford Medical Log, entry for February 15, 1876.

92. Stedman, *Stedman's Medical Dictionary*, 748.

93. Green, *Operative Hand Surgery*, I, 788–89.

94. This was Private Edward M. Spencer (b. 1850), Company D. From Philadelphia, Pennsylvania, he enlisted in the Sixth Infantry there in 1872. Records note his occupation as a cigarmaker, and he had brown eyes, dark hair, fair complexion, and a height of five feet, eight inches. He was discharged for disability March 26, 1876. U.S. Army Register of Enlistments, Sixth Infantry, P–Z, 1872, p. 210; Sixth Infantry Returns, March 1876.

95. Lord notes McMullin being one of the 103 recruits of the Seventh Infantry at the post. However, no listing or discharge of McMullin is found in the U.S. Army Register of Enlistments 1871–77, the Sixth Infantry Returns, or Fort Buford Post Returns 1875–76.

96. Becker, "History of the Stanford-Binet Intelligence Scales," 1–14.

97. Stedman, *Stedman's Medical Dictionary*, 691.

98. Flint, *Principles and Practice of Medicine*, 962–64.

99. This was First Sergeant Walter Hartford, Company E, Sixth Infantry (b. 1834). Born in Dublin, he enlisted in the Sixth Infantry on June 1, 1875, at the old American Fur Company's Fort Sarpy, Montana, at the age of forty-one. He was a former soldier and five feet, ten inches tall. No details regarding a reason for the court-martial are noted on Sixth Infantry Returns or the medical log. Hartford was discharged

June 1, 1875, at Fort Buford, reenlisted the same day, and was eventually discharged for expiration of service there May 31, 1880. U.S. Army Register of Enlistments, 1871–77, A–G, 92; Fort Buford Post Returns, June 1875.

100. Lord does not provide the first name of this soldier. During his time at the post, there were two soldiers named John Smith in the Sixth Infantry. As one of Company D was discharged in November 1875, the other Private John Smith of Company I is the soldier admitted for tonsillitis. He enlisted on August 28, 1875, at Buford. Sixth Infantry Returns, August 1875.

101. Flint, *Principles and Practice of Medicine*, 378.

102. Jameson et al., *Harrison's Principles of Internal Medicine*, 1081–84 (streptococcal pharyngitis and scarlet fever), 218 (tonsillitis), 214 and 2542–44 (rheumatic fever).

103. Flint, *Principles and Practice of Medicine*, 378.

104. This was Private Edward Jennings (Lord misspelled it Jenniger), Company C, Sixth Infantry. He was initially an unattached recruit, but was later assigned to the Sixth Infantry at Fort Buford and in the hay-cutting company there in September. Sixth Infantry Returns, September and November 1875.

105. Fort Buford Medical Log, entry for March 22, 1876.

106. Willey and Scott, *Health of the Seventh Cavalry*, 164–65.

107. Jameson et al., *Harrison's Principles of Internal Medicine*, 1279–85; Agnew, *Medicine in the Old West*, 86–88; Richardson, *Health and Longevity*, 580–87; Willey and Scott, *Health of the Seventh Cavalry*, 212–14.

108. Fort Buford Medical Log, entry of March 1, 1876.

109. Fort Buford Medical Log, entry for March 7, 1876.

110. For treatment of various symptoms associated with rheumatism in the 1870s, see Flint, *Principles and Practice of Medicine*, 956–58, 962; for modern modalities, Jameson et al., *Harrison's Principles of Internal Medicine*, 1841–45 (pericarditis); Shabetai, *Pericardium*, 167–69 (pericardiocentesis).

111. Fort Buford Medical Log, entry for March 8, 1876; also, U.S. Military Burial Registers, Fort Buford, 123.

112. This was Sergeant John W. Gilneath, Company G, Sixth Infantry (b. 1851). Born in Independence, Missouri, he enlisted in the Sixth Infantry at Fort Scott, Kansas, on February 8, 1870. He was described as having gray eyes, brown hair, fair complexion, and a height of five feet, eight inches. He reenlisted in 1875 and was discharged for disability at Fort Abraham Lincoln on January 25, 1880. U.S. Army Register of Enlistments, 1869–70, A–G, 328 and 1871–77, A–G, 278; Sixth Infantry Returns, February and June 1875.

113. Fort Buford Medical Log, entry of March 9, 1876.

114. Fort Peck (1867–79) in northeastern Montana was never an army fort. It was an important trading post established by the Durfee and Peck Trading Company, named for Campbell Kennedy Peck (1831–79), partner with Elias Hicks Durfee (1828–74), both from New York. Built on the Missouri River, the fort had a stockade with five bastions. In 1871, it was purchased from the firm and became the Fort

Peck Indian Agency, which had moved from the Milk River area. When the agency moved again in 1878, the fort was abandoned. With the building of the Fort Peck Dam and Reservoir by the U.S. Army Corps of Engineers in 1934, the original fort site now lies under water. There is a historical marker overlooking the site at the reservoir. Roberts, *Encyclopedia of Historic Forts*, 475; "Old Fort Peck," Waymarking, posted July 16, 2018, http://www.waymarking.com/waymarks/WMYRAM_Old_Fort_Peck_Fort_Peck_MT (accessed April 10, 2020).

115. This was Private Henry Puck, Company E, Sixth Infantry (b. 1849). His arm burn would have been treated the same as Private Gallagher's, as discussed in the text. Born in Schleswig-Holstein, Germany, he enlisted in the Sixth Infantry at Davenport, Pennsylvania, on January 18, 1870. He is described as having blue eyes, dark hair, and a height of five feet, six and one-eighth inches. He reenlisted at Fort Buford on January 18, 1875, and later served at the Yellowstone Depot in May 1876 during the Little Big Horn campaign. Records note he had excellent character as he continued to reenlist several times, at Fort Stevenson in 1880, Fort Douglas (Utah) in 1885, and Fort Sheridan (Illinois) in 1890, officially changing his name to Henry Rodgers that year. U.S. Army Register of Enlistments, 1860–70, P–Z, 14; 1871–77, P–Z, 37; 1878–84, P–Z, 15; 1885–90, L–Z, 292 and 1885–90, L–Z, 320; Sixth Infantry Returns, January 1875 and May 1876 for Fort Buford.

116. This was Private Edward Jennings, Company C, Sixth Infantry. Lord misspelled his last name as Jenniger in the medical log.

117. Lord did not record the first name of the injured man and initially misspelled the last name as Hines, although he recorded it as Hinds in his follow-up entries. This was Private Orange S. Hinds of Company K, Seventh Infantry. Born in Talmadge, Ohio, he enlisted in the Seventh Infantry at Chicago, Illinois, on June 11, 1875; had blue eyes, light hair, and fair complexion; and was five feet, seven and three-fourths inches tall. Hinds was discharged the following year on July 11, 1876, at Fort Shaw, Montana Territory, on certified disability. U.S. Army Register of Enlistments, H–O, 1875, p. 91; U.S. Seventh Infantry Regimental Returns, July 1876. There was a recruit named Private Robert S. Hines serving with the Sixth Infantry, Company E; however, he is not recorded as having enlisted in the regiment until May 8, 1876, at Columbus Barracks, Ohio, and therefore was not the Private Hines injured here. U.S. Army Register of Enlistments, 1871–77, H–O, 1876, p. 110; Sixth Infantry Returns, June, September, and October 1876.

118. See Green, *Operative Hand Surgery*, 962–71, for distal fingertip amputations.

119. Fort Buford Medical Log, entries for April 11 and 25, 1876.

120. Thomas J. Mitchell, from Illinois. He was appointed Fort Peck Indian Agent April 18, 1876, replacing former agent William W. Alderson, who had served in that position since September 1, 1873. Miller et al., *History of the Assiniboine and Sioux*, 86–98.

121. Joseph Leighton was the brother of Alvin C. and James Leighton. He was the Indian agency trader at Fort Peck and had declined an offer to join his brothers at

Fort Buford. "Report of the Committee of Indian Affairs to the House of Representatives," First Session of the Forty-Fourth Congress, 342.

122. Fort Buford Medical Log, entry for April 30, 1876.

123. Stedman, *Stedman's Medical Dictionary*, 634.

124. Richardson, *Health and Longevity*, 561–62; Chase, *Dr. Chase's Recipes*, 116–17; Jameson et al., *Harrison's Principles of Internal Medicine*, 2290.

125. Newly appointed agent Thomas J. Mitchell sent word that he was suffering from an attack of rheumatism. Miller et al., *History of the Assiniboine and Sioux*, 87.

126. The steamboat *Carroll* was built in Pittsburgh in 1875 and owned by Walter A. Burleigh and his son Tim B. Burleigh of Yankton, Dakota Territory. The elder Burleigh, originally from Maine, was also a physician, lawyer, and former Indian agent, and he was later elected to the U.S. House of Representatives for the Dakota Territory. The boat was 185 feet long. The *Carroll* was destroyed by a fire while at an overnight stop about fifty miles above Fort Randall during a trip to the Black Hills in 1877. Lass, *Navigating the Missouri*, 289.

127. Francis Woodbridge, Seventh Infantry (1853–91). A native of Michigan, he entered the service in 1869 and became a second lieutenant in the Seventh Infantry in February 1876. Woodbridge was assigned in March that year by the Adjutant General's Office to oversee the 103 recruits of his regiment who were at Fort Buford over the winter and served in the Terry/Gibbon column in September in the Great Sioux War. He received brevet promotion for gallantry at the Big Hole, Montana, engagement of August 1877. Promoted to first lieutenant in 1883, he retired in 1891. Despite having been ill for some time, Woodbridge was studying law in Ann Arbor, Michigan, after retiring when he was accidentally killed that year at the age of thirty-eight by an accidental gunshot from a revolver he was handling; *Saline* (Michigan) *Observer*, May 7, 1891. He and his wife, Alice Field Woodbridge (1858–1939), are buried in Woodmere Cemetery, Detroit, Michigan. Seventh Infantry Returns, May 1876; Hedren, *Great Sioux War Orders*, 83, 122; Heitman *Historical Register (1903)*, 1056; Findagrave.com.

128. This was Sergeant James Cummings, Company C, Sixth Infantry. Although an unfortunate death, this is an intriguing case. Here, Dr. Lord confirms his following of renowned Dr. Austin Flint's medical textbook by noting Flint's own description of a similar case he observed. Flint noted, aside from "irritant and corrosive poisons," the condition, although infrequent, was seen to occur after "excessive indulgence in alcoholic drinks" and "follow[ing] a debauch." However, even today, the pathogenesis of acute gastritis is not clearly understood as causes of gastric erosions are varied and include acute poisoning, trauma, severe stress, sepsis, burns, shock, chronic alcoholism, medications (aspirin and other antiarthritic medications), and failure of respiratory, renal and liver systems. Flint stated the term acute gastritis was "understood to denote gastric inflammation of such intensity as to place life in imminent danger" with death rapidly occurring as it did in this case of Sergeant Cummings. Symptoms include rapid onset of intense pain, hematemesis (vomiting of blood), and tendency of diarrhea more with poisoning. Flint noted rapid death

was "apparently by shock," although by asthenia (abnormal physical weakness/lack of energy) if the condition progressed over several days. If the patient was fortunate to survive, treatment included a gradual diet progression, avoiding acidic foods, minimal ice or ice water, opiates to quiet the stomach, or the use of salts of morphia on the tongue. Today, gastroscopy confirms the diagnosis of erosive gastritis, and treatment is directed to the system of the underlying specific cause, such as management of and surgery for bleeding, treating pneumonia, antacid regimens for prevention in stress, and fluid replacement. Sergeant Cummings's case was attributed to his debauch of alcohol along with the two small drinks of gin, the action that pushed him over the edge and started the rapidly fatal course. He was buried the following day in the post cemetery. Although Lord was the post surgeon attending Cummings, his colleague, Dr. J. A. McKinney, signed the medical record for the month relating the details of Cummings's death since Lord was transferred to the Yellowstone Depot for the Little Big Horn campaign. Flint, *Principles and Practice of Medicine*, 368–73; Jameson et al., *Harrison's Principles of Internal Medicine*, 2241–43, bleeding in, 1272; Sixth Infantry Returns, May 1876; U.S. Military Burial Registers, 1768–1921, Fort Buford, Dakota Territory, 123 and 27; U.S. Register of Deaths in the Regular Army, 1860–89, Dakota Territory, 1874–76, 31.

129. Corporal William S. Doyle, Company C, Sixth Infantry, born in 1830 in Dublin, Ireland, came to New York and was a painter described as having hazel eyes, black hair and a height of five feet, five inches. He served in the First New York Infantry during the Civil War. He enlisted in the regular army, first with the Forty-Second Infantry in 1867, then the Sixth Infantry, in which he spent the remainder of his career. Doyle continued to reenlist, serving at various posts, including Forts Buford, Leavenworth, Douglas, and Robinson, before retiring from the army as an orderly sergeant on December 13, 1890. U.S. Civil War Abstracts, in the New York Military Rosters, 1861–1900, Albany, New York, at Ancestry.com; U.S. Army Register of Enlistments, 1867, A–O, 194; 1869–70, A–O, 213; 1871–77, A–O, 29; 1878–84, A–G, 22; 1885–90, A–G, 334; Sixth Infantry Returns, January 1875, June 1876, 1880, and Post Returns for Fort Leavenworth 1880–81, Fort Douglas 1885–86, Fort Robinson 1890.

130. The *E. H. Durfee* was a sternwheeler owned by the Durfee and Peck Trading Company (partners Campbell Kennedy Peck and Elias Hicks Durfee) in association with their Northwest Transportation Company. The boat was built in Pittsburgh with dimensions listed as 206 feet in length by 35 feet wide with a carrying capacity of 497.17 tons. Lass, *Navigating the Missouri*, 253, 263, 266–67; Lass, *Steamboating on the Upper Missouri River*, 108.

131. William Wilkins Sanders, Sixth Infantry (1839–83). Born in Pittsburgh, Pennsylvania, he served in the U.S. Eighth Infantry as second lieutenant in 1860 and was promoted to first lieutenant during the Civil War. He later served as colonel of the Second Pennsylvania Cavalry. During the Indian Wars period, he was acting inspector general for the Department of Dakota in 1880, and he died in 1883 at Fort Snelling, Minnesota. Sanders is buried in Woodlands Cemetery, Philadelphia,

Pennsylvania. Heitman, *Historical Register (1903)*, 858; Sixth Infantry Returns, May and June 1976; Findagrave.com.

132. Bernard Albert Byrne, Sixth Infantry (1853–1910). Born at Newport Barracks, Virginia, the son of an army officer, he enlisted as a second lieutenant in the Sixth Infantry in 1875. Promoted to captain in 1894, then major in the Thirteenth Infantry, he later received the Medal of Honor for actions in the Philippine Islands in 1899. Byrne married Bartha Barnitz in 1892, retired in 1906, and died in 1910 in California. He is buried in Arlington National Cemetery. Heitman, *Historical Register (1903)*, 271; Arlington National Cemetery Unofficial Website, www.arlingtoncemetery.net; Arlington National Cemetery, Official Website, www.arlingtoncemetery.mil, Medal of Honor, #2 Point of Interest, Section 1, Site 707.

133. J. B. Newman, Acting Assistant Surgeon, U.S.A., replaced Assistant Post Surgeon Lieutenant Paul R. Brown. Fort Shaw Post Returns, May 1876.

134. Fort Buford, Post Returns, May 1876.

135. Hedren, *Great Sioux War Orders*, 90. Hedren notes that the infantry companies assigned to the depots were to serve as boat guards for the steamboats used during the military operations.

136. The Stanley Stockade was built for the Yellowstone expedition of 1873, which was led by former Civil War officer Colonel David Sloan Stanley (1829–1902), commander of the Twenty-Second Infantry regiment. The expedition "was designed for the protection of engineering surveyors of the Northern Pacific Railroad." Expedition troops included those from Stanley's regiment along with ten companies of the Seventh Cavalry, commanded by Lieutenant Colonel George Custer. The stockade for the transfer of supplies was "a strong bastioned stockade upon the south bank of the Yellowstone, eight miles land above Glendive Creek," easily accessed by the steamboats *Far West* and *Josephine*. The Dakota Column camped at the stockade from June 11 to June 15, 1876, during the time Lord, Major Moore, and the Sixth Infantry companies were there. Nothing remains of the stockade today, although signs indicate the original location. Chorne, *Following the Custer Trail*; Stanley, *Report on the Yellowstone Expedition*, 3 (first quotation), 5 (second quotation).

137. Hedren, *Great Sioux War Orders*, 92.

138. The last page and half of the medical record of Fort Buford for the month of May 1876 consists of fourteen entries covering the dates from May 16 to May 31. This portion has not been included here since those entries were written by Dr. McKinney, who succeeded Lord as post surgeon.

CHAPTER 4.
TO THE LITTLE BIG HORN

1. The Hunkpapa and Oglala were two of the Lakota (Teton) Sioux's seven tribes. Gray, *Centennial Campaign*, 308–20, provides an analysis of the various Sioux bands and the agencies serving them during the Indian Wars period.

2. Lazarus, *Black Hills/White Justice*, 440. The stipulations regarding railroads in the Fort Laramie Treaty of 1868 are in Article 11. One of these stipulations permitted peaceful construction of a railroad not passing over the reservation; however, the actual northern boundary was in dispute between the Indians and the U.S. government.

3. Historian M. John Lubetkin's series on the Yellowstone Surveys of 1871–73 (*The Road to War: The 1871 Yellowstone Survey*; *Before Custer: Surveying the Yellowstone, 1872*; and *Custer and the 1873 Yellowstone Survey*) and his *Jay Cooke's Gamble* regarding the Northern Pacific Railroad are considered the definitive studies of these events.

4. The published sources on the 1874 expedition are varied in style. Ernest Grafe and Paul Horsted's *Exploring with Custer: The 1874 Black Hills Expedition* is considered the definitive study of the expedition; others are *With Custer in '74: James Calhoun's Diary of the Black Hills Expedition* and Terry Mort's *Thieves' Road*.

5. Ostler, *Lakotas*, 92; see also Hutton, *Phil Sheridan*, 297–98.

6. The Indian Office (also known as the Bureau of Indian Affairs) at the end of 1875 estimated the number of roaming bands that winter to be 3,000 Sioux (430 lodges) and 400 Cheyenne (50 lodges), although this did not account for the additional summer roaming bands that were to join in the war. Gray, *Centennial Campaign*, 320.

7. Chapter 3 of Gray's *Centennial Campaign* provides the most in-depth analysis of this secret meeting. General William T. Sherman, commander of the entire U.S. Army at the time, did not attend the meeting, in part because of his long-standing political feuding with Belknap.

8. The Fort Laramie Treaty of 1868 provided no specific reservation for the Northern Cheyennes. It did allow them a choice of either the Great Sioux Reservation or the Southern Cheyenne and Arapaho Reservation, established in the Indian Territory between the Arkansas and Cimarron Rivers. Kappler, *Indian Affairs*, 2:985.

9. Hedren's *Powder River: Disastrous Opening to the Great Sioux War* is the definitive study of this engagement and its aftermath.

10. Although referred to as the Montana Column by some historians, Gibbon's column was never officially designated as such. The column numbered 409 enlisted men and 27 officers (Lieutenant Bradley's account lists 426 men total) from five companies of the Seventh Infantry and four troops of the Second Cavalry, 25 Crow scouts and 4 quartermaster scouts, 12 civilian teamsters and packers for twelve contract wagons plus twenty-four government wagons, two Gatling guns, and a 12-pounder Napoleon gun. Donovan, *A Terrible Glory*, 144; and Gray, *Centennial Campaign*, 73–74. For a listing of all the officers, see Hedren, *Great Sioux War Orders*, 83–84.

11. Troops composing Gibbon's Column started to assemble March 17 when five companies of Seventh Infantry from Fort Shaw marched toward Fort Ellis to join Second Cavalry companies stationed there. Terry's Column did not start out until May 17 from Fort Abraham Lincoln, while Crook's second deployment of the Great Sioux War did not depart until twelve days later from Fort Fetterman. As the first year of the Great Sioux War continued during the summer, Gibbon's Column would

not return to Fort Ellis until September 29 and his Seventh Infantry companies returned to their posts in early October. Crook left command of his third troop deployment of the summer on September 16 and Terry's Column returned to Fort Abraham Lincoln on September 26. Hedren, *Great Sioux War Orders*, 81–83, 113–19; Gray, *Centennial Campaign*, 72–73, 344.

12. Paulding's original diary is in the William J. Ghent Papers at the Library of Congress, Washington, D.C.

13. This incident was also noted by Lieutenant Bradley, journal entry of May 23, 1876, in *March of the Montana Column*, 119. Dr. DeWolf noted the Dakota Column had received news of this incident. Letter of June 3, 1876, in Harburn, *A Surgeon with Custer*, 113.

14. Paulding, letter of June 14, 1876, in Buecker, "Surgeon at the Little Big Horn," 39.

15. Bradley, *March of the Montana Column*, journal entry for May 16, 1876, pp. 98–102. Bradley's journal provides a detailed account of Gibbon's expedition. James H. Bradley (1844–77) was born in Sandusky County, Ohio. During the Civil War, he served with the Fourteenth Ohio Volunteers in 1861 and the Forty-Fifth Ohio Volunteers from 1862 to 1865. While in the latter regiment, he participated in the Atlanta and Nashville campaigns. He married Mary Beech, daughter of a physician from Atlanta, Georgia, and they had two daughters. Serving in the Seventh U.S. Infantry, Bradley was killed in action on August 9, 1877, at Big Hole, Montana, in the Nez Perce War. He is buried in Oakwood Cemetery, Stryker, Ohio. Heitman, *Historical Register (1903)*, 238; Findagrave.com.

16. Bradley, March of the Montana Column, journal entries of May 16 and May 24–27, 1876, pp. 98, 124, 141; Gray, *Centennial Campaign*, 82–85.

17. For more extensive analysis of the Clymer-Belknap Hearings, see Utley, *Cavalier in Buckskin*, 148–64; Hutton, *Phil Sheridan*, 305–11; Donovan, *A Terrible Glory*, 104–15; Gray, *Centennial Campaign*, 59–71; Kroeker, *Great Plains Command*, 143–52; Prickett, "Malfeasance"; Koster, "The Belknap Scandal"; and Smith, *Grant*, 593–95. A primary source is U.S. House of Representatives, *Report on Management of the War Department*. Secretary of War Belknap had been accused of accepting financial bribes benefiting himself and his wife in return for awarding the contracts for civilian post traderships at various military posts. As commandant at Fort Abraham Lincoln between 1873 and 1875, Custer's testimony also implicated President Grant's brother, Orvil Lynch Grant, as being involved in the scheme, which, of course, infuriated the president. As a result, Grant suspended Custer and ordered him to remain in Washington, D.C. The president eventually relented and allowed Custer to be involved in the planned Sioux campaign, but with the stipulation that he serve only as second in command to Terry for the Dakota Column. This decision resulted only through the diplomatic intervention of Custer's friends—Generals Terry, Sherman, and Sheridan—on his behalf.

18. The Dakota Column numbered 886 men, including all twelve companies of the Seventh Cavalry, one company each from the Sixth Infantry and Seventeenth

Infantry, and a provisional company of Twentieth Infantry manning three Gatling guns. There were 50 officers; a veterinary surgeon; 4 contract surgeons; 39 Indian scouts; more than 150 wagons; about 175 teamsters, guides, and interpreters; 35 pack mules; and more than 100 cattle. Seventh Cavalry Regimental Return, May 1876; James Calhoun, dispatch to *New York World*, June 3, 1876; C. Lee Noyes, personal correspondence with the author. For a list of the officers, see Hedren, *Great Sioux War Orders*, 98–100.

19. Although earlier studies have been done on the route and sites of the Custer Trail from Fort Abraham Lincoln to the Yellowstone Depot region for the 1876 campaign, Laudie Chorne's *Following the Custer Trail* is definitive.

20. For DeWolf's biography, including extensive annotation of his diary and letters, see Harburn, *A Surgeon with Custer*. See also n50 below.

21. Brown, "Yellowstone Supply Depot," 26. For a brief history of the Stanley Stockade, see chapter 3, n136.

22. Brown, "Yellowstone Supply Depot," 25. Earlier in the year on March 1, 1876, during initial planning of the campaign, Terry had chartered the steamboats for use during the summer operations.

23. For an in-depth review of the onset of the 1876 campaign and officer rosters/troop organization, see Hedren, *Great Sioux War Orders*. See Overfield, *Little Big Horn* for company muster rolls of officers and troops. Gray's *Custer's Last Campaign*, 134–80, provides an account of the column formations and movement; Donovan's *A Terrible Glory* is a well-researched narrative focusing on Custer and the Little Big Horn battle.

24. This was Camp No. 19 near Locate, Montana, a town that no longer exists but stood where Highway 12 crosses the Powder River, twenty-five miles east of Miles City. See Chorne, *Following the Custer Trail*, 131–45. An important note is that Dr. DeWolf's numbers in his diary identifying the camps along the expedition trail are one number higher than those provided in Chorne's study. This is because DeWolf counted Fort Abraham Lincoln as camp one, while Chorne designated the Heart River camp as first.

25. DeWolf, diary entry and letter of June 8, 1876, in Harburn, *A Surgeon with Custer*, 114–15; Terry, *Field Diary*, entry for June 9, 1876, p. 21.

26. Carroll, "Diary of Matthew Carrol," 232; Gray, *Centennial Campaign*, 107.

27. Terry, *Field Diary*, entry of June 10, 1876, p. 21. This was the controversial Reno scout, under the command of Major Marcus Reno, Seventh Cavalry; see n42.

Marcus A. Reno (1834–89) was born in Illinois and was an 1857 U.S. Military Academy graduate. He served with the U.S. First Dragoons in Oregon and Washington Territory until 1861 and during the Civil War with various cavalry units. He received brevet promotions to colonel and brigadier general. Reno married Mary Hannah Ross of Harrisburg, Pennsylvania, in 1863, although she died in 1874. They had one son, Robert Ross Reno. His second wife, Isabella, divorced him in 1889 three months before his death. Reno was appointed to the Seventh Cavalry as a major in 1868, and he and Custer were adversaries throughout their tenures in the regiment. His dismissal from the army in 1880 involved an alleged "peeping Tom" incident at Fort Meade, South Dakota, concerning the daughter of Seventh Cavalry commander, Colonel Samuel D. Sturgis. A heavy smoker and drinker most of his life, Reno died of pneumonia following surgery for tongue cancer in April 1889. For his biography, see Nichols, *In Custer's Shadow*.

28. This is Camp No. 20 in Chorne's *Following the Custer Trail*, 147. The base of operations was here June 11–15, 1876, then moved to the mouth of the Tongue River.

29. George Brinton Walker (1851–1902), born in Evansville, Indiana, graduated from the U.S. Military Academy in 1868. He served in the Sixth Infantry for most of his career, was promoted to captain in 1891, and retired as a major in the Eighteenth Infantry in 1900. Walker died at Laramie, Wyoming, and is buried in Oakhill Cemetery in Evansville, Indiana. Heitman, *Historical Register (1903)*, 997; Findagrave.com.

30. Hedren, *Great Sioux War Orders*, 89–92; Sixth Infantry Regimental Returns, May 1876; Brown, "Yellowstone Supply Depot," 26.

31. Sanford, "Fort Buford Diary, 1876-1877," entry of May 19, 1876, p. 11.

32. Sanford, " Fort Buford Diary, 1876-1877," entry of May 19, 1876, p. 11; Brown, "Yellowstone Supply Depot," 26. This was Fort Buford's post trader Alvin C. Leighton.

33. Sanford's diary entries of May 18 to June 10 cover the time Lord was at the Yellowstone Depot. See Sanford, "Fort Buford Diary, 1876–1877," 11–15.

34. Sanford, "Fort Buford Diary, 1876–1877," entries of May 19, June 8, and June 12, 1876, pp. 11, 13–14.

35. George E. Lord to the Surgeon General, May 31, 1876, Lord ACP.

36. Heski, "Camp Powell," 16. Captain Powell, commander of Company C, Sixth Infantry, was sent to establish the new depot site and arrived on June 5. Heski notes that some of the captain's company members unofficially named the depot *Camp Powell* in his honor; however, the site was always referred to as the Powder River Supply Depot.

37. For the Powder River Depot reorganized officer assignments, see Brown, "Yellowstone Supply Depot," 27.

38. Captain Edward W. Smith to G. A. Custer, Camp at Mouth of Rosebud River, June 22, 1876, in Overfield, *Little Big Horn* (quotation); Terry, *Field Diary*, entry of June 22, 1876, p. 23.

39. Hedren's *Rosebud, June 17, 1876* is the definitive history of this battle. His meticulously researched account provides a near minute-by-minute description of the fighting based on primary sources and lesser-known newspaper accounts. Magid, *Gray Fox*, 240–61, also provides an informative account of the battle.

40. Hedren, *Rosebud, June 17, 1876*, 302–3.

41. Officers known to be present for this conference included Custer; Gibbon; Gibbon's Second Cavalry commander, Major James R. Brisbin; Terry's aide, Captain Robert P. Hughes, Third Infantry; and Terry's adjutant, Captain Edward W. Smith, Eighteenth Infantry. Gray, *Centennial Campaign*, 140, 145.

42. Although Reno's scout was helpful in providing information regarding recent Indian movements, this became a source of contention between Reno and his superiors, Custer and Terry, for having disobeyed the latter's orders to not go beyond Rosebud Creek. Dr. James DeWolf's account is the only surviving primary narrative of the scout, contained in Harburn, *A Surgeon with Custer*, 116–20. For other perspectives on this controversial scout, see Hardorff, "Reno Scout"; Hedren, *Great Sioux War Orders*, 104–5; Nichols, *In Custer's Shadow*, 151–60; Stewart and Luce, "Reno Scout"; Willert, "Another Look."

43. Terry to P. H. Sheridan, June 21, 1876, War Department, and *Army and Navy Journal*, July 15, 1876; Edward W. Smith to Custer, June 22, 1876, in Overfield, *Little Big Horn*, 2–24; Secretary of War, *Annual Reports*, 1876–77, P. H. Sheridan to E. D. Townsend (AG), November 25, 1876, p. 443.

44. Bloody Knife is famously known as Custer's favorite scout. He worked for the American Fur Company before enlisting as a scout in the U.S. Army in 1868. He and Custer developed a close friendship during the Yellowstone expedition in 1873. See Innis, *Bloody Knife*; Gray, "Arikara Scouts with Custer," 443–78; Libby, *Arikara Narrative*.

45. George B. Herendeen (1846–1918) was born in Ohio. After serving in the Civil War, he worked as a cowhand in Colorado, New Mexico, and Montana. He assisted in the construction of Fort Pease on the Yellowstone and served as a scout for Custer during the Little Big Horn campaign. He died in Harlem, Montana, and is buried there. See Nichols, *Men with Custer*, 146–47; Hammer, *Custer in '76*, 219–27; and Nichols, *Reno Court of Inquiry*, 249–72, 284–88.

46. Frederick Francis Gerard (1829–1913) was a civilian interpreter with Custer during the Little Big Horn campaign. Born in St. Louis, he worked as a trader at Fort Pierre and Fort Berthold in Dakota Territory and as an interpreter at Fort Benton, Montana Territory, in 1875. He survived the Little Big Horn tragedy by hiding in the timber area with three other soldiers after the mass confusion during Reno's retreat to the bluffs. Married to an Indian woman during his earlier years, he later married Ella S. Waddell and they raised a family. He died in St. Cloud, Minnesota, and is buried in the Saint Benedict Parish Cemetery, Avon, Minnesota. His last name is often misspelled Girard. Nichols, *Men with Custer*, 119; Hammer, *Custer in '76*, 228–39; Nichols, *Reno Court of Inquiry*, 83–91, 93–105, 107–29, 131–38; Findagrave.com.

47. Mark Kellogg (1831–76) was the only newspaper reporter on the Little Big Horn campaign. Working for the *Bismarck Tribune*, he was killed near Last Stand Hill. Born in Brighton, Ontario, Canada, he was raised in La Crosse, Wisconsin, and was a newspaper reporter in Iowa and Minnesota before moving west. Sandy Barnard's biography *I Go with Custer* contains Kellogg's newspaper accounts of the Dakota Column's journey.

48. Bill Yenne's *The Other Custers* provides biographies and detailed family histories of these other Custer family members.

49. Henry Rinaldo Porter (1848–1903) was born in New York and initially attended the University of Michigan Medical School but graduated from Georgetown University Medical School in 1872. After completing a three-month internship at the Columbia Hospital for Women and Lying-In Asylum in Washington, D.C., he signed as a contract surgeon with the army and served in the Arizona Territory and then Camp Hancock in Bismarck, Dakota Territory, in 1873. There, he established a private practice, which he resumed when he left the army after the Sioux campaign. Porter and James DeWolf became good friends while at Fort Abraham Lincoln and on the subsequent Little Big Horn campaign. He married Charlotte Viets in her hometown of Oberlin, Ohio, in 1877. Porter died in 1903 while on a world tour cruise and is buried in Agra, India. The Porters' Victorian home still stands today in Bismarck, North Dakota, as a private residence. See Walker, *Dr. Henry R. Porter*; and Stevenson, *Deliverance from the Little Bighorn*.

50. James Madison DeWolf (1843–76) was born in Mehoopany, Pennsylvania. He served in the First Pennsylvania Light Artillery, Battery A, during the Civil War. Thereafter, he served as a hospital steward in the U.S. Fourteenth Infantry during the Snake Indian War in Idaho and Washington. During that time, he married Fanny Downing of Norwalk, Ohio, before graduating from Harvard Medical School in 1875. He served as an army contract surgeon at Fort Totten, Dakota, before being assigned to the Dakota Column. DeWolf was killed in Reno's retreat to the bluffs. His field diary was recovered by his friend Dr. Porter after the battle. DeWolf and his wife are buried in Greenlawn Cemetery, Norwalk, Ohio. See Harburn, *A Surgeon with Custer*.

51. Godfrey "General Godfrey's Narrative" 134; see also Noyes, "Guns 'Long Hair' Left Behind." Godfrey's 1876 diary and later narrative in 1892 are among primary sources concerning the Little Big Horn battle. Godfrey's original field diary is in the Library of Congress. The deteriorated condition of the service horses is considered to be the main reason for Custer's decision not to take them on the final trek to the Little Big Horn. Noyes's extensively researched article is widely considered to be the definitive work on Terry's Gatling detachment.

Edward Settle Godfrey (1843–1932) was born in Kalida, Ohio, and attended Vermillion Institute in Hayesville, Ohio. He served with the Twenty-First Ohio Infantry in 1861, then attended the U.S. Military Academy in 1863, graduating in 1867. Assigned to the Seventh Cavalry, he was promoted to first lieutenant the following year. After the Little Big Horn, he saw action at the Snake Creek fight in the Nez Perce campaign and later at Wounded Knee Creek in 1890. Godfrey served in Cuba and the Philippines in 1901. He rose through the ranks, becoming a brigadier general in 1907 and retiring that year. His first wife, Mary Pocock, died in 1883, and he married Ida De La Mothe Emley in 1892. Godfrey is buried in Arlington National Cemetery. Nichols, *Men with Custer*, 121–22; Heitman, *Historical Register (1903)*, 461.

52. See Gray, *Centennial Campaign*, 272.

53. Noyes, "Custer's Surgeon, George Lord," 19, n17 (quotation).

54. Gray, *Centennial Campaign*, 274.

55. S.F.O. No. 13, Headquarters, Department of Dakota, June 13, 1876, NARA, RG94. John Callahan (1853–76) was born in Salem, Massachusetts, and enlisted in the Seventh Cavalry in Boston at age twenty-one on November 5, 1872. He was assigned as hospital steward with Dr. John Williams on May 15, 1876, before being assigned to Lord. S.F.O. No. 5, Department of Dakota, Fort Abraham Lincoln, NARA, copy in WSL/LIBI; Nichols, *Men with Custer*, 48.

56. Isaiah Heylin Ashton (1849–89) was born in Philadelphia, Pennsylvania. He served as a contract physician for the army in 1875–76. He was not involved in the Little Big Horn battle, having been assigned to the supply depot. He married Kate Thompson of St. Paul in 1877. After traveling within the country and abroad, in 1882 he and his wife moved to Irvington, New York, where he established a private practice. Ashton suffered from ill health for much of his life. He was described as an "ambitious and enthusiastic physician" who cared deeply for his patients. Ashton died from peritonitis, which had developed from internal injuries sustained after being thrown from a horse-drawn wagon eight days earlier. He is buried in Sleepy Hollow Cemetery, Sleepy Hollow, New York. New York State Medical Association, *Transactions for the Year 1889*, pp. 395–96; Findagrave.com.

57. Others remaining behind at the depot were several cavalry troopers who feigned sickness because they did not want to go further with the campaign. Heski, "Camp Powell," 18.

58. DeWolf, second letter for May 14, 1876, in Harburn, *A Surgeon with Custer*, 93.

59. John Winfield Williams (circa 1839–89) was the chief medical officer for the entire expedition and also specifically tended the battery and Captain Stephen Baker's company of the Sixth Infantry (S.F.O. no. 5, AGO, NARA, photocopy in WSL/LIBI). Born in Washington, D.C., Williams was a second lieutenant in the medical department in 1862 and served as an assistant surgeon in the Fourteenth U.S. Infantry during the Civil War. He was breveted a major in 1865. Thereafter, he served in Arizona Territory and as chief medical officer for Custer's Black Hills Expedition in 1874. Williams died while still on active duty in Chalmette, Louisiana, and is buried in Chalmette National Cemetery. Heitman, *Historical Register (1903)*, 1041; Findagrave.com.

60. DeWolf, diary entry for June 22, 1876, in Harburn, *A Surgeon with Custer*, 123.

61. Godfrey, *Field Diary*, entry of June 22, 1876, p. 9, and Godfrey, "General Godfrey's Narrative," 134–35. A portion of this same evening officer's call was described differently by Benteen in his later narrative concerning the Little Big Horn. Both Godfrey's and Benteen's accounts agree that Custer invited the suggestions of his officers. However, Benteen wrote that Custer also brought up the subject of his displeasure that some officers had criticized his actions through improper channels by forwarding their concerns to the Department of Dakota headquarters rather than discussing them initially with him. When the captain then inquired about this with the insinuation that Custer had been intending his accusations directly at

him, Benteen wrote that Custer responded, "None of my remarks have been directed towards you." Benteen, "Narrative" in Graham, *Custer Myth*, 177.

62. DeWolf, diary entry of June 23, 1876, in Harburn, *A Surgeon with Custer*, 124. Historian John S. Gray also noted a comparison of several primary accounts (Lieutenant Varnum's letter, Reno's official report, the Godfrey and DeWolf diaries) being in agreement on the day's march totaling thirty-three miles. Gray, *Custer's Last Campaign*, 209.

63. Frederick W. Benteen (1834–98) was born in Petersburg, Virginia. His family moved to St. Louis in 1841 and he later served in the Missouri Volunteer Cavalry throughout the Civil War. He married Catherine Louise Norman in 1862. Appointed captain in the Seventh Cavalry in 1866, Benteen's personality conflict with Custer was well known. It originated from his accusation of Custer's alleged abandonment of Major Joel Elliott and his detachment, who were killed in the 1868 attack on Cheyenne chief Black Kettle's camp in western Oklahoma. That animosity and his alleged actions at the Little Big Horn have long been the subject of continuous debate. Benteen retired from the army in 1888 because of poor health and was breveted a brigadier general in 1890. He died in Atlanta, Georgia, and is buried in Arlington National Cemetery. See Mills, *Harvest of Barren Regrets*; Nichols, *Men with Custer*, 20–22; Graham, *Custer Myth*, chap. 4; Unger, *ABCs of Custer's Last Stand*, chap. 20.

64. Benteen, "Narrative," in Graham, *Custer Myth*, 178.

65. Stevenson, *Deliverance from the Little Bighorn*, 12.

66. Stedman, *Stedman's Medical Dictionary*, 430; Chase, *Dr. Chase's Recipes*, 220. Dysentery can be acute or chronic and, aside from acid water, can result from several other causes including parasites, amebic microorganisms, bacteria, inflammatory diseases of the intestines (Crohn's disease or ulcerative colitis), and abnormal growths such as benign or malignant tumors.

67. Flint, *Principles and Practice of Medicine*, 439–43, 453–54. As to treatment of the diarrheal pain and cramping symptoms during this era, Flint's textbook noted this to include "in chalk mixture, a grain of opium, a sixth or quarter of grain of a salt of morphia in mint water, or five grains of Dover's powder combined with two or three grains of aromatic powder . . . such as anise, ginger, cloves, mint, etc., or a few drops of chloroform." Any of the remedies chosen could be repeated in six to eight hours if needed. Dover's Powder (named after the eighteenth-century English physician Dr. Thomas Dover) was a combination of ipecac and opium used as a pain reliever or to induce sweating to impede a cold or when fevers occurred. For antidiarrheal use of ipecac and opium, see Chase, *Dr. Chase's Recipes*, 363. It was recommended that opium be used only temporarily due to its known effects of impairing bowel function in the form of constipation. Additional palliative measures included a restricted diet and fluid replacement.

68. Jameson et al., *Harrison's Principles of Internal Medicine*, 133–35, 297, 3344–45; Roy and Irvin, *Sports Medicine*, 474, 480. Similar to the "summer or trail colic"

syndrome, these other conditions (e.g., dehydration, very early heat exhaustion, and fatigue) include several of the same symptoms, such as anorexia (lack of appetite), weakness, lethargy, and confusion.

69. Benteen consistently asserted that Custer's forced marches resulted in the fatigue of the troops, which therefore contributed to the defeat at the Little Big Horn, in addition to being a violation of orders to await the arrival of Gibbon. This was debated by officers involved in the battle and by later historians. Noyes, "Galloping to Their Doom?," addresses the debate, offering evidence and sound reasoning for disputing Benteen's assertions.

70. Godfrey, *Field Diary*, entry of June 24, 1876, pp. 9–10. The Sun Dance was a summer spiritual ceremony held by the Sioux to renew and unify tribal culture. The sighting of this campsite, which showed signs of having been abandoned only a few days prior, indicated that roaming factions of Indians were on the move and further confirmed the direction of movement toward the Little Big Horn Valley.

71. Busby, Montana, is a modern-day town approximately twenty-three miles east of the southern portions of the Little Big Horn Battlefield.

72. Charles Albert Varnum (1849–1936) was Custer's chief of Indian scouts for the Sioux campaign and also served in the same capacity during the Nez Perce campaign in 1877. Born in New York, he resided in Massachusetts and later Florida after his parents moved there in 1866. He graduated from the U.S. Military Academy in 1872 and was appointed second lieutenant in the Seventh Cavalry. Varnum served under Custer in the 1873 Yellowstone and 1874 Black Hills expeditions. He was later at Wounded Knee and White Clay Creek actions in 1890. During his career, he was a professor of military science at the University of Wyoming and University of Maine. He served in the Spanish-American War and in Cuba. He was later promoted to colonel and retired in 1907. Varnum died in San Francisco, California, was survived by his wife, Mary, and is buried in San Francisco National Cemetery. Carroll, *Custer's Chief of Scouts*; Nichols, *Men with Custer*, 337–38; Heitman, *Historical Register (1903)*, 985; Findagrave.com.

73. Mitch Boyer (1837–76) was born at Fort Laramie of mixed parents, an Indian mother and French Canadian father. Boyer served as a guide, interpreter, and scout for the army until his death at the Little Big Horn. His biography is told by Gray in *Custer's Last Campaign*. See also Nichols, *Men with Custer*, 29–30. Boyer's skeletal remains buried in the field at Little Big Horn were identified in 1989 through superimposition photography by archaeologists. Scott, *They Died with Custer*, 320–22.

74. Charles Alexander Reynolds (1842–76) was born in Kentucky, although he grew up in Illinois and Kansas, two states in which his father practiced medicine. He attended Abington College in Illinois (present-day Eureka College in Illinois); however, he left to serve in the Civil War with the Tenth Kansas Infantry. After the war, Reynolds became a scout and hunter in the upper Missouri country. He served with the Yellowstone and Black Hills expeditions. He was referred to as "Lonesome Charley," as he often kept to himself, but he was cordial and well liked by almost

everyone who met him. He was killed during Reno's retreat to the bluffs. Brininstool, *Troopers with Custer*, 305–22; Nichols, *Men with Custer*, 277.

75. Varnum to Walter Camp, April 14, 1909, in Hammer, *Custer in '76*, 60.

76. The accounts of these early morning reconnoiters at the Crow's Nest on June 25, as described by those who were there, are contained in multiple sources. Graham, *Custer Myth*, 20–23, 31–33, 342 (including Varnum's letter of July 4, 1876, to his parents); Hammer, *Custer in '76*, 59–60 (Varnum's 1909 interview); Gray, *Custer's Last Campaign*, 220–41.

77. Nichols, *Reno Court of Inquiry*, 560.

78. Nichols, *In Custer's Shadow*, 171; Gray, *Custer's Last Campaign*, 245, 299 (quotation).

79. Walker, *Dr. Henry R. Porter*, 55–56; Noyes, "Custer's Surgeon, George Lord," 18.

80. "Reminiscences of the Massacre on the Little Big Horn," *Minneapolis Tribune*, May 16, 1897. Dr. Porter also related this same incident several years earlier in 1886 with the *St. Louis Globe Democrat*, Dustin Collection (catalog no. 5261), WSL/LIBI. Lord's use of the term "not much" here is a synonym for unlikely, hardly, or not quite. Word Hippo Thesaurus, www.wordhippo.com (accessed October 10, 2020).

81. Unger, *ABCs of Custer's Last Stand*, 54–55, offers discussion and speculation on these theories. Potential reasons range from Custer's and Benteen's mutual dislike for each other to the belief that Benteen would likely not see any Indians that far south, or that Reno's battalion would potentially need two surgeons since he would be attacking the village first.

82. Nichols, *Reno Court of Inquiry*, 403 (Benteen testimony); Graham, *Custer Myth*, 227 (Benteen statement to the *New York Herald*, August 8, 1876). Roger Darling's *Benteen's Scout* provides the definitive study of that assignment. Gray, *Centennial Campaign*, 301–6 offers analysis on Benteen's opinions about that action.

83. Gray, *Custer's Last Campaign*, 253–55 (Varnum's sighting), 257, 273–75 (Gerard's sighting). Some historians maintained that interpreter Fred Gerard saw the fleeing Sioux Indians at the lone tepee. However, Gray has established that Gerard's sighting was a second one that occurred not at the lone tepee, but rather beyond that location at a ridge overlooking the Little Big Horn Valley. The lone tepee was located about 6.5 miles from the village. Gray, *Centennial Campaign*, 300.

84. Gray, *Custer's Last Campaign*, 275.

85. Gray, *Centennial Campaign*, 301.

86. Reno to E. W. Smith, July 5, 1876, in Overfield, *Little Big Horn*, 44 (quote); Nichols, *Reno Court of Inquiry*, 561 (Reno's testimony).

87. Nichols, *Reno Court of Inquiry*, 140 (Varnum testimony).

88. Gray, *Custer's Last Campaign*, 272.

89. Overfield, *Little Big Horn*, 44 (quote) in Reno's official report to Capt. Edward W. Smith, Eighteenth Infantry, July 5, 1876.

90. Location of the skirmish line is discussed in Moore, *Where the Custer Fight Began*, 121–32. See also Donahue, *Where the Rivers Ran Red*, 225–38, for his analysis of the "Skirmish Line of Horror."

Notes to Chapter 4

91. Nichols, *Reno Court of Inquiry*, 284, 564. For a biography, see Innis, *Bloody Knife*.
92. Nichols, *Reno Court of Inquiry*, 196, 205, 212 (Porter's testimony).
93. Nichols, *Reno Court of Inquiry*, 562 (quote). This is an interesting, intended metaphor of words, as Reno was obviously referring to the timber being his and his command's death site had they stayed at that location any longer. At the Court of Inquiry in 1879, some officers supported Reno's assessment of this situation, while others were of the opinion that his decision should have been to remain in the timber area for a defensive fight.
94. Nichols, *Reno Court of Inquiry*, 197 (quote).
95. For all the accounts of DeWolf's death, see Harburn, *A Surgeon with Custer*, 130–40. For accounts of Hodgson's death, see Hardorff, *Custer Battle Casualties II*, 93–98; and Barnard, *Ten Years with Custer*, 296. Benjamin Hubert Hodgson (1848–76) was born in Philadelphia and was an 1870 U.S. Military Academy graduate. He joined the Seventh Cavalry shortly thereafter. Hodgson and DeWolf became good friends on the campaign. Reno, a close friend also, was so distraught over Hodgson's death that he ordered a detail of soldiers to retrieve the officer's body during a lull in the fighting.
96. Godfrey, *Field Diary*, entry for June 25, 1976, p. 12. This notation of Benteen's arrival is contained within Godfrey's description of events starting with his June 24 entry and continuing to his entry for June 26. Donovan, *A Terrible Glory*, 257–59.
97. John Gray has established this time as about 4:10 P.M. while Custer was engaged in his fight around Medicine Tail Coulee and Last Stand Hill. Gray, *Centennial Campaign*, 302, 306.
98. Gall's account, *Detroit Free Press*, Saturday, June 26, 1886, p. 4. Gall (circa 1840–94) was born in South Dakota of the Hunkpapa Sioux. He was one of the Lakota leaders at the Battle of the Little Big Horn. In the 1880s, he lived on the Standing Rock Indian Reservation and converted to Christianity. He died on the reservation and is buried in the Saint Elizabeth Episcopal Cemetery in Wakapala, South Dakota; Findagrave.com. Michno, *Lakota Noon*, 78, also relates this Indian push coming from the southeast direction.
99. There are numerous Indian accounts, although, again, the one used in this description is taken from Hunkpapa Sioux warrior chief Gall's account in the *Detroit Free Press*, Saturday, June 26, 1886, p. 4; Gall's account is discussed in Michno, *Mystery of E Troop*, 64–66. Michno's meticulously researched book provides an excellent analysis of his interpretations of this controversial portion of the battle. In another book, *Lakota Noon*, Michno also presents a concentrated look at the Indian accounts of their movements during the battle, as does Hardorff, *Indian Views of the Custer Fight*. Donahue, *Where the Rivers Ran Red*, 173–75, 185–97, 203–5, 271–72, 276 also provides some additional well-researched analysis regarding these last stages of the battle.
100. The regimental (headquarters) staff members included Custer, Lord, Adj. First Lieutenant William W. Cooke, Sergeant Major William H. Sharrow, chief trumpeter Henry Voss, interpreter Mitch Boyer, guide Boston Custer, and newspaper correspondent Mark Kellogg. Nichols, *Men with Custer*, xvi.

101. Donahue is uncertain whether Lord accompanied the headquarters staff to the end or fled the destruction of the Calhoun Hill area, Donahue, *Where the Rivers Ran Red*, 325n25. Regardless, Lord made it to Last Stand Hill during the active fighting at both locations.

102. For unknown reasons, Porter declined the offer from Reno of a revolver, which is strange since he was an experienced fighter, having been involved with Crook in Arizona in 1872–73. He was also a regular hunter on the campaign. Likewise, DeWolf, a veteran of combat in both the Civil War and Snake Indian War, was experienced with firearms. His April 21 and June 8 letters to his wife during the expedition (in addition to Porter's July 28, 1876, letter to DeWolf's wife, Fannie, concerning his death) confirm that DeWolf carried a revolver during the campaign and battle. Nichols, *Reno Court of Inquiry*, 189; Harburn, *A Surgeon with Custer*, 77, 122–23, 136.

103. Thomas Weir (1838–76), an Ohio native, grew up in Albion, Michigan, and graduated from the University of Michigan in 1861. Weir was a decorated Civil War veteran, serving with the Third Michigan Cavalry. He was also a close friend of the Custers. Debate among historians has continued for years in reexamining the controversy over his dispute with Benteen and Reno regarding the attempt to go to Custer's aid near the end of the battle. Some historians claim that Weir planned to tell Custer's widow, Libby, the details of this episode, but he died later that year of alcohol abuse or "fatigue and exposure" brought on by the Sioux campaign. Kenneth Hammer, "Interview with Winfield S. Edgerly," in *Custer in '76*, 55–57; Graham, *Custer Myth*, 215–17; Nichols, *Men with Custer*, 350–51.

104. Godfrey, "General Godfrey's Narrative," 43. In later years, Dr. Porter considered this the most accurate account of the action at the Reno-Benteen entrenchment, although not without some personal bias on the dispute between Godfrey and Reno. Walker, *Dr. Henry R. Porter*, 60.

105. Stevenson's *Deliverance from the Little Big Horn* provides an in-depth account of Porter's actions after he established the field hospital. Details are also in Porter's testimony in Nichols, *Reno Court of Inquiry*. Gray, *Centennial Campaign*, 276–83, provides extensive analysis from primary sources of the number of wounded men treated on their July 5 arrival at Fort Abraham Lincoln. Gray noted that a total of 54 soldiers were wounded by the end of the day on June 26. Then 42 patients were transported on the *Far West* on July 3, although only 38 ultimately arrived at Fort Lincoln, owing to deaths and dropping off a couple of sick men at the Powder River depot hospital and Fort Buford en route.

Chapter 5.
Aftermath

1. Holmes Offley Paulding to his mother, letter of July 2, 1876, in Buecker, "Surgeon at the Little Big Horn," 42–43. Lieutenant Bradley's Montana journal ends abruptly

after his July 26 entry. His account of the initial discovery is in a letter to the editor of the *Helena* (Montana Territory) *Herald*, July 25, 1876, in Bradley, *March of the Montana Column*, 171–74, wherein he stated finding 197 bodies, even though Paulding noted in his letter the discovery of 200 bodies. Gibbon noted in his official report to Terry covering the entire year's Sioux campaign to Terry (via Terry's Department of Dakota assistant adjutant Major George D. Ruggles) that Bradley stated the initial account was 194. Gibbon to Ruggles, October 17, 1876, in Overfield, *Little Big Horn*, 85. Among later reviews and summaries, Gray has asserted a total of 263 killed in action June 25–26. Gray, *Centennial Campaign*, 287.

2. Bradley's scouting party consisted of twelve men of the Seventh Infantry. Interview with Charles F. Roe, December 8, 1910, Walter Camp Field Notes, folder 43, BYU Library, cited in Hammer, *Custer in '76*, 250n3.

3. Interview with Charles F. Roe, December 8, 1910. The supposed dead buffalo sighting was made by second lieutenant Charles F. Roe (1848–1922), Second Cavalry regimental adjutant, who also led one of the scouting parties. In Gibbon's Montana column, Roe was a friend and mess mate of Dr. Paulding (Paulding letter to his mother, April 24, 1876, in Buecker, "Surgeon at the Little Big Horn," 37). Born in Highland Falls, New York, he graduated from the U.S. Military Academy in 1868. Roe oversaw the reburials and construction of the Custer Battlefield monument in 1881. *Army and Navy Journal* 19, no. 7 (September 17, 1881): 145. He resigned from the army in 1888 to enter real estate but returned to service in the New York State Militia the following year. Roe was appointed brigadier general of the volunteers from New York during the Spanish-American War. He died in his original hometown and is buried in Woodlawn Cemetery in Bronx, New York. Heitman, *Historical Register (1903)*, 842; Findagrave.com.

4. Godfrey, "General Godfrey's Narrative," 376 (quotation).

5. Paulding to his mother, letter of June 28, 1876, in Buecker, "Surgeon at the Little Big Horn," 40.

6. Paulding, letter to his mother, July 2, 1876, p. 43. Paulding also noted that he knew Dr. Porter very well from the time they spent at Fort Abraham Lincoln the year before. Paulding, letter to his mother, July 8, 1876, p. 45.

7. Paulding, letter to his mother, July 8, 1876, p. 44.

8. J. W. Williams, Asst. Surgeon to the Surgeon General, July 6, 1876, mouth of Big Horn River, M.T., Lord ACP.

9. Paulding, letter to his mother, July 8, 1876, in Buecker, "Surgeon at the Little Big Horn," 44. Italics in the original.

10. Interview with Richard E. Thompson, February 14, 1911, from Walter Camp Field Notes, folder 51, BYU Library, in Hammer, *Custer in '76*, 247.

11. Extract of letter of 2nd Lieut. R. E. Thompson 6th Infantry relative to recognition of the body of Asst. Surg. Geo. E. Lord, U.S.A., officially reported "Missing in Action" since battle of "Little Big Horn," June 25, 1876, NARA, RG 94 AGO, File 4473, ACP 1876, and copy in Lord ACP.

12. First Lieutenant Thomas W. Lord, RQM, 20th Infantry to Adjutant General, U.S. Army, August 14, 1876, Washington, D.C., NARA, RG 94 AGO, File 4473, ACP 1876, and copy in Lord ACP.

13. Captain O. E. Michaelis to Lieut. T. W. Lord, September 29, 1876, St. Paul, Minnesota, NARA, RG 94, 5467, ACP 1876, copy in WSL/LIBI. The trader was James Coleman, an associate of trader John Smith. Both had followed the Dakota Column and traveled on the *Far West* up the Yellowstone River. Heski, "Camp Powell," 16–17. See also Harburn, *A Surgeon with Custer*, 225n76.

14. Noyes, "Custer's Surgeon, George Lord," 18.

15. Documentation of Smith being at these locations when Lord was present is found in DeWolf's letter to his wife, Fannie, June 21, 1876, in Harburn, *A Surgeon with Custer*, 122; and Chorne, *Following the Custer Trail*, 152, 182.

16. Interview with Richard E. Thompson, February 14, 1911, in Hammer, *Custer in '76*, 247–48.

17. The Casualties List of the Commissioned Officers reported to the Adjutant General's Office on July 15, 1876, dated July 17, 1876, lists First Lieutenant George E. Lord as "Missing in action with Sioux Indians, on Little Big Horn River." A later document amends the file, noting (handwritten) that Lord was "Killed June 25, 1876 in action on Little Big Horn River." Lord ACP.

18. Michno, *Mystery of E Troop*, 185. The published literature concerning the burials and care for the wounded is vast. In addition to Michno's review of the various accounts and those already cited of Godfrey and Benteen, see also Hardorff, *Custer Battle Casualties* and *Custer Battle Casualties II*; and historian Fred Dustin's reviews and Colonel Michael V. Sheridan's report, both in Graham, *Custer Myth*.

19. P. H. Sheridan to M. V. Sheridan, May 16, 1877, AGO, WSL/LIBI. Custer's remains were reburied at West Point, New York; Second Lieutenant John Crittenden's were left where he fell on the field, at the request of his father; and Captain Keogh's were transported to Fort Hill Cemetery in Auburn, New York, per a request in his will. Those of Dr. DeWolf were returned to Norwalk, Ohio, the hometown of his wife. The other officers' remains were transported at government expense and reburied at Fort Leavenworth. Although the purpose of the expedition was not to rebury the remains of the enlisted men, this was done because many were exposed due to the elements and the original shallow graves, a consequence of lack of adequate tools and necessary time during the initial burials.

20. M. V. Sheridan to P. H. Sheridan, July 20, 1877, full report in Graham, *Custer Myth*, 374–75 (both quotations).

21. Graham, *Custer Myth*, 368, 375, 377.

22. Michno, *Mystery of E Troop*, 213.

23. Michno, *Mystery of E Troop*, 180, 213.

24. Michno, *Mystery of E Troop*, 215–16. This excerpt is from Owen J. Sweet's original "Report on the Custer Battlefield, May 15, 1890," copy in WSL/LIBI.

25. *Uniform Regulations of the Army of the United States 1861*, 10–11; and Jacobsen, *Regulations and Notes for the Uniform of the Army of the United States, 1872*, 7.

26. General Owen J. Sweet to Walter M. Camp, January 13, 1913, copy in WSL/LIBI-00312_11329–11331, cited in Hardorff, *Custer Battle Casualties II*, 41.

27. Interview with Major Sam'l Burkhardt Jr., January 16, 1913, in Hammond, *Custer in '76*, 252.

28. Letter to M. V. Sheridan, July 14, 1977, Sheridan Papers, LOC, cited in Noyes, "Custer's Surgeon, George Lord," 20n29.

29. Harburn, *A Surgeon with Custer*, 158.

30. J. H. Baxter, Chief Medical Purveyor, U.S.A., SGO to John S. Billings, April 2, 1885, A.M.M. (American Medical Museum) No. 160 Miscellaneous Section, NARA, copy in National Museum of Health and Medicine.

31. Interview with Charles DeRudio, February 2, 1910, in Hammer, *Custer in '76*, 87; General Edward S. Godfrey to Walter M. Camp, May 3, 1909, in Hardorff, *Custer Battle Casualties*, 40.

32. Captain William Sanders, Sixth Infantry, Commanding Fort Buford, to the Adjutant General, Washington, D.C., July 29, 1876, copy in Lord ACP.

33. Sanders to Adjutant General, July 29, 1876.

34. "Foundation Acquires Surgeon's Kit from Battle of Little Big Horn," AMEDD Museum Foundation, http://www.ameddmuseumfoundation.org/foundation-acquires-surgeons-kit-from-battle-of-little-big-horn/ (accessed April 28, 2018).

35. "Original U.S. Battle of Little Big Horn Army Surgical Kit of Dr. George Edwin Lord," International Military Antiques, https://www.ima-usa.com/products/original-u-s-battle-of-little-big-horn-army-surgical-kit-of-dr-george-edwin-lord-kia?variant=38445334789 (accessed April 28, 2018).

36. Harburn, *A Surgeon with Custer*, 152.

37. *Harrisburg* (Pennsylvania) *Telegraph*, May 11, 1877; also *Oakland (California) Tribune*, May 22, 1877. Lieutenant Frederick Schwatka (1849–92) was born in Galena, Illinois, but was raised in Oregon, where he attended Willamette University. An 1871 graduate of the U.S. Military academy and a second lieutenant in the Third Cavalry, he studied law and also earned a medical degree from Bellevue Hospital Medical College in New York City in 1871. He was a participant in the Battle of Slim Buttes and served on an army discovery expedition in 1879 investigating the lost Sir John Franklin Canadian Arctic Expedition of 1845. Resigning from the army after his return, he led several private exploring expeditions in Alaska and Mexico. He died of an accidental overdose of laudanum while self-treating a stomach disorder. Richard C. Davis, "Schwatka, Frederick," in *Dictionary of Canadian Biography*, vol. 12, University of Toronto/Université Laval, 2003, http://www.biographi.ca/en/bio/schwatka_frederick_12E.html (accessed October 13, 2020).

38. T. W. Lord to the Surgeon General, U.S. Army, Washington, D.C., November 28, 1887, copy in Lord ACP.

39. Major Charles R. Greenleaf, Surgeon, U.S. Army, to 1st Lieut. T. W. Lord, December 6, 1887, copy in Lord ACP.

40. Major James Morrow Walsh (1840–1905), a native of Ontario, was one of the original officers of the North-West Mounted Police and commander of Fort Walsh (named for him) in present-day Saskatchewan. He became friends with Sitting Bull and attempted to convince the chief and his followers to return to the United States in 1877. See Roderick C. MacLeod, "Walsh, James Morrow," in *Dictionary of Canadian Biography*, vol. 13, 1071–72, http://www.biographi.ca/en/bio/walsh_james_morrow_13E.html (accessed March 5, 2022); also Anderson, *Sitting Bull's Boss*.

41. *Army and Navy Journal*, March 8, 1879, p. 549.

42. Aside from the mentioned later searches by Major Walsh in response to rumors, one other example is noted by Godfrey. After the battle, a dead Seventh Cavalry horse shot in the head and a carbine near the carcass were discovered near the mouth of Rosebud Creek. Godfrey noted, "We conjectured that some man had escaped . . . killed his horse for meat . . . An Indian would not have left the carbine." Godfrey, "General Godfrey's Narrative," 146. A controversial book proposing there was a survivor is John Koster, *Custer Survivor: The End of a Myth, the Beginning of a Legend*.

43. Nichols, *Reno Court of Inquiry* (Benteen testimony), 437–38 (both quotations).

44. "The Romance of Dr. Lord," *Lewiston* (Maine) *Evening Journal*, April 3, 1907, copy in the Bowdoin College Library Archives, Brunswick, Maine.

45. "The Romance of Dr. Lord," (all three quotations).

46. "The Romance of Dr. Lord." Among the listed former schoolmates of Lord who wrote to the *Lewiston Evening Journal* were Samuel W. Ingalls, P. L. Wyman, and Mr. and Mrs. Henry M. Packard, all of Auburn, Maine. Ingalls and the Packards were still recorded as living in the Auburn/Lewiston area three years later. U.S. Census, 1910, Auburn, Androscoggin, Maine.

Epilogue

1. Heitman, *Historical Register* (1903), 642.

2. Post Returns, Fort Snelling, December 1877, NARA.

3. George Sykes (1822–80) was born in Dover, Delaware and graduated from the U.S. Military Academy in 1838. With the Third Infantry, he saw service in the Second Seminole Indian War and Mexican American War. During the Civil War, Sykes was appointed major in the U.S. Fourteenth Infantry in 1861, was promoted to brigadier general of volunteers in 1862, and was given command of the Union V Corps of the Army of the Potomac. In 1863, he was assigned to Kansas for the remainder of the war. He returned to the regular army and was later appointed colonel in command of the Twentieth Infantry. Sykes oversaw the regiment for twelve years, serving as commander at Fort Snelling much of that time. He died at Fort Brown, Texas, in 1880 and is buried at the West Point cemetery at the U.S.

Military Academy. Heitman, *Historical Register* (1903), 941; Eicher and Eicher, *Civil War High Commands*, 521.

4. J. N. Coe, "Twentieth Regiment of Infantry," 669.

5. U.S. Census, 1880, Brownsville, Cameron, Texas; Ancestry.com.

6. Post Returns, Fort Brown, 1877–81; Fort Leavenworth, 1881–83; Fort Supply, 1884, NARA.

7. Coe, "Twentieth Regiment of Infantry," 671.

8. Post Returns, Fort Assinniboine, March 1886–Sept 1887, NARA.

9. Heitman, *Historical Register* (1903), 642.

10. Thomas's father, Reverend Lord, died in 1884 and his mother Mary in late 1888. Both are buried in Riverside Cemetery in Oshkosh, where his adopted sisters lived for the remainder of their lives. It is unknown whether Thomas attended either of his parents' funerals.

11. U.S. Department of the Interior, *Register of the Department of the Interior*, 141.

12. Frank Young Commagere (unknown–1892), was a native of Ohio. He was for a while a cadet at the Naval Academy. During the Civil War, he served with the Fourteenth Ohio Infantry in 1861, became a lieutenant in the Sixty-Seventh New York Infantry in 1862, and later served as major in the U.S. Colored Troops Sixth Cavalry until the end of the war. Commagere served as a lieutenant in the Seventh Cavalry from 1866 until resigning in 1868. He married Mary Victoria O'Flynn (unknown–1903) in 1869. Thereafter, he became a journalist in Washington, D.C., writing for the *National Tribune*. He and his second wife, Anna M. Commagere, are buried in Arlington National Cemetery. Heitman, *Historical Register (1903)*, 319; U.S. Civil War Soldier Records, and Profiles, 1861–65, U.S. City Directories, 1822–1995, and U.S. Veterans' Gravesites, 1775–2019, all per Ancestry.com; Findagrave.com.

13. U.S. Register of Civil, Military, and Naval Service, 1863–1959, Patent Office, 1905, p. 680; U.S. National Cemetery Interment Control Forms, 1928–62, Ancestry.com; Findagrave.com.

14. Last Will and Testament of Anita M. Commagere, May 21, 1896, Wills and Probate Records, District of Columbia, 1737–1953, Ancestry.com.

15. *Evening Star* (Washington, D.C.), June 6, 1896; July 24, 1896; August 8, 1896; and March 6, 1897.

16. *Evening Star* (Washington, D.C.), March 6, 1897 (both quotations).

17. U.S. Census, 1900, Washington, D.C. The census lists the household members at the 933 New York NW address as Willis B. Magruder, age 40, a government clerk; his wife, Susan H. Magruder, age 34; their son, Willis B. Magruder, age 14; their African American servant, Charlotte Estes, age 34; and three boarders: John A. Holmes, age 26, a stenographer; Lord, age 56 at the time; and D. W. Magruder, age 23, also a government clerk, likely a relative. Lord had been living at the Magruder house since the prior year. Washington, D.C., City Directory, 1899, Ancestry.com.

18. Marshall Hall is located near Bryan's Road in Charles County, Maryland, almost directly across the Potomac River in view of George Washington's historic

Mount Vernon home in Virginia. It is the site of the colonial plantation and contains the ruins of the Marshall family mansion house. Marshall Hall is part of Piscataway National Park, overseen by the National Park Service. William Marshall established the original plantation on the site in 1690 after purchasing land from the Piscataway Indians. Thomas Marshall built the mansion home about 1725. It was owned by a succession of family descendants until being sold in 1867. During the Victorian era, it became a popular picnic and summer entertainment site with docks and wharfs built by the Mount Vernon and Marshall Hall Steamship Company, which purchased the property to ferry tourists for sightseeing on the Potomac River. In the 1920s, the Marshall Hall Amusement Park with a roller coaster was established on the site and was accessible by both land and ferry service. The amusement park closed in 1980 and the National Park Service acquired the site, in part at the urging of the Mount Vernon Ladies' Association to preserve the original views from both historic sites. The original colonial Marshall Hall house was destroyed by fire later that year, the cause suspected as arson. The ruins of the brick mansion and a separate small original kitchen house are preserved and can be visited by the public. Marshall Hall, Historical Marker Database at http://www.marshallhall.org; and National Park Planner at https://npplan.com/parks-by-state/maryland-national parks/piscataway-park-park-at-a-glance/piscataway-park-marshall-hall/ (accessed January 28, 2020).

19. "Yields Up Its Dead, Body of Capt. Lord Found in the Potomac Fully Identified," *Evening Star* (Washington, D.C.), Saturday, April 18, 1903, p. 17. The details presented here were drawn from this newspaper account.

20. "Yields Up Its Dead," 17.

21. Arlington National Cemetery official website, www.arlingtoncemetery.mil (accessed January 29, 2020).

22. Fort Myer was built during the Civil War as one of the fortifications defending Washington, D.C. It is located next to Arlington National Cemetery on the former estate grounds of Robert E. Lee and his wife, Mary Anne Custis Lee, who had abandoned the land and mansion house when Lee resigned his commission to join the Confederate Army. Initial portions of the fortification started in 1861 were named Fort Cass and two years later were expanded and named Fort Whipple. In 1881, the post was renamed for the late commander of the U.S. Army and Navy Signal School of Instruction, Brigadier General Albert J. Myer. The fort is a National Historic Landmark and was renamed Joint Base Myer–Henderson Hall when the fort merged in 2005 with the nearby Marine Corps post of the latter name. Michael, *Fort Myer*, and Gavan et al., *History of Fort Myer*, available at HathiTrust Digital Library, www.hathitrust.org (accessed January 29, 2020).

23. "Placed at Rest, Remains of Capt. Lord Buried in Arlington Cemetery," *Evening Star* (Washington, D.C.), Wednesday, April 22, 1903, p. 6.

24. Last Will and Testament of Thomas W. Lord, Probate Date, June 3, 1903, District and Probate Court, Probate Records, District of Columbia, 1737–1952, Ancestry.com (accessed July 26, 2020). His will was drawn and signed on January 20, 1894.

25. Washington, D.C., City Directory, 1888 to 1901 (inclusive), Ancestry.com (accessed Jan. 28, 2020). The city directories listed Lord as living at the following locations for the successive years mentioned: Ebbitt House in 1888; 735 13th Northwest in 1891–92; 2223 14th NW in 1893; 608 12th NW in 1895–96; 911 H NW in 1897–98; and the Magruder House in 1899 until his death in 1901.

Bibliography

Archival Materials
National Archives and Records Administration, Washington, D.C.
Fort Buford Medical Log, August 1875 to May 1876, pp. 229–68, copy in microfilm roll 4293, State Historical Society of North Dakota Archives, Bismarck, North Dakota.
Fort Buford, RG 98, Records of the U.S. Army Commands, Sent 1867–94, copy in microfilm roll 4287, State Historical Society of North Dakota Archives, Bismarck, North Dakota.
George E. Lord, Service File, Letters Received, Adjutant General's Office, RG 94, File 3231, Appointment, Commission and Personal Branch File (ACP) 1875.
Thomas W. Lord, RG 94, Carded Medical Records, Volunteers: Mexican and Civil Wars, 1846–65, Entry 534 for Thomas W. Lord.
Will of June 1903, District of Columbia, Washington, D.C., 1–5.

National Archives and Records Administration, New York, New York
Examining Board Report for George E. Lord (classical exam portion), NARA, RG 112, Army Medical Board, New York City, N.Y., 1874, 1875, and 1876, Entry 323, No. 26 (George E. Lord), 128–29.

National Archives and Records Administration, Washington, D.C., and Other Records
Returns from U.S. Military Posts, 1800–1916.
 Camp Hancock Post Returns, 1872–77, Microfilm Publication M617, roll 451.
 Fort Abercrombie Post Returns, 1858–77, Microfilm Publication M67, roll 1.
 Fort Abraham Lincoln Post Returns, 1872–80, Microfilm Publication M617, roll 628.
 Fort Arbuckle Post Returns, 1850–70, Microfilm Publication M617, roll 38.
 Fort Assinniboine Post Returns, 1879–91, Microfilm Publication M617, roll 42.
 Fort Brown Post Returns, 1887–1902, Microfilm Publication M617, roll 153.

Fort Buford Post Returns, 1866–79, Microfilm Publication M617, roll 158.
Fort Buford Post Returns, 1880–95, Microfilm Publication M617, roll 159.
Fort Douglas Post Returns, 1866–75, Microfilm Publication M617, roll 325.
Fort Garland Post Returns, 1873–83, Microfilm Publication M617, roll 395.
Fort Gibbon Post Returns, 1899–1906, Microfilm Publication M617, roll 402.
Fort Hamilton Post Returns, 1860–76, Microfilm Publication M617, roll 443.
Fort Hayes Post Returns, 1865–75, Microfilm Publication M617, roll 469.
Fort Leavenworth Post Returns, 1851–69, Microfilm Publication M617, roll 611.
Fort Leavenworth Post Returns, 1870–90, Microfilm Publication M617, roll 612.
Fort McKeen Post Returns, 1872, Microfilm Publication M617, roll 1522.
Fort Omaha Post Returns, 1874–75, Microfilm Publication M617, roll 880.
Fort Pembina Post Returns, 1870–81, Microfilm Publication M617, roll 899.
Fort Randall Post Returns, 1867–1879, Microfilm Publication 617, roll 989.
Fort Rice Post Returns, 1871–78, Microfilm Publication M617, roll 1006.
Fort Ripley Post Returns, 1866–77, Microfilm Publication M617, roll 1027.
Fort Sheridan Post Returns, 1887–96, Microfilm Publication M617, roll 1159.
Fort Sill Post Returns, 1869–75, Microfilm Publication M617, roll 1173.
Fort Sill Post Returns, 1876–87, Microfilm Publication M617, roll 1174.
Fort Snelling Post Returns, 1861–73, Microfilm Publication M617, roll 1196.
Fort Snelling Post Returns, 1874–84, Microfilm Publication M617, roll 1197.
Fort Stevenson Post Returns, 1876–83, Microfilm Publication M617, roll 1228.
Fort (Camp) Supply, Indian Territory, 1868–79, Microfilm Publication M617, roll 1243.
Fort Supply, Indian Territory, 1880–94, Microfilm Publication M617, roll 1244.
Fort Wayne Post Returns, 1861–73, Microfilm Publication M617, roll 1401.
Fort Yates Post Returns 1875–84, Microfilm Publication M617, roll 1476.
Whetstone Indian Agency Post Returns, June 1870–April 1872, Microfilm Publication M617, roll 1424.
Office of the Quartermaster General, 1818–1905 (RG 92).
Seventeenth Infantry Regimental Returns, 1872–80, Microfilm Publication M665, roll 184.
Seventh Infantry Regimental Returns, 1874–84, Microfilm Publication M665, roll 83.
Sixth Infantry Regimental Returns, 1869–78, Microfilm Publication M665, roll 70.
Twentieth Infantry Regimental Returns, 1874–81, Microfilm Publication M665, roll 212.
Twenty-Second Regimental Returns, 1874–81, Microfilm Publication M665, roll 228.

Bibliography

U.S. Army Register of Enlistments, 1798–1914, Microfilm Publication M233.
U.S. Appointments of U.S. Postmasters 1832–1971 (RG 28), Microfilm Publication M841, 145 rolls.
U.S. Register of Post Traders, ACP Branch, Records of the Adjutant General's Office, RG 94.
U.S. Burial Registers of Military Posts, Camps, Stations, 1768–1821.
U.S. Census Records, 1840–1940.
U.S. City Directories, 1822–55.
U.S. Civil War Pension Index, General Index to Pension Files, 1861–1934, Microfilm Publication T-288.
U.S. Civil War Soldier Records and Profiles, 1861–65.
U.S. College Student Lists, 1763–1921.
U.S. National Homes for Disabled Volunteer Soldiers, 1866–1938.
U.S. Records Department of Veteran Affairs, 1773–2007.
U.S. Register of Civil, Military, and Naval Service, 1863–1959.
U.S. Register of Deaths in the Regular Army, 1860–89.
U.S. Select Military Registers, 1862–1985.
U.S. Compiled Marriages for Belfast, Hallowell and Pittsdon (Maine), 1748–1875 (for Thomas N. Lord and Mary E. Tupper).
California Death Index, 1905–39.
Dictionary of Deceased American Physicians, 1804–1929.
Maine Marriage Records, 1713–1922, Maine State Archives.
Massachusetts Town and Vital Records, 1620–1988.
Massachusetts Birth, Marriage, and Death Records, 1700–1850.
Missouri Death Records, 1850–1931, St. Louis, 1896–1904.
National Cemetery Administration, U.S. Veterans' Gravesites, 1775–2019.
Ohio Deaths, 1908–32, 1930–2007.
Probate Records, District of Columbia, 1801–1930.
Wills District of Columbia, Washington, D.C., 1903.
Wisconsin Marriage Records, 1838–1911.
Findagrave.com.
Fold3.com.

Dyer Memorial Library & Archives, Abington, Massachusetts
Catalogue of the Abington High School, 1849–1912. Boston: Fort Hill Press, 1912.
Osgood, Gilman, and Joseph M. Murphy, ed. *A Record of the Golden Anniversary Reunion of the Abington High School Association, November 15, 1923, and Catalog, 1874–1923 and 1915–1927.* Abington, Mass.: Franklin Print, 1927.
The Selectmen's Annual Report of the Receipts and Expenditures of the Town of Abington for the Financial Year ending Feb. 1, 1867: Also, the Annual Report of the School Committee for 1866–67. Abington, Mass.: Rockwell & Rollin, Printers, 1867.

The Selectmen's Annual Report of the Receipts and Expenditures of the Town of Abington for the Financial Year ending Feb. 1, 1868 of the School Committee for 1867–68. Abington, Mass.: Rockwell & Rollin, Printers, 1868.

George J. Mitchell Department of Special Collections and Archives, Bowdoin College Library, Brunswick, Maine

Academic Transcripts for Bowdoin College, Years 1862–63 for the class of 1866.
Catalogue of Bowdoin College and the Medical School of Maine, 1835, 1863–68, 1912.
General Catalogue of Bowdoin College and the Medical School of Maine, 1794-1912.

Special Collections, Galter Library, Northwestern University Feinberg School of Medicine, Chicago, Illinois

Chicago Medical College Catalogue, *1869–70* and *1870–71*.

Androscroggin Historical Society, Auburn, Maine

Records of "The First Congregational Society of Auburn," Book 1, 1844–71.

Auburn Public Library, Auburn, Maine

Biographical information on Reverend Thomas Newman Lord, Conference of the Congregational Churches in Maine.
History of West Auburn Congregational Church, West Auburn (Minot), Maine.

White Swan Library, Little Bighorn Battlefield National Monument

First Lieutenant Thomas W. Lord, RQM, 20th Infantry to Adjutant General, U.S. Army, Washington, D.C., August 14, 1876, containing extract of letter from 2nd Lieutenant R. E. Thompson, 6th Infantry, RG 94, 4666, ACP 1871.
O. E. Michaelis, Captain of Ordnance, to T. W. Lord, September 29, 1876, RG 94, 5467, ACP 1876.
Philip H. Sheridan and Michael V. Sheridan Letters (photocopies of letters from the National Archives and Records, Administration, Records of the War Department, Adjutant General's Office).

NEWSPAPERS

Army and Navy Journal. 1873, 1879
Bismarck Tribune
Bowdoin Daily Sun
Chicago Tribune

Daily Oklahoman
Evening Star (Washington, D.C.)
Harrisburg (Pennsylvania) Telegraph
Lewiston (Maine) Evening Journal
Minneapolis Daily Tribune
National Tribune (Washington, D.C.)
Oakland (California) Tribune
Oshkosh (Wisconsin) Daily Northwestern
Saline (Michigan) Observer

PUBLISHED MATERIALS

Agnew, Jeremy. *Medicine in the Old West: A History, 1850–1900*. Jefferson, N.C.: McFarland, 2001.

Album of Genealogy and Biography, Cook County, Illinois. Chicago: Calumet Press, 1909.

Anderson, Ian. *Sitting Bull's Boss: Above the Medicine Line with James Morrow Walsh*. Surry, British Columbia: Heritage House, 2000.

Arey, Leslie B. *Northwestern University Medical School: 1859–1979*. Evanston. Ill.: Northwestern University, 1959. Revised and extended edition, 1979.

Ashburn, Percy M. *A History of the Medical Department of the United States Army*. Boston: Houghton Mifflin, 1992.

Atkins, Annette. *Harvest of Grief: Grasshopper Plagues and Public Assistance in Minnesota, 1873–89*. St. Paul: Minnesota Historical Society Press, 1984.

Baker, Robert Orr. *The Muster Roll: A Biography of Fort Ripley, Minnesota*. St. Paul, Minn.: H. M. Smyth, 1970.

Barnard, Sandy. *I Go with Custer: The Life and Death of Reporter Mark Kellogg*. Bismarck, N.Dak.: Bismarck Tribune, 1996.

———, ed. *Ten Years with Custer: A 7th Cavalryman's Memoirs*. Terre Haute, Ind.: AST Press, 2001.

Barry, James P. "Fort Wayne," in *Old Forts of the Great Lakes: Sentinels in the Wilderness*. Lansing, Mich., Thunder Bay Press, 1994.

Bartlett, Richard A. *Yellowstone: A Wilderness Besieged*. Tucson: University of Arizona Press, 1988.

Becker, Kirk A. "History of the Stanford-Binet Intelligence Scales: Content and Psychometrics," in *Stanford-Binet Intelligence Scales*, Fifth Edition, Assessment Service Bulletin, Number 1. Itascia, Ill.: Riverside/Houghton Mifflin, 2003.

Billings, John S. *A Report on Barracks and Hospitals, with Descriptions of Military Posts, War Department Circular No. 4*. Washington, D.C.: War Department, Surgeon-General's Office, Government Printing Office, 1870.

———. *A Report on the Hygiene of the United States Army, with Descriptions of Military Posts, Circular No. 8.* Washington, D.C.: War Department, Surgeon-General's Office, Government Printing Office, 1875.

Billroth, Theodor. *General Surgical Pathology and Therapeutics, in Fifty Lectures: A Text-Book for Students and Physicians.* New York: D. Appleton, 1871.

Biographical Sketches of the Leading Men of Chicago. Chicago: Wilson & St. Clair, 1868.

Bordin, Ruth. *The University of Michigan: A Pictorial History.* Ann Arbor: The University of Michigan Press, 1867.

Bradley, James H. *The March of the Montana Column: A Prelude to Disaster, The Journal of Lieutenant James H. Bradley, 1876.* Edited by Edgar I. Stewart. New edition. Norman: University of Oklahoma Press, 1961.

Brininstool, E. A. *Troopers with Custer: Historic Incidents of the Battle of the Little Big Horn.* New York: Bonanza Books, 1952. Reprint, Lincoln: University of Nebraska Press, 1988.

Brodhead, Michael J. "Natural History along the Parallel of 49° North." Edited by Richard Grossinger. *IO Productions* (Cape Elizabeth, Maine) 13 (Spring 1972): 270–84.

Brown, Lisle G. "The Yellowstone Supply Depot." *North Dakota History* (State Historical Society of North Dakota) 40 (Winter 1973): 24–33.

Brust, James S., Brian C. Pohanka, and Sandy Barnard. *Where Custer Fell: Photographs of the Little Bighorn Battlefield Then and Now.* Norman: University of Oklahoma Press, 2005.

Buecker, Thomas R., ed. "A Surgeon at the Little Big Horn: The Letters of Holmes O. Paulding." *Montana: The Magazine of Western History* 32, no. 4 (Autumn 1982): 34–49.

Carroll, John M. *Custer's Chief of Scouts: Varnum.* Lincoln: University of Nebraska Press, 1987.

———. "Surgeon George Lord: A Brief History." *Little Big Horn Associates Research Review* (Boaz, Ala.) 1 (September 1984): 7–14.

Carroll, Matthew. "Diary of Matthew Carroll, Master in Charge of Transportation for Colonel John Gibbon's Expedition Against the Sioux Indians, 1876." In *Contributions to the Montana Historical Society*, 2:229–40. Helena, Mont.: State Publishing, 1896.

Chambers, Lee. *Fort Abraham Lincoln Dakota Territory.* Arglen, Pa.: Schiffer Publishing, 2008.

Chase, A. W. *Dr. Chase's Recipes or Information for Everybody—An Invaluable Collection of Over One Thousand Practical Recipes.* Rev. ed. Chicago: Thompson and Thomas, 1900. Originally published 1867.

Chicago Medical Society. *History of Medicine and Surgery and Physicians and Surgeons of Chicago.* Chicago: Biographical Publishing, 1922.

Chorne, Laudie J. *Following the Custer Trail.* Bismarck, N.Dak.: Trails West, 2001.
Cleaveland, Nehemiah, and Alpheus Spring Packard. *History of Bowdoin College with Biographical Sketches of Its Graduates.* Boston: James Ripley Osgood, 1882.
Clow, Richmond L. "The Whetstone Indian Agency, 1868–1872." *South Dakota History* 7, no. 3 (June 1977): 291–308.
Coe, J. N. "Twentieth Regiment of Infantry." *The Army of the US Historical Sketches of Staff and Line with Portraits of Generals-in-Chief.* Edited by Theophilus Rodenbough and William Haskin. New York: Maynard, Merrill, 1896.
Coleman, Sister Bernard, Sister Veronica LaBud, and John Humphrey. *Old Crow Wing: History of a Village.* Duluth: College of St. Scholastica, 1967. Reprint, Brainerd, Minn.: Evergreen Press, 2000.
Coolidge, Austin J. *History and Description of New England.* Boston, John B. Mansfield, 1859.
Cross, John R. "Whispering Pines: Their Lives in Front of Them—the Class of 1866." *Bowdoin Daily Sun*, September 21, 2016.
Cutright, Paul R., and Michael J. Brodhead. *Elliott Coues: Naturalist and Frontier Historian.* Urbana: University of Illinois Press, 1981.
Darling, Roger. *Benteen's Scout to the Left: The Route from the Divide to the Morass, June 25, 1876.* El Segundo, Calif.: Upton and Sons, 2000.
DeLee, Jesse C., David Drez Jr., and Mark D. Miller. *Orthopaedic Sports Medicine: Principles and Practice.* 2 vols. Philadelphia: Saunders, 2003.
Delo, David M. *Peddlers and Post Traders: The Army Sutler on the Frontier.* Salt Lake City: University of Utah Press, 1992.
De Trobriand, Philippe. *Military Life in Dakota: The Journal of Philippe Regis de Trobriand.* Translated by Lucile M. Kane. Lincoln: University of Nebraska Press, 1982. Reprint of 1951 edition.
Donahue, Michael. *Where the Rivers Ran Red: The Indian Fights of George Armstrong Custer.* Montrose, Colo.: San Juan Publishing, 2018.
Donovan, James. *A Terrible Glory: Custer and the Little Bighorn, the Last Great Battle of the American West.* New York: Little, Brown, 2008.
Eicher, John H., and David J. Eicher. *Civil War High Commands.* Stanford: Stanford University Press, 2001.
Flint, Austin. *A Treatise on the Principles and Practice of Medicine, Designed for the Use of Practitioners and Students of Medicine.* 3rd ed. Philadelphia: Henry C. Lea, 1868.
Frazer, Robert W. *Forts of the West.* Norman: University of Oklahoma Press, 1965.
Friedberg, Stanton A. "The Memorable Life of Hosmer A. Johnson, Early Midwestern Laryngologist." In *Ann Otol Rhinol Laryngol*, 92:470–72. Chicago: Rush–Presbyterian–St. Luke's Medical Center, 1963.

Gavan, Paul A., Eugene C. Orth, John W. Gorn, and staff of the *Fort Myer Post*. *The History of Fort Myer, Virginia: 100th Anniversary*. Fort Myer, Va.: Fontana Lithograph, 1963.

Gillett, Mary C. *The Army Medical Department, 1865–1917*. Washington, D.C.: Center of Military History, U.S. Army, 1995.

Godfrey, Edward S. *The Field Diary of Lieutenant Edward Settle Godfrey*. Edited by Edgar I. Stewart, Jane R. Stewart, and Carl S. Dentzel. Portland, Ore.: Champoeg Press, 1957.

———. "General Godfrey's Narrative (Custer's Last Battle)." In W. A. Graham, *The Custer Myth: A Source Book of Custeriana*, 125–49, 376–77. New York: Bonanza, 1953. Reprint, Mechanicsburg, Pa.: Stackpole, 1995.

Golant, A., R. M. Nord, N. Paksima, and M. A. Posner. "Cold Exposure Injuries to the Extremities." *Journal of the American Academy of Orthopedic Surgery* 16 (December 2008): 704–15.

Grafe, Ernest, and Paul Horsted. *Exploring with Custer: The 1874 Black Hills Expedition*. 3rd ed. Custer, S.Dak.: Golden Valley Press, Dakota Photographic, 2005.

Graham, W. A. *The Custer Myth: A Source Book of Custeriana*. New York: Bonanza, 1953. Reprint, Mechanicsburg, Pa.: Stackpole, 1995.

Gray, John S. "Arikara Scouts with Custer." *North Dakota History* 35 (December 1968): 443–78.

———. *Centennial Campaign: The Sioux War of 1876*. Fort Collins, Colo.: Old Army Press, 1976. Reprint, Norman: University of Oklahoma Press, 1988.

———. *Custer's Last Campaign: Mitch Boyer and the Little Bighorn Reconstructed*. Lincoln: University of Nebraska Press, 1991.

———. "Medical Service on the Little Big Horn Campaign." *Westerners Brand Book* 24 (January 1968): 81–88.

Green, David P. *Operative Hand Surgery*. New York: Churchill Livingston/ Elsevier, 1988 (2nd ed.), 2016 (7th ed.).

Greene, Jerome A. *Fort Randall on the Missouri, 1856–1892*. Pierre: South Dakota State Historical Society Press, 2005.

Hammer, Kenneth, ed. *Custer in '76: Walter Camp's Notes on the Custer Fight*. New edition/reprint. Norman: University of Oklahoma Press, 1990.

Harburn, Todd E., ed. *A Surgeon with Custer at the Little Big Horn: James DeWolf's Diary and Letters, 1876*. Norman: University of Oklahoma Press, 2017.

Hardorff, Richard. *The Custer Battle Casualties: Burials, Exhumations and Reinternments*. El Segundo, Calif.: Upton and Sons, 1989.

———. *The Custer Battle Casualties II: The Dead, the Missing and a Few Survivors*. El Segundo, Calif.: Upton and Sons, 1999.

———. *Indian Views of the Custer Fight: A Source Book*. Norman: University of Oklahoma Press, 2005.

———. "The Reno Scout." *Little Big Horn Associates Research Review* 2 (December 1977): 3–12.
Jameson, J. Larry, Anthony Fauci, Dennis Kasper, Stephen Hauser, Dan Longo, and Joseph Loscalzo. *Harrison's Principles of Internal Medicine*. 2 vols. 20th ed. New York: McGraw-Hill, 2018.
Hedren, Paul L. *Great Sioux War Orders of Battle: How the United States Army Waged War on the Northern Plains, 1876–1877*. Norman: Arthur H. Clark and University of Oklahoma Press, 2011.
———. *Powder River: Disastrous Opening of the Great Sioux War*. Norman: University of Oklahoma Press, 2016.
———. *Rosebud, June 17, 1876: Prelude to the Little Big Horn*. Norman: University of Oklahoma Press, 2019.
———. "The Sioux War Adventures of Dr. Charles V. Petteys, Acting Assistant Surgeon." *Journal of the West* 32 (April 1993): 29–37.
———. "Sitting Bull's Surrender at Fort Buford: An Episode in American History." Williston, N.Dak.: Fort Union Association, 1997.
Heitman, Francis B. *Historical Register and Dictionary of the United States Army, from Its Organization September 29, 1789 to March 2, 1903*. Washington, D.C.: U.S. Government Printing Office, 1903.
Herman, Gwyn S., Laverne A. Johnson, and Chris Grohndal. *Habitats of North Dakota Woodlands*. Fargo, N.Dak.: North Dakota Studies, North Dakota Center of Distance Education, 2008.
Heski, Thomas M. "Camp Powell: The Powder River Supply Depot." *Research Review, Journal of the Little Big Horn Associates*, 17, no. 1 (Winter 2005): 13–24.
Houghton, Edwin B. *The Campaigns of the Seventeenth Maine*. Portland, Maine: Short and Loring, 1885.
Hutchins, James S., ed. *Army & Navy Journal on the Battle of the Little Big Horn and Related Matters, 1876–1881*. El Segundo, Calif.: Upton and Sons, 2003.
Hutton, Paul Andrew. *The Custer Reader*. Lincoln: University of Nebraska Press, 1992. Reprint, Norman: University of Oklahoma Press, 2004.
———. *Phil Sheridan and His Army*. Norman: University of Oklahoma Press, 1985.
Huxley, Thomas Henry. *Lessons in Elementary Physiology*. 3rd ed. London: Macmillan, 1869.
Innis, Ben. *Bloody Knife: Custer's Favorite Scout*. Fort Collins, Colo.: Old Army Press, 1973. Reprint edited by Richard E. Collin, Bismarck, N.Dak.: Smoky Water Press, 1994.
———. *Interments at Fort Buford 1866 to 1895*. Second Printing. Williston, N. Dak.: Fort Buford 6th Infantry Regiment Association, 2006.
———. *Sagas of the Smoky-Water*. Williston, N.Dak.: Centennial Press, 1985.

Jacobsen, Jacques Noel, Jr., ed. *Regulations and Notes for the Uniform of the Arm of the United States, 1872.* 2nd ed. Staten Island, New York: Manor Publishing, 1981.
Kappler, Charles J. *Indian Affairs: Laws and Treaties.* Washington, D.C.: Government Printing Office, 1904.
Kelly, Carla. *Fort Buford: Sentinel at the Confluence.* Williston, N.Dak.: Fort Union Association, 2009.
Kimball, Maria Brace. *A Soldier-Doctor of Our Army: James Peleg Kimball, Late Colonel and Assistant Surgeon-General, U.S. Army.* Boston: Houghton Mifflin, 1917. Reprint, Cambridge, Mass.: Riverside Press, 1971.
Kime, Wayne R. *The Black Hills Journals of Colonel Richard Irving Dodge.* Norman: University of Oklahoma Press, 1996.
Koster, John. "The Belknap Scandal: Fulcrum to Disaster." *Wild West: The American Frontier* (June 2010): 58–64.
Kroeker, Marvin E. *Great Plains Command: William B. Hazen in the Frontier West.* Norman: University of Oklahoma Press, 1976.
Lass, William E. *A History of Steamboating on the Upper Missouri River.* Lincoln: University of Nebraska Press, 1962.
———. *Navigating the Missouri: Nature's Highway, 1819–1935.* Norman: Arthur H. Clark, 2008.
Lazarus, Edward. *Black Hills / White Justice: The Sioux Nation versus the United States, 1775 to the Present.* New York: Harper Collins, 1991.
Lepley, John G. "'Old Reliable': The Steamboat Benton on the Upper Missouri." *Montana: The Magazine of Western History* 30, no. 3 (Summer 1980): 42–51.
Libby, Orin G., ed. *The Arikara Narrative of Custer's Campaign and the Battle of the Little Bighorn.* Norman: University of Oklahoma Press, 1998.
Lubetkin, M. John. *Custer and the 1873 Yellowstone Survey.* Norman: Arthur H. Clark, 2013.
———. *Jay Cooke's Gamble: The Northern Pacific Railroad, the Sioux, and the Panic of 1873.* Norman: University of Oklahoma Press, 2006.
MacLeod, Roderick C. "Walsh, James Morrow," in *Dictionary of Canadian Biography*, 13:1071–72. Toronto, Ontario: University of Toronto Press, 1994.
Magid, Paul. *The Gray Fox: George Crook and the Indian Wars.* Norman: University of Oklahoma Press, 2015.
Matsen, William E. "The Battle of Sugar Point: A Re-examination." *Minnesota History* 50, no. 7 (Fall 1987): 269–75.
Mattison, Ray H. "The Army Post on the Northern Plains, 1865–1885." *Nebraska History* 35 (1954): 17–43.
McChristian, Douglas C. *Regular Army O! Soldiering on the Western Frontier, 1865–1891.* Norman: University of Oklahoma Press, 2017.

Bibliography

Merrill, Georgia Drew, ed. *History of Androscoggin County*. Boston: Ferguson, 1891.
Michael (Kupic), John. *Fort Myer*. Charleston, S.C.: Arcadia, 2011.
Michno, Gregory. *Lakota Noon: The Indian Narratives of Custer's Defeat*. Missoula, Mont.: Mountain Press, 1997.
———. *The Mystery of E Troop: Custer's Gray Horse Company at the Little Bighorn*. Missoula, Mont.: Mountain Press, 1994.
Miller, David, Dennis Smith, Joseph R. McGeshick, James Shenley, and Caleb Shields. *The History of the Assiniboine and Sioux Tribes of the Fort Peck Indian Reservation, Montana, 1800–2000*. Poplar, Mont.: Fort Peck Community College, 2008.
Miller, Frank E., ed. *Domestic Medical Practice: A Household Adviser in the Treatment of Diseases, Arranged for Family Use*. Chicago: Domestic Medical Society, 1912.
Millett, Larry, *Lost Twin Cities*. Minneapolis: Minnesota Historical Society, 1992.
Mills, Charles K. *Harvest of Barren Regrets: The Army Career of Frederick William Benteen, 1834–1898*. Lincoln: University of Nebraska Press, 1985.
Mock, Cary J. "Rainfall in the Garden of the United States Great Plains, 1870–1889." *Climatic Change* 44 (2000): 173–95.
Moore, Donald W. *Where the Custer Fight Began: Undermanned and Overwhelmed; The Reno Valley Fight*. Battle of the Little Big Horn Series, no. 10. El Segundo, Calif.: Upton and Sons, 2011.
New York State Medical Association. *Transactions of the New York State Medical Association for the Year 1889*. Vol. VI, edited by Edward Dunham. New York: J. H. Vail, 1890.
Nichols, Ronald H. *In Custer's Shadow: Major Marcus Reno*. Fort Collins, Colo.: Old Army Press, 1999.
———, ed. *Men with Custer: Biographies of the 7th Cavalry*. Hardin, Mont.: Custer Battlefield Historical and Museum Association, 2000.
———. *Reno Court of Inquiry: Proceedings of a Court of Inquiry in the Case of Major Marcus A. Reno at the Battle of the Little Big Horn River on June 25–26, 1876*. Hardin, Mont.: Custer Battlefield Historical and Museum Association, 2007.
Noyes, C. Lee. "Custer's Surgeon, George Lord, among the Missing at Little Bighorn Battle." *Greasy Grass* 16 (May 2000): 13–20.
———. "Galloping to Their Doom?" *Wild West, The American Frontier* 33, no. 1 (June 2020): 22–23.
———. "The Guns 'Long Hair' Left Behind: The Gatling Gun Detachment at the Little Big Horn." *English Westerners' Brand Book* 33, no. 2 (Summer 1999): 1–24.

———. "The Tragedy of Dr. George E. Lord." *Little Big Horn Newsletter* 34, no. 5 (July 2000): 4–6.

Ostler, Jeffrey. *The Lakotas and the Black Hills: The Struggle for Sacred Ground.* New York: Penguin, 2010.

Overfield, Loyd J., II, ed. *The Little Big Horn, 1876: The Official Communications, Documents and Reports with Rosters of the Officers and Troops of the Campaign.* Lincoln: Arthur H. Clark and University of Nebraska Press, 1971.

Petersen, Edward S. "Surgeons of the Little Big Horn." *Chicago Westerners' Brand Book* 31 (August 1974): 41–43.

———. "George Edwin Lord: Surgeon at the Little Big Horn." Unpublished paper, 1973, submitted to Bowdoin College Alumni Association. Copy in George Lord file, George J. Mitchell Department of Special Collections and Archives, Bowdoin College Library, Brunswick, Maine.

Plante, Trevor K. "Lead the Way: Researching U.S. Army Indian Scouts, 1866–1914." *National Archives* 41, no. 2 (Summer 2009).

Prickett, Robert C. "The Malfeasance of William Worth Belknap, Secretary of War." *North Dakota History* 17, no. 1 (January 1950): 5–51, 97–100.

Putz, Paul M. "Missouri Riverboat Wreckage Downstream from Yankton, South Dakota." *Nebraska History* 64, no. 4 (1983): 521–41.

Quine, William E. "Edmund Andrews." *Surgery, Gynecology and Obstetrics* (December 1922): 824–27.

Raines, Rebecca Robbins. *Getting the Message Through: A Branch History of the U.S. Army Signal Corps.* Washington, D.C.: Center of Military History of the U.S. Army, 1996.

Register of Officers and Agents, Civil, Military, and Naval in the Service of the United States, 1863–1959. Washington: Government Printing Office; digitalized books, Oregon State Library (77 volumes), Ancestry.com, 2014.

Reports upon the Survey of the Boundary between the Territory of the United States and the Possessions of Great Britain from the Lake of the Woods to the Summit of the Rocky Mountains. Northern Boundary Commission (1872–76). Washington, D.C.: Government Printing Office, 1878.

Richardson, Joseph G. *Health and Longevity.* New York: Home Health Society, 1912.

Roberts, Robert B. *Encyclopedia of Historic Forts: The Military, Pioneer, and Trading Posts of the United States.* New York: MacMillan, 1988.

Roy, Steve, and Richard Irvin. *Sports Medicine: Prevention, Evaluation, Management, and Rehabilitation.* Englewood Cliffs, N.J.: Prentice-Hall, 1983.

Sanford, Wilmot P. "The Fort Buford Diary of Pvt. Sanford, 1874–1875." Edited by Ben Innis. *North Dakota History* 33, no. 4 (Fall 1966): 335–75.

———. "The Fort Buford Diary of Private Sanford, 1876–1877." Edited by Michael E. Hill and Ben Innis. *North Dakota History* 52, no. 3 (Summer 1985): 2–40.

Bibliography

Scott, Douglas D., P. Willey, and Melissa A. Connor. *They Died with Custer: Soldiers' Bones from the Battle of the Little Bighorn.* Norman: University of Oklahoma Press, 1998.
Scott, Kim Allen. *Yellowstone Denied: The Life of Gustavus Cheyney Doane.* Norman: University of Oklahoma Press, 2015.
Shabetai, Ralph. *The Pericardium.* Boston: Kluwer Academic Publishers, 2003.
Skinner, Ralph B., John E. Libby, and Daphne W. Merrill. *History of Auburn, 1869–1969: 100 Years a City.* Auburn, Maine: Auburn Historical Commission, 1968.
Smith, Jean Edward. *Grant: A Biography.* New York: Simon and Schuster, 2002.
Solberg, Winton U. *Reforming Medical Education: The University of Illinois College of Medicine, 1880–1920.* Urbana: University of Illinois Press, 2009.
Sperry, F. M. ed. *A Group of Distinguished Physicians and Surgeons of Chicago: A Collection of Biographical Sketches of Many of the Eminent Representatives, Past and Present, of the Medical Profession of Chicago.* Chicago: J. H. Beers, 1904.
Stanley, David S. *Report on the Yellowstone Expedition of 1873.* Washington, D.C.: U.S. War Department, Government Printing Office, 1874.
Stedman, Thomas Lathrop. *Stedman's Medical Dictionary.* 23rd ed. Baltimore, Md.: Williams and Wilkins, 1976.
Stepenoff, Bonnie. *Working the Mississippi.* Columbia: University of Missouri Press, 2015.
Stephenson, Larry W. *Wayne State University School of Medicine, 150 Years, 1868–2018.* Detroit: Wayne State University Press, 2019.
Stevenson, Joan Nabseth. *Deliverance from the Little Big Horn: Doctor Henry Porter and Custer's Seventh Cavalry.* Norman: University of Oklahoma Press, 2012.
Stewart, Edgar I. *The March of the Montana Column: A Prelude to the Custer Disaster; Lt. James H. Bradley's Diary.* Norman: University of Oklahoma Press, 1991.
Stewart, Edgar I., and Edward S. Luce. "The Reno Scout." *Montana: The Magazine of Western History* 10, no. 3 (Summer 1960): 22–28.
Terry, Alfred H. *Field Diary of General Alfred H. Terry: The Yellowstone Expedition, 1876.* 2nd ed. Bellevue, Neb.: Old Army Press, 1970.
Transactions of the American Medical Association. Vol. XXVIII. Philadelphia: American Medical Association, 1877.
Turchen, Lesta V., and James D. McLaird. *The Black Hills Expedition of 1875.* Mitchell, S.Dak.: Dakota Wesleyan University Press, 1975.
Unger, Arthur C. *The ABCs of Custer's Last Stand: Arrogance, Betrayal and Cowardice.* Battle of the Little Big Horn Series, no. 4. El Segundo, Calif.: Upton and Sons, 2004.
Uniform Regulations for the Army of the United States 1861: Illustrated with Contemporary Official War Department Photographs. Washington, D.C.: Smithsonian Institution, 1961.

U.S. Department of the Interior. *Register of the Department of the Interior: Containing Appointees of the U.S. Patent Office (Corrected to January 23, 1893)*. Washington, D.C.: Government Printing Office, 1893.

U.S. House of Representatives. *Report of the Committee on Indian Affairs*, First Session of the 44th Congress. In Miscellaneous Documents of the House of Representatives, vol. 5, no. 167. Washington, D.C.: Government Printing Office, 1876.

———. *Report of the Committee on Indian Affairs*, First Session of the 44th Congress. In Miscellaneous Documents of the House of Representatives, vol. 285. Washington, D.C.: Government Printing Office, 1876.

———. *Report on Management of the War Department, Rep. Heister Clymer, Chairman of the Committee*. H.R. Rpt. No. 79, 44th Cong., Washington, D.C.: Government Printing Office, 1876.

U.S. Sanitary Commission, Frederick Law Olmsted, Secretary. *Report of a Committee of the Associate Medical Members of the Sanitary Commission on the Subject of Venereal Diseases, with Special Reference to Practice in the Army and Navy*. New York: John F. Trow, 1862.

U.S. War Department. *Annual Reports of the War Department: The Messages and Documents Communicated to the Two Houses of Congress at the Third Session of the Forty-Fifth Congress, Report of Lieutenant Edward Maguire, Corps of Engineers, June 30, 1878, Expeditions and Surveys in the Department of the Dakotas*. Vol. II, part III, appendix QQ. Washington, D.C.: Government Printing Office, 1878.

———. *Regulations for the Medical Department of the Army, 1863*. Washington, D.C.

———. *Revised United States Army Regulations 1861 with an Appendix Containing the Changes and Laws Affecting Army Regulations and Articles of War to June 25, 1863*. Washington, D.C.

———. *War of the Rebellion: A Compilation of the Official Records of the Union and Confederate Armies*. 128 parts in 70 vols, and atlas. Washington, D.C.: Government Printing Office, 1880–1901.

Utley, Robert M. *Cavalier in Buckskin: George Armstrong Custer and the Western Military Frontier*. Norman: University of Oklahoma Press, 1988.

———. *Sitting Bull: The Life and Times of an American Patriot*. 1st ed. New York: Holt Paperbacks, 2008.

Vaughn, J. W. "Dr. George E. Lord, Regimental Surgeon." *New York Westerners' Brand Book* 9, no. 2 (1962): 25–26, 30–31, 34–36.

Walker, L. G., Jr. *Dr. Henry R. Porter: The Surgeon Who Survived Little Bighorn*. Jefferson, N.C.: McFarland, 2008.

Warner, George E., Charles M. Foot, Edward Neill, and John Fletcher Williams. *History of Ramsey County and the City of St. Paul*. Minneapolis: North Star, 1881.

Willert, James. "Another Look at the Reno Scout." *Research Review: The Journal of the Little Big Horn Associates* 14 (Summer 2000): 17–31.
Willey, P., and Douglas D. Scott. *Health of the Seventh Cavalry: A Medical History*. Norman: University of Oklahoma Press, 2015.
Yenne, Bill. *The Other Custers: Tom, Boston, Nevin, and Maggie in the Shadow of George Armstrong Custer*. New York: Skyhorse, 2018.

Index

Abenakis, 4
Abington, Mass.: 12, 14; North Abington High School, 12–13, 20
acting assistant surgeons, 26, 36
Adams Hall, 15
Æneid (Virgil), 8
agency system (U.S. Indian), 30–31, 96
American Fur Company, 62
American Medical Association, 16, 18
American Revolution, 54
American West, 43, 131, 142
Anabasis (Xenophon), 8
Andrews, Edmund, 17, 20–22, 26, 55, 151n61
Androscoggin County, Maine, 4, 6
Androscoggin River, 3
Androscoggins, 4
Ann Arbor, Mich., 15
Apaches, 53
Appleton Hall, 9, 149n37
Arikara scouts, 105, 111–12
Arizona Indian Wars, 53, 109
Arlington National Cemetery, 138, 140
Army and Navy Journal, 133–34, 195n3, 198n41
Army Medical Department, 33, 41, 49, 53, 129
Army Medical Examining Board, 34, 37, 44, 48–50, 52, 54–55, 134
Army Medical Museum, Washington, D.C., 128–29, 132; Foundation at Fort Sam Houston, Tex., 129–30
Army of the Potomac, 6

Arnold's Greek and Latin Prose, 8, 10
Ashton, Isaiah, 108, 189n58
Assiniboines, 39
Auburn (and West Auburn), Maine, 3–5, 134, 147n16

Bakersfield, Maine, 4
Bannister, John, 163n103
Bates College, 8, 148n34
Belknap, William W., 66, 97, 169n27
Benteen, Frederick, 110–12, 114, 117–18, 120, 123, 133–34, 190n63
Biddeford, Maine, 2, 43, 46, 47–48
Big Horn Expedition, 98
Big Horn River, 105
Big Muddy Creek, Dak. Terr., 70, 171n37
Big White Clay, Nebr., 31
Billings, John S., 128, 165n2, 197n30
Billroth's General Surgical Pathology, 20, 152n78
Bismarck, Dak. Terr., 32, 48, 64–65, 70–74, 94, 98, 166n7
Bismarck Tribune, 105, 123, 133
Black Hills, 30; and Black Hillers, 97
Black Hills Expedition of 1874, 57, 97, 183n4; of 1875, 58
Bloody Knife, 105, 116, 187n44
Boston, Mass., 1, 12
Boughton, J. Ottinger, 31
Bowdoin College (Brunswick, Maine), 2–3; requirements, expenses, and curriculum, 8–11, 13, 16, 20, 24, 41, 136, 148–49n34, 149n35

219

Boyer, Mitch, 111–12, 191n73, 193n100
Bradley, James H., 101, 121–23, 184n13, 184nn15–16
Brainard, Daniel, 15In61
Breckinridge, Minn., 40
British Northern Boundary Survey Commission, 37–39
bronchitis, 36
Brown, Joseph B., 50, 52, 54, 162n89
Brown, Josette, 138
Brown, Paul, 69, 171n33
Brunswick, Maine, 2, 8–9
Bucolics (Virgil), 8
Buford Minstrels, 77, 84
Burgoyne, John, 54
Burkhardt, Samuel, 128, 197n27
Busby, Mont., 111, 191n71
Butler's Analogy, 10
Byford, William H., 17, 20–21, 26, 151n61
Byne, Charles C., 57, 164n108
Byrne, Bernard A., 94, 103, 182n132

Cabin John Bridge (Georgetown, Va.), 139
Caesar's Bridge model, 13, 150n45
Calhoun, James, 107, 123
Calhoun Ridge, 122
Callahan, John, 108
Camp, Walter, 125, 128
Camp Hancock, Dak. Terr., 109
Camp King, Cape Elizabeth, Maine, 4
Camp Reno, Mont. Terr., 43
Canada, 34, 37
Carroll, John M., 50
Carroll, Mont. Terr., 64–65, 166n9
catarrh (colds), 36
Chamberlain, Joshua Lawrence, 11
Chancellorsville, Va., Battle of, 6–7, 142
Chandler, Zachariah, 97
Cheyennes (Northern Cheyennes), 97, 99, 105, 121, 183n8

Cheyenne River Indian Agency, 22, 32, 109
Chicago, Ill., 15, 34
Chicago Medical College, 15; building, 20–21, 23, 54; curriculum and textbooks, 19–20; founding, 16–18
Chicago Tribune, 39, 133
chloroform, 41, 78; use and comparison with ether, 175n64
Christianity, 30
Cicero's Select Orations, 8
Civil War, 5–7, 7, 9, 11, 30, 32, 34, 109, 142
Clark, Elbert Judson, 22–23, 25, 108–9, 153n82
Clark, Lucien, 140
Cleveland, Grover, 138
Cleveland, Ohio, 23
Clymer-Belknap Hearings, 102, 184n17
Coleman, John, 125, 196n13
Commagere, Anna M., 138–39, 199n12
Commagere, Frank Y., 138, 199n12
Congregational Church, 2, 3–4, 146n13
consumption. *See* tuberculosis
Cooke, William W. 115, 118, 122–24, 193n100
Coues, Elliott, 33–35, 41, 43–44, 48, 155n18
Coulson Packing Company, 102, 185n22
Craft, David L., 65, 70, 73, 168n22
Crane, Charles H., 34, 37, 52
Craven, John, 80, 81, 84, 175n86
Crazy Horse, 96, 98, 105
Crittenden, John J., 123, 196n19
Crook, George, 53; Battle of the Rosebud, 109, 114, 131; and Powder River fight, 97–99
Crowell, William Henry Harrison, 64, 167n13
Crow scouts, 105, 111–12, 115
Crow's Nest, 112, 115, 192n76

Index

Crow Wing (Old Crow Wing and River), Minn., 29, 154n3
Custer, Boston, 107, 123, 193n100
Custer, George Armstrong, 57; body located, 125, 133, 135; at Crow's Nest, 112, 113–14; leads 1874 Black Hills Expedition, 97; route to the Little Big Horn 109–11; on Last Stand Hill, 118–19, 120–23; and start of Little Big Horn expedition, 98, 102, 104–5
Custer, Tom, 107, 122–23
Cummings, James, 93–94, 180n128

Dakota column, 97–98, 100, 102–3, 105, 108, 125; total deployment composition, 184–5n18, 185n19
Dakota Sioux uprising, 28, 30, 32
Dakota Territory, 30–32, 38–39, 97
Dale, Alfred, 56, 164n103
Dalton's Human Physiology, 20, 152n77
Dammon [Damon], Betsy Jackson, 1–2, 143n2
Dammon [Damon], Chandler, 1, 143n2
Davis, Nathan S., 17–18, 21, 26, 151n61
Day, Russel H., 71, 190, 172n41
Deep Ravine, 127–28
Delta Kappa Epsilon (DKE) fraternity, 11, 149n41
Department of Dakota, 34, 37, 39, 41, 44, 53–54, 61, 87, 125, 137
Department of Texas, 137
Department of the Missouri, 137
Department of the Platte, 97–98
DeRudio, Charles, 129
Detroit, Mich., 15, 38, 39
Detroit Medical College, 15, 18, 151n54
Devil's Lake, Dak. Terr., 39
DeWolf, James M., 18, 20, 48, 52, 99, 102; chosen for Little Big Horn medical staff, 107–9, 111–13; killed at Little Big Horn, 119, 131, 142, 185n20, 187n50, 196n19

diabetes mellitus, 80, 82, 85
diarrhea, 36, 110–11, 190n67
Dick, Abraham, 81, 84–90, 176n87
Divide (Little Big Horn–Rosebud), 112
Division of the Missouri, 97
Dodge, Richard Irving, 58, 164n109
Dover's Powder, 83
Doyle, William S., 94, 181n129
DuBose, E. W., 164n110
dysentery, 36, 110–11

Eaton, Mary Montgomery, 14, 44, 56, 137, 140–41, 150n50
Eaton, Theodore Horatio, Jr., 140–41, 150n50
Eaton, Theodore Horatio, Sr., 14, 141, 150n50
Ebbit House (Washington, D.C.), 132, 201n25
Ether, 84, 175n64
Evening Star, 139–40

Farmington, Maine, 2
Farquhar, Francis U., 38
Felton's Greek Reader, 8
First World War, 129
Flint, Austin, 54, 80, 82, 93, 180–81n128
Flint's Principles & Practice of Medicine, 20, 54, 80, 86, 93, 110–111, 180–81n128
Fort Abercrombie, Dak. Terr., 38, 157n41
Fort Abraham Lincoln, Dak. Terr., 32, 43, 57–59, 64, 74, 98–99, 102, 109, 123
Fort Assiniboine, Mont. Terr., 138
Fort Benton, Mont. Terr., 39, 44, 94
Fort Brown, Tex., 137
Fort Buford, Dak. Terr., 32, 39, 42–44, 60; daily life, hospital, and medical log during Lord's tenure, 61–99, 104, 123, 129, 165n2
Fort Dufferin, Manitoba, 39, 158n78
Fort Ellis, Mont. Terr., 60, 100

Fort Fetterman, Wyo. Terr., 98
Fort Laramie, Wyo. Terr., 58
Fort Laramie Treaty of 1868, 30, 57, 96, 154n7, 182n21, 183n8
Fort Leavenworth, Kans., 126
Fort Myer, Washington, D.C., 140, 200n22
Fort Peck, Mont. Terr., 90; and Indian agency, 93, 94, 128, 178n114
Fort Pembina, Dak. Terr., 38, 157n39
Fort Randall, Dak. Terr., 31; and hospital, 32, 33, 35–36, 47
Fort Rice, Dak. Terr., 71, 172n42
Fort Ripley, Minn., 27–29, 32, 148, 154n1
Fort Sam Houston, Tex., 130, 197n34
Fort Shaw, Mont. Terr., 69, 93, 171n34
Fort Snelling, Minn., 25, 32, 34, 37, 42, 44, 48, 55–57, 60–61, 124
Fort Stevenson, Dak. Terr., 32, 42, 170, 171n39
Fort Supply, Indian Terr., 127–28
Fort Totten, Dak. Terr., 3, 39
Fort Union, Dak. Terr., 62, 73
Fort Wayne, Mich., 14–15, 25, 150n49
Forty-Third Regiment, 14
Forty-Ninth parallel, 37–38
Fredericksburg, Va., Battle of, 6–7
frostbite, 79–80, 175nn69–70

Gall, 193nn98–99
Gallagher, James, 84, 176–77n88
Garden Coulee, Dak. Terr., 73–74, 173n48
Gardiner, Maine, 3
gastritis, 93, 180–81n128
Gates, Horatio, 54
Gatling gun battery, 107, 188n51
Georgetown, Va., 139
Georgetown University Medical School, 53
Georgics (Virgil), 8
Gerard, Frederick, 105, 115, 187n46, 192nn83–84

German Theatre Comique, 77
Gibbon, John, 98, 100–103, 105, 109, 121, 183nn10–11, 186n41
Gilneath, John W., 90, 178n112
Glendive Creek, 95, 102, 103
Godfrey, Edward, S., 110, 120, 122–23, 129, 188n51, 189n61
Goff, James, 5
gonorrhea, 83–84
Government Insane Asylum, Washington, D.C., 78
Grand Army of the Republic posts, Washington, D.C., 140
Grand Lodge of the Order of United Workmen of the State of Michigan, 141
Grant, Ulysses S., 37, 97
Gray, Henry, 152–53n77
Gray, John R., 107
Gray's Anatomy, 20, 152–53n77
Great Sioux Reservation, 30, 96–97
Great Sioux War, 23, 53; causes and start of, 97
Greek readers and grammar, 8
Greene, Oliver D., 40
Greenleaf, Charles R., 132
Groesbeck, Stephen W., 64, 66, 69, 70, 74, 165n6
Gross' Surgical Anatomy, 20, 152n77
Gurley, Charles L., 74, 77, 173n51

Hall, John D., 94
Hamline Methodist Episcopal Church (Washington, D.C.), 140
Harbach, Abram A., 38–39, 157n38
Harrington, Henry, 122–23, 126, 134
Hartford, Walter, 6, 177n99
Hartley, John, 33, 155n20
Harvard Medical School, 18, 53
Haven, Leslie, 108
Hazen, William B., 64–66, 69, 71, 74, 165n5
Head, James F., 25, 34, 36, 48–49, 50

Index

Heart River hunting camp (Dak. Terr.), 58–59, 164n112
Herendeen, George, 105, 187n45
Hinds, Orange S., 91, 179n117
Hodgson, Benjamin, 116, 193n95
Hoffman, George H.C., 52
Hooper, Annah, 46
Hooper, Annie M. F., 42–47, 55, 134
Hooper, Edward H. C., 46
Hooper, Tristam, 46
Humbert, James, 64, 166n10
Hughes, Robert P., 123, 186n41
Hunkpapa Sioux, 96, 182n1
Huxley's Lessons in Elementary Physiology, 20, 152n78

Iliad (Homer), 54
Indian hemp (*Apocynum cannabinum*), 84
Invalid Reserve Corps (Veteran Reserve Corps), 7, 14
Isham, Ralph N., 17, 22, 151n61

Jacob, Richard T., 70, 73–74, 171n36
Jennings (Jenniger) Edward, 87, 90, 178n104, 179n116
Johnson, Andrew, 69, 170n30
Johnson, Hosmer Allen, 15–18, 20–22, 26, 151n55
Jordan, Walter B., 172n44

Kellogg, Mark, 105, 123, 164n110, 187n47, 193n100
Keogh, Miles, 122–23, 196n19
Kibbee, Mrs. H. E., 138
Kimball, James, 49, 162n87

Lacquiparle County, Minn., 56
Lake Forest College (Ill.), 16–17
Lake of the Woods, Minn., 37–38
Lake Superior and Mississippi Railroad, 42
Lambourne, Thomas, 68, 170n29
languages, 10, 49

Last Stand Hill (Custer Hill), 118–20, 122–23, 126–29, 137
Leech Lake, Minn., 29–30
Legendre's Geometry, 10
Leighton, Alvin C., 73, 172n44
Leighton, James, 172n44, 179n121
Leighton, Joseph, 92, 179n121
Lewiston, Maine, 2, 5, 8, 134
Lewiston Evening Journal, 2, 134, 198nn44–46
Lewiston Falls Academy, 4–7, 11, 24
Little, Edward, 5, 147n20
Little Big Horn, Battle of, 59; and "Montana Harry's" tale, 135, 198nn44–46; sequence of events, 115–20, 133–34
Little Big Horn column, 105; route, 109–11, 123; selection of medical staff, 108–9; total deployment and personnel, 106
Little Big Horn River and valley, 105, 111–15; at Medicine Tail Coulee, 118, 121
Little Missouri River, 102
Limerick, Maine, 37, 42, 46
Lind University (Ill.), 16–17
Lister, Joseph, 55
Lone Tepee, 114–115, 192n83
Lord, George Edwin, 1; early life, 2–6; at Bowdoin College, 8–11; at North Abington (Mass.) High School, 12–13, 16; at Chicago Medical College 15, 19, 20, 22, 24–25; application for army contract physician, 26–27; at Fort Ripley and Whetstone Agency Post, 30–31; at Fort Randall, 31–36; with Northern Boundary Survey Escort, 37–44; romance with Annie Hooper, 42–48; before Army Medical Examining Board, 48–55; and Minnesota grasshopper plague, 56–57; at Fort Abraham Lincoln, 58–59; at Fort Buford and Medical Log, 66–93;

Lord, George Edwin (*continued*)
at Yellowstone Depot, 93–94, 99, 103–4; chosen for Little Big Horn medical staff, 107–9; with Little Big Horn column, 110–12; death on Last Stand Hill, 118–20; body found, 122–27; surgical cases preserved, 128–31; personal uniform, sword, chapeau, 132; survival rumor misinterpretation, 133–34; "Romance of Dr. Lord" tale, 134–35; obituary, 136
Lord, Julia Allen, 1–2, 132, 138, 140, 145–46n11
Lord, Mariah Holmes, 1–2, 132, 138, 145–46n11
Lord, Mary Damon (Dammon), 1, 143n2
Lord, Mary Montgomery Eaton. *See* Eaton, Mary Montgomery
Lord, Mary Tupper, 1–3, 132, 138, 144n5, 145n10, 199n10
Lord, Robert Newman, 1, 143n2, 145n8
Lord, Thomas Newman, 1–4, 37, 46, 132, 138, 144n5, 145nn8–10, 146n12, 199n10
Lord, Thomas William, 1, 3–4; Civil War enlistment, 6; wounded at Chancellorsville, 7, 14–15, 25–26, 34, 44, 48, 55, 123–24; donates brother's pocket surgical case, 128–29; donates brother's uniform, sword, chapeau, 132–33; at Fort Brown and other posts, 137–38; Commagere will controversy, 138–39; death and burial, 139–40; last will and testament, 141–42, 144nn5–6, 147n24
Loyal Legion Post, Washington, D.C., 140
Ludlow, William, 71, 172n40

Macon, Ga., 138
Maghee, Thomas H., 52
Magruder, Susan, 139, 141–42, 199n17
Magruder, Willis B., 142, 199n17
mania/mental health problems. *See* Mario, Edwin
Manitoba, Canada, 29, 34, 39
Manley, John A., 30, 154n4
Mario, Edwin, 78–79, 175n62
Marshall, Thomas, 139
Marshall Hall, 139–40, 199–200n18
Massachusetts General Court, 4
McAllister, Charles, 74, 174n52, 174n56
McKinney, John A., 64, 66, 70, 79, 90, 93–95, 167n14
McMullin, Charles, 177n95
medical pannier, 131
Medical School of Maine, 8, 15, 19, 148–49n34
Medicine Tail Coulee, 118, 193n97
Merchants Hotel (St. Paul, Minn.), 41, 44, 161n81
Mercy Hospital (Chicago, Ill.), 17, 20–22, 25
metacarpal phalangeal dislocations, 84
Michaelis, Otho E., 123–25
Minneapolis Daily Tribune, 40, 112
Minnesota, 28, 30, 37
Minnesota grasshopper plagues, 56–57
Milk River, Mont. Terr., 43, 160n69
Minot, Maine, 4
Mississippi River, 28–29, 38
Missouri River, 30–32, 42, 45, 60–62, 73, 77, 90
Mitchell, Thomas, 92, 128, 179n120
Monmouth, Maine, 2
Montana column, 98, 100–103, 105, 109; total deployment and composition, 183nn10–11
Montana Harry, 135, 198nn44–46
Montana Territory, 30, 39, 43, 48, 61, 97–98, 138
Moore, Beverly, 48
Moore, Orlando H., 63–64, 94, 103, 167n12
Mount Vernon Estate, Va., 139
Mouse River, Dak. Terr., 38

Index

Mulligan, George P., 83, 176n82
Murdock, Daniel H., 73, 103, 173n46
mutual imbecility, 85, 177n97

Napier, John, 54
Nash, Francis O., 40–42, 158–59n53
National Museum of Health and Medicine, 129, 131–32
Neal, Anson, 140
Nebraska Territory, 31–32, 98
Neisseria gonorrhoeae, 83. *See also* gonorrhea
Newburyport, Mass., 2
Newman, J. B., 94, 182n33
New Ulm, Minn., 56
New Valley Troupe, 77
New York City, 14, 44, 49
New York Metropolitan Life Insurance Company, 141
New York Westerners Brand Book, 7
Northern Boundary Survey, 34, 39; and escort, 42, 45, 61, 124
Northern Boundary Survey Commission, 37, 39, 40, 44, 48
Northern Pacific Railroad, 29, 31, 38, 42, 96–97, 102
North Platte River Agency, Nebr., 30
Northwestern University Feinberg School of Medicine, 17. *See also* Chicago Medical College
North Yarmouth, Maine, 8, 146n12
Nowlan, Henry J., 123, 125–26
Noyes, C. Lee, 25, 45–46, 108, 125

Odyssey (Homer), 10
Ojibwe (Chippewas), 28–30
Old Bear, 99
Old Orchard Beach, Maine, 45–46
Oshkosh, Wisc., 138
Otis, Elwell S., 32, 66, 155n17, 169n25

Packard, Henry M., 2
Paley's Evidences and *Paley's Natural Theology*, 10

Palmer House Hotel (Chicago), 133
Panic of 1873, 97
Paulding, Homes O., 57–60; journal describing Gibbon's Montana column, 100–101, 109, 121–23, 195n3
Pejepscot Purchase, 4
Penny, Charles G., 69, 74, 170n31
pericarditis, 81, 88–90
Petersen, Edward S., 50
Petteys, Charles, 53, 162n95
piles (hemorrhoids), 92
Pine Ridge Reservation, Nebr., 31
Poland, Maine, 4
Ponca Indian Agency, Nebr. Terr., 32
Porter, Henry R., 48, 53; chosen for Little Big Horn medical staff, 107–9, 110–12; on Lord at Little Big Horn, 113, 116, 119–20, 123, 131, 142
Porter, James, 122–23, 126, 134
Potomac River, 139–40
Potter, Edward, 139
Powder River, 30, 95, 98, 102–3, 123, 125
Powder River Expedition (1876), 53, 98–99
Powder River Supply Depot, 103–4, 108, 186n36
Powell, James W., 70, 103, 171n35
Puck, Henry, 90, 179n113

Quaking Asp River, Mont. Terr., 43, 48, 160n67

Red Cloud's War, 30
Red River (Dakota-Manitoba), 29, 34, 38
Reed, Harry Armstrong, 107, 123
Reily, William Van Wyck, 123
Reinhart, I. J., 52
Reno, Marcus A., 39–42, 103, 105, 112–13, 114–16, 118–20, 135, 185–86n27, 187n42
Reno-Benteen Hill, 116, 119, 121, 123
Reno Court of Inquiry, 116, 133
Reno Creek, 113

Revolutionary War, 4
Reynolds, Charley, 111, 191n74
Reynolds, Joseph, 98
rheumatic fever and rheumatic heart disease, 81
rheumatism, 80–82, 84–87, 175nn72–73
Richardson, William, 65, 169n23
Richmond, Va., 14
Roberts, Thomas A., 7
Rockford, Ill., 22
Rocky Mountains, 37, 39, 56
Rosebud, Battle of the, 105, 114
Rosebud Creek, 100, 103, 105, 109, 125, 131
Rush Medical College (Chicago), 16, 151n61
Rutter, David, 17, 151n61

Saco River, Maine, 46
Sallust, 8
Sanders, William W., 94, 129, 181n131
Sanford, Wilmot P., 104, 174n54
Saratoga, Battle of, 54
Schaefer, Eugene, 84, 177n90
Schwatka, Frederick, 131, 197n37
Scott, Douglas, 81, 87, 217
Scott, Steve, 75, 174n53
Second Cavalry, 98
Seventeenth Maine Infantry, 6; and Battles of Fredericksburg and Chancellorsville (1863), 6–7; Regimental Association, 140
Seventh Cavalry, 39; assignments at Little Big Horn, 112, 121, 125; deployment personnel at Little Big Horn, 105; regimental band, 102, 104; rheumatism and tonsillitis, 81, 87, 97–98
Seventh Infantry, 75, 93
Sheridan, Michael V., 126–28
Sheridan, Philip H., 97–98, 126
Sitting Bull, 62, 96, 102; and Sun Dance Camp, 111, 191n70, 133

Sioux: Dakota, 28, 30, 32; Lakota, 30, 31, 39, 57–58, 62, 74, 95–98, 100–101, 105, 111, 121, 182n1
Sixth Infantry, 39, 43, 59, 74, 77, 95, 103, 173n49
"Slide" (Missouri River), 77, 174n57
Slim Buttes, Battle of, 131
Smith, Algernon E., 123
Smith, Edward H., 186n41
Smith, John (soldier), 86, 178n100
Smith, John (sutler), 125, 196n13, 196n15
Smith, William, 64, 166n11
Smyth's Algebra, 8
Snake Indian War, 53
Socrates, 54
Spencer, Edward, 84–85, 177n94
Spotted Tail, 31
Spotted Tail Agency, 131
Stafford, Joseph S., 163n103
Stanley Stockade, 95, 102–4, 182n136, 185n21
State Historical Society of North Dakota, 130
steamboats: *Benton*, 65, 167–68n16; *Carroll*, 93, 180n126; *Durfee*, 94, 181n130; *Far West*, 73, 102–5, 123, 172–73n45; *Fontenelle*, 42, 45, 159n62; *General Meade*, 65, 169n24; *Josephine*, 65, 71, 73, 94–95, 102–3, 168n21; *Key West*, 64, 66, 69–71, 93, 102–3, 166n8
Stevenson, Joan Nabseth, 110
St. Louis, Mo., 32
St. Paul, Minn., 25–26, 28, 32, 37–38, 40, 42, 44, 55–56, 71, 125
Sturgis, James (Jack), 122–23, 126, 133–34
Sturtevant House Hotel, New York City, 49, 161n85
surgeon general, 27
Sweet, Owen J., 127–28
Sweet Grass Hills, Mont. Terr., 43, 48, 160n68

Swift Bear, 31
Sykes, George, 137–38, 198n3
syphilis, 36, 87
Terry, Alfred H., 98, 100–102, 105, 121, 123, 125
Third Army Corp (Army of the Potomac), 6
Third Cavalry, 98
Thompson, Richard E., 59, 123–25, 195nn10–11
Tongue River, 101, 103
tonsillitis, 86–87, 90
Topsham, Maine, 3
Townsend, Thomas G., 65, 168n20
trail colic, 110–11
Treponema pallidum, 87. *See also* syphilis
tuberculosis (consumption), 30
Tupper, James, 3
Tupper, Mary E. *See* Lord, Mary Tupper
Turtle Mountain, Dak. Terr., 38–39, 158n44
Twentieth Infantry, 25–26, 30, 38–39, 56, 137
Twentieth Maine Volunteer Infantry, 11
Twenty-Second Infantry, 31–32
Twenty-Third Infantry, 57
Twenty-Fifth Infantry, 127
Twining, William J., 38, 45, 158n44, 160n69

Union Army, 7
Union Pacific Railroad, 30
University of Michigan Medical School, 15, 151n54
Upham's Mental Philosophy and Upham's *Treatise of the Will*, 10
U.S.A. General Hospital, Annapolis, Md., 7
U.S. Army, 25, 37, 57

U.S. Census of 1850, Biddeford, Maine, 2
U.S. Census of 1880, Brownsville, Tex., 137
U.S. Patent Office, Washington, D.C., 138, 140

Varnum Charles, 111–12, 114–115, 191n72
Vaughn, J. W., 7
venereal disease, 64–65, 83, 87, 167n15, 168n19
Veteran Reserve Corps, 7, 14. *See also* Invalid Reserve Corps
Virchow's Cellular Pathology, 20, 152n77

Wagner, Arthur L., 73, 77, 93, 173n47
Walker, George B., 93, 103, 186n29
Walsh, James, 133, 198nn40–41
Washington, D.C., 6, 27, 87, 102, 129, 138–39, 141
Washington Territory, 53
Weeds, James F., 33, 155n19
Weir, Thomas, 120, 194n103
Whetstone agency/post, Dak. Terr., 30–31, 154n10
Willey, P., 81, 87, 217
Williams, John, 109, 123, 125, 189n59
Windler, H., 130
Winne, Charles Knickerbacker, 27, 154n93
Winnebago, Ill., 23
Winnebago (HoChunk) Indian Reservation, 28
Winthrop, Maine, 3
Wiscasset, Mass., 2
Woodbridge, Francis, 93, 180n127
Wood's Materia Medica and Pharmacology, 20, 152n77
Woods Trail, Minn., 29
Woolrich, Maine, 8
Wyoming Territory, 30, 97–98

Yale University, 11
Yankton and Yankton Agency, Dak. Terr., 32, 65, 168n17
Yates, George, 122–23
Yellow Medicine County, Minn., 56
Yellowstone Depot, 95–96, 102–3, 105, 185nn21–22
Yellowstone River, 60–61, 94, 95, 100–101, 102–3, 105
Yellowstone Survey Expeditions (1871, 1872, 1873), 38, 96

www.ingramcontent.com/pod-product-compliance
Lightning Source LLC
Chambersburg PA
CBHW020759230426
43666CB00007B/767